ALSO BY GLYN WILLIAMS

The British Search for the Northwest Passage in the Eighteenth Century
The Expansion of Europe in the Eighteenth Century
The Great Map of Mankind (with P. J. MARSHALL)
Terra Australis to Australia (with ALAN FROST)
Ruling Britannia (with JOHN RAMSDEN)
The Voyages of Captain Cook
The Great South Sea

FRONTISPIECE: Commodore George Anson.
Oil by unknown artist, probably 1744–1745.

THE PRIZE OF
ALL THE OCEANS

*The Triumph and Tragedy
of Anson's Voyage
Round the World*

GLYN WILLIAMS

HarperCollins*Publishers*

HarperCollins*Publishers*
77–85 Fulham Palace Road,
Hammersmith, London W6 8JB

www.**fire**and**water**.com

Published by HarperCollins*Publishers* 1999
1 3 5 7 9 8 6 4 2

A catalogue record for this book
is available from the British Library

ISBN 0 00 257125 0

Set in Postscript Linotype Adobe Caslon by
Rowland Phototypesetting Ltd, Bury St Edmunds, Suffolk

Printed and bound in Great Britain by
The Bath Press, Bath

FOR SONIA AND JAN

CONTENTS

ILLUSTRATIONS

The endpapers show the track of the *Centurion* round the world.
From *Anson's Voyage* (*British Library*)

MAPS AND FIGURES

'The most desirable prize that was to be met with in any part of the globe ... she had on board 1,313,843 pieces of eight, and 35,682 oz. of virgin silver.'

A Voyage Round the World by George Anson (1748)

PREFACE

COMMODORE GEORGE ANSON'S VOYAGE OF 1740–44 holds a
unique and terrible place in British maritime history. The misadventures
of this attempt by Royal Navy ships to sail round the world make a
dramatic story of hardship, disaster, mutiny and endurance. Only one of
Anson's squadron, the flagship *Centurion*, completed her mission. The
other vessels were wrecked, scuttled, or forced back in shattered condition.
Out of more than 1,900 men who sailed from Spithead in September
1740, almost 1,400 died, most from disease or starvation. There were
circumstances of particular horror about the departure from England, for
crammed on board Anson's ship as soldiers were hundreds of disabled
veterans from past wars, almost all of whom died before the ships reached
their destination of the South Sea.

With crews ravaged by scurvy, Anson's ships were battered by relentless storms as they attempted to round Cape Horn. The ships' logs for
those weeks are filled with desperate entries as the ships struggled to
keep afloat. Two of the six men-of-war in the squadron turned back,
their captains to face later accusations of desertion. A third, the *Wager*,
was wrecked on a desolate island off the coast of Chile in circumstances
in which all discipline vanished. Amid scenes of defiance and violence
most of the crew mutinied, and split into groups to attempt their escape.
Led by the gunner, the largest of these groups made a small-boat voyage
through the Strait of Magellan that stands as a remarkable feat of seamanship. The remaining three ships reached an uncertain safety at the old
buccaneer haunt of Juan Fernández, but when they put to sea again their
depleted crews totalled less than the normal complement of a fourth-rate
man-of-war. The tale of disaster was not yet finished, for in the crossing
of the North Pacific scurvy struck once more, many of the crew were
marooned for weeks on the island of Tinian, and when Anson reached

the coast of China in November 1742 he was left with one ship and a handful of men, some of whom had 'turned mad and idiots'.

The most extraordinary part of the voyage was still to come, for despite his losses Anson was determined to seize the treasure galleon that made the annual voyage from Acapulco to Manila. Laden with Peruvian silver, she was 'the Prize of all the Oceans'. In June 1743 Anson intercepted the *Nuestra de Señora de Covadonga*, and in a 90-minute action forced her surrender. After refitting at Canton he returned home the next year to find himself compared with Drake, and his exploits with the long-remembered feats of arms against the Spain of Phillip II. The casualties were forgotten as the public celebrated a rare triumph in a drab and interminable war. Descriptions of the voyage filled the newspapers and periodicals; doggerel verses and popular ballads were composed in Anson's honour; a half-dozen narratives on the voyage were published; and in 1748 the long-awaited authorised account appeared under the name of Richard Walter, chaplain on the *Centurion*, and became a best-seller.

Walter's volume has formed the basis of all accounts of Anson's voyage from the mid-eighteenth century to the present. The book, more fully illustrated than any similar work up to that time, was both a stirring story of adventure at sea and an exhortation to further Pacific enterprise. Here I have relied on it for detail not available elsewhere, but that use has been constrained by the discovery of evidence that seems to show that Richard Walter played only a preliminary part in the writing of *A Voyage Round the World by George Anson*, and that the book as published was partly the work of an author who never sailed on the voyage. This loss, if such it is, has been more than compensated for by the wealth of material that has been brought to light in recent years. The private papers and diaries of those involved with the genesis of the voyage – ministers, admirals, ex-factors of the South Sea and East India companies – show that it was envisaged as something more than a predatory raid into the *Mar del Sur*. With its underlying motives of overthrowing Spanish rule in Chile and Peru, and cultivating commercial links with the replacement governments, it represented the beginning of more ambitious British designs in the Pacific. Admiralty files in the Public Record Office and National Maritime Museum allow one to follow, almost day by day, the preparations for the voyage: the problems in manning the ships; the concern about scurvy; the delays in fitting out the ships; the curious and rather suspect role of the two agents-victuallers who were to sail on the expedition. Most heart-rending among the other documents dealing with the preparations are those from Chelsea Hospital describing the age and disabilities of more than 40 of the individual pensioners sent to their deaths, along with many of their comrades, on Anson's ships. The feel of doom that seems to hang over the 'Secret Expedition' appears justified when records in Paris show that at an early stage French agents in London knew about the voyage, and sent their information to the Spanish government.

For the voyage itself more than twenty official logs survive, together with several private journals, the latter generally much less inhibited than those handed in to the Admiralty. These are supplemented by the captains' letters home; especially important are those written by Captain Legge and Captain Murray, the two who turned back. The wreck of the *Wager* produced its own flurry of narratives, and to them we can now add a long and previously unknown letter from the ship's detested captain, David Cheap, whose continuing refrain was 'je ne regrette rien'. As far as possible, I have tried to let the participants tell their own stories; rather like the trench memoirs of a later and greater war the shipboard accounts vary from those that struggle to convey the horrors of the voyage, to others that are so understated as to be almost nonchalant. So Lawrence Millechamp begins his description of the action against the galleon with the words, 'The particulars of the action that ensued are hardly worth mentioning.' Here I tried to put the taking of the *Covadonga* into perspective by reference to the voluminous documentation in the Spanish archives, which shows a ship ill-equipped and ill-prepared for her encounter with the *Centurion*. The frustrations and quarrels of Anson's stay at Canton before returning home are illuminated by 'A little Secret History' about those events, written by an East India Company supercargo at Canton. Since the highly critical account of the Chinese in the authorised account of the voyage helped to shape changing British perceptions of China in the mid-eighteenth century, this is a fascinating manuscript which for the first time attempts to explain the Company and Chinese side of events.

The homecoming, after initial celebrations and promotions, was bedevilled by a three-year dispute over prize money, and here the mass of legal documents among the Hartwell Papers and the records of the High Court of Admiralty has been found invaluable. Anson's huge share of the prize money helped to buttress his position as the new force in naval affairs, which until his death in 1762 were dominated by his work at the Board of Admiralty. Further documents in the Public Record Office and the British Library show that Anson had hoped to mount a follow-up expedition to the Pacific in the first year of peace in 1749. High diplomacy stifled the plans for this second voyage, and Anson had to wait for another war before the government agreed to send a force which in 1762 captured Manila.

The continuing interest in the Pacific soon bore a different fruit in the voyages of Cook and his contemporaries. Anson's successors in the Pacific were for the most part men of peace rather than of war. For them Anson's voyage, with its heavily armed ships, diseased crews and unrealistic objectives, was an object-lesson in how not to do things. Across the generations the grim story of the voyage, with its appalling losses, continues to haunt the imagination, but perhaps the most lasting impression is of Anson's own fortitude in the face of all the odds. This was the commander who had watched helplessly while his crews died in their hundreds 'like rotten sheep', who hauled ropes alongside his men and tended them when they were ill; but who never wavered in his determination to come home triumphant.

In one sense this book has been a long time in the writing. My first research into Anson's voyage began during summer visits to Guernsey in the early 1960s. Through the kindness of the de Sausmarez family I was given access at Sausmarez Manor to the journals and other papers of Philip Saumarez, who had sailed with Anson as an officer on the *Centurion* (and who anglicised his name on joining the Royal Navy). That was the beginning of sporadic research and occasional publication on the voyage. Diversions to other subjects took me away for years at a time, until some intervention, some chance discovery, brought me back again. The last of these was the recent surfacing of records relating to the voyage that were not even known to exist – the personal testimony of the senior East India Company supercargo at Canton during Anson's troubled stay there. His 'little Secret History' and other papers formed the last piece of the jigsaw, and the fact that they are housed in Portland, Oregon, a city where I spend time each year, seemed to carry some sort of message. Whether that message has been correctly interpreted or not, this book is the result. Over the years of working on Anson's voyage I have accumulated many debts to archivists, librarians and colleagues; and I hope that I have acknowledged these in other places. Here I shall confine my thanks to those who have helped in the last year or so with the task of turning a set of good intentions and miscellaneous notes into a book: Giles Gordon and Professor Peter Hennessy for steadfast encouragement and good cheer; Dr Nicholas Rodger for letting me see in advance his entry on Anson for *The New Dictionary of National Biography*; and Dr Pieter van der Merve for notes on Anson memorabilia at Shugborough. Ed Oliver drew the maps. I owe a special debt of thanks to Sir James Watt, who was more generous with his time and with his detailed advice on the medical aspects of the voyage than I had any right to expect. Those errors that remain are of course my own.

GLYN WILLIAMS
January 1999

I

A South Sea Venture

'I saw it was a voyage to cover some adventure I was not let
into, as well as to annoy the Spanish navigation in those seas.'
Admiral Sir John Norris, November 1739

LONDON IN THE SUMMER OF 1739 was tense with excitement at the
prospect of war with Spain. For two years the government of Sir Robert
Walpole had struggled to contain rising anti-Spanish feelings stirred up
by a parliamentary opposition looking for a chance to overthrow the
powerful First Minister. Walpole's opponents found their opportunity in
the public outrage that greeted exaggerated reports of Spanish atrocities
against British trading vessels in the Caribbean. The wealth of that region
had long fired the imagination of Europe. Huge amounts of silver shipped
up the Pacific coast from Peru crossed the narrow isthmus of Panama to
await shipment to Spain on the treasure fleet from Portobelo. Farther
north, Asian luxury goods brought to Acapulco on the Manila galleon
were sent overland to Vera Cruz, where they were loaded together with
Mexican silver onto the flota sailing for Europe. These cargoes of precious
metals were supplemented by indigo, cotton, dye-woods, hides, sugar and
tobacco – truly 'the wealth of the Indies'.

To tap this silver lifeline, legally or otherwise, had been the ambition
of generations of English merchants, pirates and privateers. By the 1730s
the fragile equilibrium reached at the Treaty of Utrecht in 1713, when the
newly formed South Sea Company had been awarded the coveted asiento,
the right to supply slaves to Spanish America, had all but broken down.
Spanish officials suspected that the concession served as a cloak for smugg-

ling, and they were equally irritated by the private traders engaged in illicit trade, especially British vessels working out of their base at Jamaica in the heart of the Spanish Caribbean. Incident followed incident as private Spanish coastguard vessels, the notorious guardacostas, intercepted foreign vessels, seized their cargoes and beat up their crews. In Britain the old hatred of Spain was not far submerged. Pamphlets, newspapers and cartoons extolled the glorious days of Drake and his contemporaries, and reminded readers of the horrors of the Spanish Inquisition. Petitions from the merchants of London and the great trading cities poured into Parliament. A merchant skipper, Captain Jenkins, arrived at the House of Commons with a bottle containing his ear (lopped off, he claimed, by guardacostas), to add a dramatic note to the uproar.

In the midst of this agitation the attempts by the British and Spanish governments to reach a sensible negotiated settlement of their differences foundered, with the South Sea Company proving an awkward stumbling block. In June 1739, well before the formal declaration of hostilities in October, the British Admiralty sent ships to lie in wait off Cadiz for the Caribbean-bound flota, and the next month Admiral Edward Vernon was ordered to the West Indies to harry Spanish shipping. These early thrusts were a sign that the forthcoming war was expected to be a maritime one in which Britain would use its superior seapower to full advantage. There would be no more of the costly and often inconclusive continental campaigns that had marked the War of the Spanish Succession against the France of Louis XIV. The butcher's bill of Marlborough's battles would be replaced by an altogether more alluring tally of territory and trade gained from the Spanish enemy. In the parliamentary debates of November 1739 speaker after speaker urged the ministry to attack Spanish America, where 'we can make them feel most sensibly the weight of our resentment: it is by conquests in that part of the world where we can most effectually secure or enlarge our navigation, and it is there where they can least resist us.'

No scheme was too madcap for consideration, and the files of ministers bulged with plans for attacks on all parts of Spain's overseas empire: Havana, Vera Cruz, Cartagena and Darien in the Caribbean; Panama and Lima in the South Sea; Manila, far distant across the North Pacific.

But if the list of objectives seemed endless, resources were not. The Royal Navy was more impressive on paper than on the high seas. Its ships had deteriorated during the years of peace; it had seen little fighting for a generation; its organisation and some of its senior officers were of doubtful quality. The First Lord of the Admiralty was Sir Charles Wager, 73 years old at the outbreak of war; the Admiral of the Fleet was Sir John Norris, almost eighty. Both had been fine fighting seamen in their time. Putting their decisions into effect was the secretary of the Admiralty, Josiah Burchett, about 72 years old, who had held his post since 1694. At the Navy Board the dominant figure was the surveyor, Sir Jacob Acworth, in post since 1715 and now about seventy years old. Age did not necessarily mean decrepitude, and these men had served the navy well, but their tenacious grip on naval affairs had its drawbacks. If nothing else, it was a depressing reminder for ambitious younger officers of the continuing importance of seniority and longevity in the navy of the Walpole era.

The Admiralty's first priority, as always, was the defence of home waters, and then the protection of British trade, especially in the Mediterranean and Baltic. Extra funds in 1738 had enabled it to prepare eighty line-of-battle ships for sea, but their deployment was hindered by the uncertainty as to whether if war came France might join on Spain's side. If ships could be spared to attack the Spanish overseas empire, then the main target zone would be the Caribbean. In addition to the general considerations of wealth and accessibility that pointed to the West Indies as the main theatre of overseas operations, there was a more specific reason. In November 1739 Vernon secured an unexpected success when he captured Portobelo with a mere half-dozen ships; and the thunderous popular acclaim at home that greeted this minor victory prompted the government to dispatch powerful forces to the Caribbean.

All this was the public and predictable face of war, discussed at length in Parliament, and in pamphlets and newspapers. Less public, and certainly less predictable, were decisions taken by British ministers at this time to send forces to a more distant and exotic region − the Pacific. Ever since Drake's voyage in the *Golden Hind*, and his capture of a treasure ship off the coast of Peru, the South Sea had exercised a powerful hold over the English imagination. At one level it promised to be an

'Inexhaustible Fountain of Gold'; at another it was the jousting ground of satirical and utopian writers. To the accounts of the imaginary travellers of Defoe and Swift were added the narratives of actual voyagers, from William Dampier to Captain George Shelvocke, whose books did much to shape English perceptions of 'the Great South Sea'. Most English seamen venturing through the Strait of Magellan or around Cape Horn were raiders, preying on Spanish trade. Some were officially authorised as privateers, most brought their commissions, as one buccaneer boasted, 'on the muzzle of our Guns'. Such enterprise was private rather than government-sponsored; only John Narborough (in 1669) and William Dampier thirty years later took naval vessels into the Pacific, on what proved to be half-hearted and unsuccessful reconnaissance expeditions. But there had also been glimpses of a more official interest. Norris's papers from the War of the Spanish Succession, when he was a vice-admiral, contain details of the Lima trade and its possible exploitation, while Wager during a short-lived bout of hostilities with Spain in 1727 found time while cruising off Cadiz to write to Sir Robert Walpole, wondering whether the ships sent to the Caribbean might not have been better employed in the South Sea in attacks on Lima or Panama. Other letters of that year suggest that the government may have had 'the Project of a Settlement in the South Seas' in mind. Whether it did or not, the war was over before any such scheme could be put into operation.

In 1739 something altogether more purposeful and elaborate began to emerge in secret discussions. As early as 3 June 1739 the Cabinet Council had on its agenda consideration of proposals from Wager for operations in the Caribbean and in the South Sea. The latter began to take firmer shape in September when two separate South Sea schemes were put before a small group of ministers. First was a proposal to send two fifty-gun ships to the Philippines to seize the treasure ship or ships coming across the North Pacific from Acapulco. The Acapulco or Manila galleon – the name changed depending on whether she was on her westbound or eastbound run – was the fabulous 'Prize of All the Oceans', the target of foreign predators in the South Sea, and had twice been taken by the English (by Thomas Cavendish in 1587 and by Woodes Rogers in 1709).

Admiral Sir John Norris. Oil by George Knapton, c. 1735.

Secondly, a quite different scheme envisaged raiding operations along the coasts of Chile and Peru by ships sent round Cape Horn, on the grounds that 'many national advantages may be gained and great riches acquired by sending ten sail of men-of-war with fifteen hundred or two thousand land forces with them into the South Seas round Cape Horn'.

Wager and Norris were the sponsors rather than the originators of these projects. The proposals came from a handful of men with first-hand experience of the regions that had been selected as targets. The suggestions for attacks on Spanish America came from two former factors of the South Sea Company, Hubert Tassell and Henry Hutchinson. Tassell had served as a Company factor in Havana in the 1730s, while Hutchinson had not only been in the Company's employ at Portobelo and Panama, but also knew Lima. Although neither man was still in the employ of the South Sea Company – and Hutchinson had been in dispute with the Company for several years over his accounts – between them they brought an unusual degree of recent knowledge to the discussions on the proposed South Sea expedition. The twists and turns of those discussions can be followed in the pages of the private diary kept by Norris. Never published, it is a frank and detailed source of information about the preparations for war in the latter half of 1739.

On 11 September Tassell and Hutchinson wrote to Walpole suggesting that a squadron of eight men-of-war carrying 1,500 soldiers should be sent around Cape Horn to attack the coasts of Chile and Peru, and at the end of the month they put their plan in person to Wager and Norris. To anyone who had read Daniel Defoe or Woodes Rogers twenty-five years earlier, much of this had a familiar ring. The squadron was to conquer Chile with the aid of its disaffected inhabitants, plunder the great treasure-house of Lima and perhaps establish a government there that was well-disposed to Britain, and then attack Panama. Smaller craft might be detached from the squadron to fortify Juan Fernández, once the island haunt of the buccaneers. Hutchinson had in his possession a manuscript coasting pilot of the South Sea coast from Cape Horn to California, compiled from his and others' observations. He claimed close knowledge of the state of Spanish defences in the South Sea: those of

Panama and Lima he described as consisting of little more than low brick walls and a few hundred soldiers whose military experience was confined to parades and processions.

Government reaction to these proposals was cautious. Both Wager and Norris were doubtful about the wisdom of sending soldiers by ship into the South Sea, and thought that an attack on Panama would be better mounted across the isthmus, Henry Morgan style; but in mid-October they decided to go ahead with a raiding expedition of about three ships along the coasts of Chile and Peru. With that agreed, on 18 October Wager and Norris met James Naish, a former supercargo of the East India Company whose experience of trading in China and the Eastern Seas dated back to 1713. He seems to have known Wager for some time, and had already discussed with him the possibility of capturing Manila. Now he produced detailed proposals, and he also volunteered to accompany the force. If naval ships reached Manila the following summer by way of the Cape of Good Hope, they could capture the annual galleon or galleons from Acapulco, carrying silver worth £2,000,000, he claimed. In addition to this alluring prospect, Naish stressed the wider implications of a predatory expedition to the Pacific. The conquest of the Philippines, at the centre of a network of trade extending across the North Pacific from Siam to Japan, would give British merchants in the East a great advantage over their European rivals. Naish himself, after an eight-year dispute with the East India Company over allegations of private trade, smuggling and fraud, had just received £30,000 in settlement that summer. Clearly, he had money to invest; and despite his agreement not to do anything to damage the Company's trade monopoly, he might not have been over-scrupulous about his observance of this undertaking. His attitude to his former employers was shown in his warning to Wager not to reveal to the East India Company any hint of an attack on Manila, for that would be a sure way of passing the news on to the Spaniards. Lacking a professional intelligence service, the government could obtain information about regions as remote from normal British commercial and diplomatic activity as the Philippines and Peru only from private individuals such as Naish, Tassell and Hutchinson. It was not altogether reassuring that two of the three had been in dispute with their employers over financial matters, and that in the schemes they pressed upon ministers private gain competed with public interest for pride of place.

Wager and Norris evidently caught some of Naish's enthusiasm, despite a frosty comment by the Duke of Newcastle, who as Secretary of State for the Southern Department was responsible for overseas operations, that 'this was a small affair, and that greater matters had been under consideration'. By the end of October ministers agreed in principle to send an expedition of three or four warships and a regiment of 1,000 soldiers to take Manila. Naish was to be 'the King's chief agent' on the expedition, responsible among other things for victualling the ships. It soon became clear that commitments elsewhere made it difficult both to send an expedition to Manila, and to raise land forces of any size to go round the Horn and into the South Sea. Instead of the eight ships carrying 1,500 or 2,000 troops that Hutchinson had in mind, only three or four ships and a couple of hundred soldiers could be spared. Norris's diary makes it clear that Newcastle and his fellow Secretary of State (for the Northern Department), the Earl of Harrington, had reservations about both the Manila and South Sea expeditions. Norris himself was beginning to suspect that trade as well as war might be involved. He was not informed of the time of at least one meeting to discuss details of the South Sea squadron – an oversight, he was assured – and when he asked Wager whether trading goods were to be carried on the ships he was referred to Tassell. Finally, after a further fortnight of uncertainty, Sir Robert Walpole came to a decision. The First Minister concluded that there were not enough forces for an attack on Manila, but that the expedition to the South Sea should go ahead, with six ships and 500 land forces. This ran against the opinion of his First Lord of the Admiralty, for Wager had made clear his preference for an expedition to Manila rather than one to the South Sea. Among the reasons put forward by Walpole for his choice was the possibility that a naval force reaching the Pacific side of the isthmus of Panama would be able to link up with British troops coming overland from the Caribbean.

At Wager's suggestion George Anson, an experienced naval officer 42 years old, had been chosen for the Manila expedition; and on the abandonment of that project he was given command of the Cape Horn expedition. The younger son from a minor county family, the Ansons of Shugborough, Staffordshire, Anson had entered the navy in 1712, at the age of fourteen. His career was typical of someone who had joined the service just as a long period of war was coming to an end and a long period of peace beginning. He saw action as a lieutenant at the Battle of Passaro in 1717 during a brief outbreak of hostilities with Spain, and in 1724 a combination of meritorious service and good connections – for his aunt was married to the Earl of Macclesfield, then Lord Chancellor – brought him promotion to captain and command of a frigate stationed at Charleston, South Carolina. Much of his time in colonial waters was spent in routine patrols against smugglers and others trying to evade the system of imperial trade regulation, but by his second spell of duty in South Carolina, which began in 1732, the deterioration in Anglo-Spanish relations was having an impact. Almost immediately, he was involved in the case of two British merchant vessels intercepted and looted by guardacostas from Havana, and in 1734 he took the *Squirrel* to Georgia to offer the colonists there protection against possible Spanish raids. In his periods of shore leave he became well-known in the convivial society of the colonial capital, Charleston. Contemporary accounts suggest that he was a hard drinker, but that above all he was known for his love of gaming. From 1726 onwards he began investing his winnings in land purchases, and by the time he left the colony he held more than 12,000 acres, including a lot in Charleston itself, and land just outside the city limits that was to be become the capital's first suburb, called Ansonborough. The fullest account of Anson during this period (by a woman) hints at a character that was not altogether easy to read. 'Mr Anson is far from being an anchorite, though not what we call a modern pretty fellow, because he is really so old-fashioned as to make some profession of religion: moreover, he never dances, nor swears, nor talks nonsense. As he greatly admires a fine woman, so he is passionately fond of music.' In 1735 Anson left South Carolina for the last time and was placed on the half-pay list. Like many of his peacetime contemporaries his career in the navy came to a halt. After two and a half years he was re-employed, this time to command a 60-gun ship, the *Centurion*, on trade protection duties once more, but this time along the Guinea coast. As war with

Spain approached, the *Centurion* was ordered to the West Indies, but then brought back to Spithead.

It was at Spithead that Anson was informed in November 1739 of his appointment, first to command the Manila expedition, and then the South Sea enterprise. There is no indication of the reasons for Wager's choice of Anson. The records show nothing in his long years of unspectacular service to draw attention, favourable or otherwise, to himself. He was one among dozens of steady naval officers whose abilities had not been given a chance to shine during their peacetime service. Again, connection may be the answer, for there is some evidence that Anson already had as patron the powerful figure of the Lord Chancellor, Lord Hardwicke, whose daughter he was to marry in 1748. And Hardwicke was certainly present at several ministerial meetings in November and December that discussed the proposed South Sea expeditions. Perhaps more to the point, Anson seems to have been one of Norris's protégés: when in 1734 the admiral was appointed commander-in-chief Anson wrote him a letter of congratulation from American waters in which he hoped that Norris would 'continue that share of Patronage you have hitherto been pleased to honour me with'. Whether Anson's appointment was the result of good judgement, chance or influence, it was in retrospect a decisive moment – not only for Anson and the men who sailed with him to the South Sea, but in the long term for the navy.

Norris's diary shows that Anson's instructions were drawn up personally by Wager, who showed a first draft of them to Walpole in late December. Altered in several places, they were in finished form by the end of January 1740, although they were not handed to Anson until June. One of the amendments deleted an instruction giving Anson discretion to go on from capturing Callao, the port of Lima, to attack the capital itself; and in general the instructions were more cautious than the original proposals put before ministers by Tassell and Hutchinson. Those had concluded with recommendations that were breathtaking in their scope, for among the hopes pinned on the projected expedition was 'to settle some island in the South Sea; to succeed in a descent on Peru; to take two men-of-war and the Lima fleet; to take Panama and their treasure; to take several valuable towns; to take the Acapulco ship; and to induce

the Peruvians to throw off their obedience to the King of Spain'. Choice
of the route home was left to Anson, but Wager pointed out that if he
got as far north as Acapulco he might very well decide to return by way
of China. Here, for the first time, the notion of a voyage round the world
by Anson and his ships appeared.

Even after the modification of its instructions, the enterprise under
Anson's command was still clearly something more than a plundering
raid. Raids on Spanish American ports and shipping in the South Sea,
and the capture of the Acapulco galleon, were the routine buccaneering
and privateering objectives of an earlier era; but the decision to take 500
soldiers, the hope that Callao could be captured and used as a base, and
the clauses that dealt with the encouragement of rebellion in Peru and
the establishment there of a government sympathetic towards British
merchants had wider implications. A draft manifesto drawn up before
Anson sailed promised British protection, freedom of trade and religious
liberty to all who rose against the Spanish crown. There was even a
suggestion that if the wealthy Creole inhabitants failed to rise in rebellion,
then an attempt might be made to win over the mulattos and oppressed
black slaves by offering them their freedom. By the standards of the time
this was an incendiary proposition, and one that in the end failed to find
its way into Anson's official instructions. Although the possibility of
rebellion within the Spanish colonies had often been mentioned in earlier
proposals, Anson's instructions reveal the first awareness in government
circles that the most promising opening for British merchants would
come if Spain's American empire, with or without outside help, moved
towards independence.

At the same time, as Anson was preparing his ships for sea, Wager
signified his approval for another expedition that hoped to reach the
Pacific, but by way of a Northwest Passage. A year later, in June 1741,
two naval vessels commanded by Captain Christopher Middleton sailed
for the icy waters of Hudson Bay to search its west coast for a passage
through to the Pacific. Though the scheme was advanced long before
the outbreak of hostilities with Spain, the promoters of the expedition
were able to turn the war to their advantage as they reminded Wager
that ships coming through a northern passage would give officials in New

Spain no warning that foreign raiders were on their coast. They would be able to seize the Acapulco galleon and destroy Spanish coastal trade before any alert could be given. Once in the North Pacific, Middleton was to negotiate alliances with native rulers, take possession of lands not under foreign control and, when he arrived off California, look out for Anson.

The fitting out of Anson's squadron and the approval of the smaller discovery expedition to Hudson Bay under Captain Middleton resurrected plans dating back to Elizabethan times for a twin approach to the Pacific by a southern and a northern route. It was no longer a matter of projects advanced by gadfly promoters or by memorialists with dubious buccaneering backgrounds. The South Sea schemes of the autumn of 1739 had found their way to the heart of government. With Wager and Norris acting, in a sense, as guarantors, ministers from Walpole downwards were directly involved. Norris's private diary shows that between late September and the end of December he was closeted, usually with Wager, and often with senior ministers, in no fewer than twenty meetings to discuss the South Sea enterprises. It is a moot question whether this number of meetings was evidence of government commitment or of government irresolution. Although the decision not to go ahead with the Manila venture and to reduce the size of the Cape Horn expedition disappointed their promoters, what was agreed in late 1739 was still impressive – not a couple of small privateering vessels, but a naval squadron and land forces of some power. If the instructions given to Anson and Middleton are taken at face value, then for the first time British warships were to be used as instruments of commercial imperialism in the Pacific. At the very least, the expedition should wreak havoc along the South Sea coasts of Spanish America; and with luck and determination the great Acapulco treasure galleon might be taken. But the expedition was more than a buccaneering venture writ large, for if the reports of Tassell and Hutchin-

OPPOSITE: 'A New & Exact Map of the Coast, Countries and Islands within ye Limits of ye South Sea Company'. Herman Moll, 1711. Moll's map shows the range of British ambitions in the South Sea in the first half of the eighteenth century. Its insets, mostly taken from the charts of the buccaneers and privateers, show many of the places associated with Anson's voyage thirty years later: the Strait of Magellan, the islands of Chiloé and Juan Fernández, and Acapulco.

son were correct, then the arrival of Anson's ships might well lead to the collapse of Spanish authority throughout Chile and Peru. This 'Enterprize of a very singular Nature', as the authorised account of the voyage later called it, might leave Britain masters of the wealth of South America. The wheel, it seemed, had come full circle since Defoe's gloomy prediction in the years following the disillusionment of the South Sea Bubble in 1720 that future activity in regions as distant as the Pacific would have to rely on 'the little Adventures of single Men, and the small Undertakings of a few'.

Time would show that the hopes that prompted the sending of Anson to the Pacific were as unrealistic as those behind earlier ventures. The projects advanced so eagerly by Tassell, Hutchinson and Naish paid little attention to the likely reactions in Old and New Spain to foreign incursions into 'the Spanish lake'. Anson's sailing instructions revealed more immediate difficulties. In one hand he held orders to destroy Spanish American towns and shipping; in the other exhortations to gain the confidence of all Spanish Americans ready to rebel against viceregal rule. A commission of enquiry sent to Peru at this time was providing disturbing evidence for the Spanish government of discontent in its American empire, but there was little likelihood that any substantial section of the colonial population would welcome the successors of Drake and the buccaneers with open arms. The problem remained that explained by Henry St John in 1711, when a similar scheme was contemplated during the War of the Spanish Succession: 'the prospects of opening a new trade with the Spaniards and of attacking their colonies at the same time tend to be repugnant one to another.'

In other ways the precedents for sending a squadron of armed vessels around Cape Horn were not encouraging. The nearest parallel was the Dutch fleet commanded by Jacques l'Hermite, which survived the voyage into the Pacific in 1623–4 in reasonably good shape, but did little once it had arrived. Whether the route used was through the Strait of Magellan or round the Horn, at some stage ships sailing in company were invariably scattered by gales and weakened by scurvy. Even if they managed to rendezvous in the South Sea, they had by then lost much of their fighting effectiveness. As a rule of thumb the more men carried on board the greater the problems of health, provisioning and discipline. Some of the most effective voyages into the South Sea were made by lightly crewed ships – the buccaneering craft of the English in the 1680s, and the French trading vessels of the first decade of the eighteenth century. The buccaneers in particular obeyed no central direction; ships sailing together were a rarity, and even when this happened the partnership was usually a temporary one. Wind and weather, caprice and greed were more important in determining a course of action than formal agreements. Anson's ships would sail under very different assumptions, subject to a rigid command structure and with instructions to keep company whatever the circumstances. After they arrived in the South Sea it was by no means clear how and where they would find food for 2,000 men once their provisions were exhausted. There were trade goods on board, but their exchange for food would depend on the goodwill of the local populace. Given that the squadron would be sailing into uncharted waters and along enemy coasts, there was an easy optimism about some of the arrangements that boded ill for the venture.

The squadron put under Anson's command at the beginning of 1740 consisted of the flagship *Centurion* (1,005 tons, 60 guns, 400 men), *Argyll* – replaced in late March by *Gloucester* (853 tons, 50 guns, 300 men), *Severn* (853 tons, 50 guns, 300 men), *Pearl* (600 tons, 40 guns, 250 men), *Wager* (599 tons, 24 guns, 120 men), *Tryal* (200 tons, eight guns, 70 men). Two merchant vessels, the *Anna* and *Industry*, would carry supplies. On 10 January Anson was appointed commander-in-chief of the squadron with the rank of commodore, the customary one for an officer in command of a detached squadron, placing him above a captain but below a rear-admiral. For Anson to see his ships' names on an official commission was one thing; to get the vessels to sea, manned and in fit condition for a voyage to the other side of the world was another. With large forces fitting out for the Caribbean and for home waters, naval dockyards and victualling departments were strained to the utmost in the first full year of the war. Anson's squadron at Portsmouth came low on the priority list, and only in June 1740 were some major repairs agreed by the Board of Admiralty (a new mainmast and foremast for the *Centurion*, and a new mainmast for the *Severn*). Other alterations hinted at problems to come. To accommodate the officers accompanying the troops, extra cabins would have to be built – four in the *Centurion*, and two in the gun room of the *Pearl*, for example. Such encroachments on the limited space aboard would not be popular with the sea officers and crew, but even more serious were the implications of the extra provisions being taken on board for the long voyage. As Captain Legge of the *Pearl* pointed out, the weight of these provisions made his ship ride so low in the water that the ports would have to be caulked up. He suggested that scuttles should be cut to let in more air, and although this seems to have been done on some of the ships, carpenters had to cut still more scuttles as an emergency measure when the ships reached the South Atlantic.

Anson despaired at the slowness of the work, and spent long hours waiting at the Admiralty in vain attempts to have a personal word with Wager about the delays. At Portsmouth he struggled with bureaucrats great and small. A letter to the Navy Board in London was necessary before the quayside storekeeper would agree to supply him with a chest of signals – essential given the command role of the *Centurion* and the number of ships in his squadron. Another request from Anson for soap to wash 216 dirty sheets sent on board his ships met with a puzzled response from the board, which pointed out that it had no precedent to guide it. The affair of the dirty sheets rumbled on for some time, until an emphatic refusal by the Lords of the Admiralty to supply soap settled the matter. It must have seemed a trivial matter in comparison with some of the complaints reaching the Admiralty at this time, such as the report from the captain of the *Cambridge* that the bedding sent on board 'was stuffed with the pinions of pigeons with the rotten flesh upon them, and such trash as tanners' pits afford'.

Anson's grumble that some men just picked up by his pressgang had been taken out of the *Centurion*'s tender and sent on board another ship was shrugged aside by the Admiralty. In July the only response to his request for more men was an order to make up his complement with men discharged from hospital, drafts brought in by the pressgang, and marines quartered in the neighbourhood. On the *Pearl* Captain Legge complained that his surgeon was too ill to do duty, and that he had no surgeon's mate to look after the sick, 'who fall ill very fast'. How many of those who sailed with Anson were pressed men is difficult to tell. Lists among Norris's papers show that at the end of February 1740 there were 65 pressed men on the *Centurion*, 61 on the *Pearl* and three on the *Severn*; but at this time the ships were so far short of their complement that these figures probably underestimate the final totals. In the muster lists Anson sent at regular intervals to the Admiralty, figures of pressed men are given only for the *Centurion* herself; on the day of sailing he had 67 on board. This bare figure reveals nothing about the calibre of the pressed

The *Centurion*, a model made for Anson in 1747.

men, whether they were experienced seamen taken from merchant ships, or landmen pressed on shore. What we do know is that Anson's problem in finding men for his ships was a microcosm of the navy's manning difficulties in these months. Sir Chaloner Ogle's fleet being prepared at Portsmouth for the West Indies consisted of thirty ships of the line with accompanying transports, and his requirements of provisions, munitions and above all men were colossal. Cabinet meetings were dominated by the manning problem. At a meeting of the Cabinet Council on 6 May 1740 an exasperated Walpole complained, 'What has been the burden of my song in every Council these four months – Oh! seamen, seamen, seamen!' Two weeks later the First Minister lamented that a third of the navy's ships were 'absolutely useless' for want of men.

The manning crisis that confronted the navy at the beginning of every major war was exacerbated by the severe winter of 1739–40, among the worst of the century. The consequent shortage of foodstuffs and their high cost when available led to malnutrition in many parts of the country. Among those coming on to the navy's books at this time there would have been many whose resistance to infections had been weakened by their low body store of essential foods. In the spring of 1740 the sick lists grew faster than the muster rolls of new recruits, so that in the five months from February to June the navy received 3,627 additional men, but sent 4,875 into the hospitals. One of most overcrowded of these was at Gosport, which served the ships at Portsmouth. During the winter of 1739–40 its 380 beds were soon full, and the overflow was crammed into taverns and lodging houses in the poor streets surrounding the hospital. In April 1740 the admiral commanding at Portsmouth, Philip Cavendish, described the 'deplorable condition' of the sick, crowded twenty or thirty into these private premises, often with broken windows and no heating, 'two or three in a Bed of different Diseases, without proper Nurses or people to look after them'. It was here that Anson was told to look for men, and where the sick from his ships were sent for treatment. Captains with a reputation for dash and daring could usually secure volunteers eager for prize money; but few officers, and certainly not Anson, had had time to build such a reputation at this early stage of the war. If a letter of 13 June from Portsmouth was correct, rumours of his destination in fact deterred potential volunteers. It may have been this that prompted Anson ten days later to ask the Admiralty about the regulations for the distribution of prize money, and in particular 'how plunder and money arising from ransomed towns is to be shared'. Whatever use Anson was able to make of such information as a recruiting ploy, the fact remains that throughout July his ships were still 170 short of their full complement. Just as worrying, there were 140 sick among the crews. Only from the *Gloucester* was there good news, for her captain, Richard Norris (son of Sir John), had been allowed to take his previous crew from the *Adventure* to his new command on a one-to-one basis. These were men who wanted to continue serving under his command, or so Sir John told the Admiralty, and accordingly 220 men from the *Adventure* joined the *Gloucester*. On all Anson's ships there was a constant seepage of men: some were sent ashore to hospital, and others deserted. Among the latter was one who joined the *Wager* on 13 March, and 'ran' at the end of the month. Given the fate of the ship this act of desertion probably saved his life; it certainly saved him from much banter on the voyage, for his name was (William) Robinson Crusoe.

Up to this point there was nothing out of the ordinary about Anson's problems. Fleets fitting out for sea in the eighteenth century needed a nucleus of experienced topmen, but they were also accustomed to receiving their share of human flotsam and jetsam, men with neither aptitude nor enthusiasm for life at sea. It was one of the grim achievements of the Georgian navy that this unpromising material was knocked into shape; but nothing could be done with the pitiful procession of pensioners from Chelsea Hospital who in early August straggled on board Anson's ships in place of the regiment of regular soldiers he had expected. This was no last-minute expedient, though it seems to have taken Anson by surprise. Norris's journal reveals that as early as 7 December 1739 'invalids' were being considered for the expedition, while an entry for 8 January 1740 records the decision to send 500 of them. On 31 January instructions were drawn up placing the five companies of invalids selected for the voyage under the command of Lt.-Col. Mordaunt Cracherode. In a military context the term 'invalid' had a specific connotation, of soldiers rendered unfit by illness, wounds or age from active service, but often regarded as suitable for garrison or reservist duties. Years later the authorised account of the voyage written under Anson's supervision reflected his outrage as he watched the old soldiers, most over 60 years old, some over 70, come on board – many on stretchers. The more Anson learned about these veterans the more his horror and indignation grew. Out of the 2,000 out-pensioners at Chelsea Hospital, he claimed that the 500 selected were the oldest and weakest – this presumably on the grounds that whatever the method of selection those chosen were being sent to almost certain death. As the authorised account put it, they were doomed to 'uselessly perish by lingring and painful diseases; and this too, after they had spent the activity and strength of their youth in their Country's service'.

In the narratives of Anson's voyage the invalids are anonymous figures; but in the ships' muster books they are listed by name. The records of Chelsea Hospital in the preceding years afford a brief glimpse of some of them as they came before the hospital's governing board applying for a pension or some other benefit. Entries on 42 of those who sailed with Anson have been found, and although this sample does not quite bear out the assertions of the authorised account about the extreme age of the invalids selected, it is enough to reveal a tragic story. The average age of the invalids traced was 55 years, and all were disabled in some way. Many had been wounded in action, usually in the Marlborough wars in Spain or Flanders; some had suffered accidents in the course of duty; others again were ill or simply 'worn out'. Among those sent on the ships were: Neil MacNeil, 56 years old, 'wounded in the Right Thigh at del Rey cut on the nose and in the forehead at Brihengel and on the left side of his belly also the left leg hurt by a bombshell at Saragossa'; Denis Bryan, 54 years old, stabbed through the left hand by a boat hook, wounded in the right arm and in the right leg; John Bridgeman, 53 years old, dim-sighted and rheumatic; Charles Ross, 53 years old, 'convulsion fitts and hard of hearing'; George Walker, 55 years old, rheumatic, weak in both legs, 'bruised' at Gibraltar, 'worn out'; Edward Butler, 70 years old, 'a Hurt in his Back worn out'. Erratic spellings make it difficult at times to sort out the Beards and Bairds, Pools and Poles, Dixons and Dicksons, so not all identifications can be accepted as reliable. Thomas Butler poses a particular problem, for there were no fewer than three invalids with this name, and it is not known which was the unfortunate one sent on the *Centurion* to die at sea. None would have been much of an asset to the fighting strength of the expedition. One Thomas Butler was 57 years old, 'much disordered . . . cannot lift his right arm to his head'; another was 60 years old, 'cut on the crowns of his head a bad cut at Villa Vicioso'; the third was 65 years old, 'shot above the Elbow in Rt. Arm at Namur Cut in the Forehead and Shot in the head at Landen'. There are some particularly poignant entries: Robert Pole, 41 years old (among the youngest of those sent), a man 'bred to the law', but now 'paraletick & very infirm'; and Sergeant Samuel Rogers, 58 years old, 'his Right Eye dim a scarr over that Eyebrow a Pistula in the inside of his thigh . . . was Sir Cha Wager's Cabin Boy when he took the galleons'. That far-off relationship – for it was in 1708 that Rear-Admiral Wager (as he was then) seized the Spanish treasure fleet at Cartagena – was not enough to save Sergeant Rogers from duty and death on the *Gloucester*.

The records of Chelsea Hospital show that its secretary was respon-sible for the task of raising the five companies from among the out-pensioners (after which he sent a memorial to the governing board of the hospital stressing his 'extraordinary service' in doing so). Of those ordered to Portsmouth, only 259 arrived on the ships; for most of those able to walk had deserted. Eighty had disappeared into the streets of Portsmouth the night before they were to have embarked. In London the Lords Justices, the collective head of government during the King's absence on the continent, were inexorable. When they heard that Anson had discharged three of the invalid officers, weak with 'age and infirmity', they immediately ordered them back on board again. The fact that two of the three do not reappear on the ships' muster books suggests that whatever the state of their health they had managed to put a good distance between themselves and the squadron at Spithead. Among the deserters some turned up at intervals before the governing body of the hospital, pleading for their pensions to be restored, and the decision in March 1741 by the relevant minister (the Secretary at War) that this should be done could be taken as an implicit admission that the original decision to send them on Anson's ships was wrong.

The officer commanding the invalids, Lt.-Col. Cracherode, left the

Centurion at Canton in December 1742 to return home. By then he had not only been 'long ill', but he had no men left to command. The muster books of the *Centurion* tell the terrible tale of the fate of the invalids who sailed on the flagship. On 5 August 1740 sixty-three arrived on board; within a week Anson had discharged twenty-three of the feeblest, leaving forty who actually sailed on the *Centurion*. By mid-1741 thirty-six of these unfortunates had died; by October 1742 only one (Acting Captain Alexander Crowden) was still alive. The muster books of the *Gloucester* show that all sixty invalids who sailed on her had perished by mid-1741. The last two survivors, the officers Captain Alexander Douglas and Lieutenant Edward Columbine, died on 13 June and 29 June 1741, less than eleven months after coming on board at Spithead.

To help the invalids storm the bastions of Spanish America three companies of marines arrived in Portsmouth, so raw that most of them had never fired a musket. They had nothing in common with the prestigious Royal Marines of a later era, but were soldiers (often raw recruits), raised to serve with the navy. They were thought fit for shipboard service on the grounds advanced by a minister the previous year: 'In fighting a ship there is no part of the land discipline required but that of loading and firing a musket, and a country fellow from the plough may be in three days taught to do this.' The writer of the authorised account of the voyage put it differently – the marines were 'useless by their ignorance of their duty'. Again, sickness bedevilled the whole undertaking. Throughout May Philip Cavendish complained to the Admiralty that the marines being sent to him were 'growing sick very fast . . . we shall be undone with these new Marines, being devoured with the Itch, Pox and other Distempers'. On 22 May the Lords Commissioners of the Admiralty reported to the Cabinet Council that the marines at Portsmouth 'were so bad, from size, youth, and sickness . . . that they were useless'. On 6 July Sir John Norris wrote from Portsmouth that of 143 marines ordered on board Anson's ships by the Admiralty, only 97 were still in quarters, and of these 66 were sick. It is little surprise that once at sea, the mortality rate among the marines was almost as shocking as that of the invalids. By mid-1741 out of the 82 embarked on board the *Centurion* ten months earlier, 69 had died. On the *Gloucester* the figures were even worse. Of the 46 marines who sailed from Spithead only two were still alive in mid-1741. The authorised account put the number of marines who sailed on the voyage at 210, but the ships' muster books show that the correct figure was 300. This increase of almost 100 men to the number generally thought to have sailed with Anson makes the final toll of casualties even greater than previous estimates.

The invalids and marines were not distributed evenly between the ships of the squadron. The largest number were assigned to the smallest ship, the *Wager*. More than a half of these were invalids, and the ship's muster book suggests that Captain Kidd was more reluctant than Anson to authorise discharges on grounds of health. Only seven out of the 84 invalids sent on board the *Wager* were discharged before sailing, whereas on the flagship Anson discharged more than a third who came on board. The overall figures for the *Wager* show that the invalids and marines far outnumbered the hundred or so crew members, an imbalance that might have had some bearing on the fate of this unlucky ship. The *Wager* was also to carry the greater part of the trade goods. Valued at £15,000, they were under the control of the agents victuallers, Hubert Tassell and Henry Hutchinson.

The position of Tassell and Hutchinson, and the victualling arrangements for the expedition in general, gave rise to considerable uneasiness among the officials at the Victualling Board. The board was under orders from the Admiralty to contract with such victuallers for the supply of Anson's squadron 'as may be most capable of performing the same'. Only Tassell and Hutchinson seem to have responded to this, but their estimates were regarded as unsatisfactory by the Victualling Board. There were several problems. Provisions for the expedition must suffice for twelve months, an unusually long period, and some would be carried on the two merchantmen, the *Anna* and *Industry*. Most foodstuffs – butter and cheese, for example – would not keep anywhere near this length of time, so substitutes were needed. Furthermore, Tassell and Hutchinson would be responsible for securing provisions over and above the twelve months' supply if, as was likely, the ships were still at sea after that time. All this made the question of settling an overall price extraordinarily difficult, especially given the high cost of most basic foodstuffs in the summer of 1740. Tassell and Hutchinson put forward 18d. per man per day as their lowest offer, a costing that appalled the board, which pointed out that this 'farr exceeded the price given on any Contract subsisting with this Board'. The board was negotiating at a disadvantage, for as it complained to the Admiralty they were 'intire strangers' as to the destination of the expedition. Anson thought that given the difficulties of provisioning in a distant part of the world the estimate 'was not dear'. For their part, Tassell and Hutchinson argued that 'it was very uncertain at what Places Provisions could be procured from . . . that probably they should be obliged to buy Provisions in an Enemys Country, so that the risque was very great'. In the end the Admiralty ordered the Victualling Board to accept the contractors' offer, and in addition to let them have an advance of £10,000 to purchase trade goods. The agreement was for the length of the voyage and set out the weekly allowance per man. The list, as accepted by the Victualling Board, included substitutes for beer, butter and cheese.

7 lbs biscuit, flour or bread
7 pints wine, or ½ pint brandy
1 lb fresh beef or turtle and 3 lbs jerked beef
2 lbs pork
1 quart peas or equivalent
3 pints barley meal
1½ lbs jerked beef or 1 lb sugar

This allowance, after deductions for wastage and spoilage, amounted to about 4,000 calories a day, and in terms of protein represented a better diet than many manual workers on land received. The Victualling Board also made arrangements to send with the expedition four portable copper ovens for baking bread, which could be used on shipboard or on shore; and Anson was directed to make certain that his men knew how to set up and dismantle these. Missing from the allowance, however, were vegetables, other greenstuffs and fruit. The assumption which explained this omission from the standard scales of the period was that such perishables would be obtained as and when ships reached port. For Anson's squadron of crowded ships and distant destinations this was a questionable assumption.

The use of private contractors by the Victualling Board was standard practice, but in other ways the role of Tassell and Hutchinson on the Anson expedition was far from standard. Their official position on the ships was as agents victuallers, but the trade goods carried on board complicated their role. Valued at £15,000 the amount seemed excessive if the goods were simply to be exchanged for provisions. As Anson was later to argue through the medium of the authorised account, it was difficult to visualise a situation in which this amount of trade goods would be needed. In a friendly port he would use bills of exchange in the usual way; in an enemy port he would seize what he wanted. Anson suspected that Tassell and Hutchinson had their own agenda in mind, but his remonstrances were disregarded by 'some considerable persons' in the government, who authorised payment for two-thirds of the cost of the goods, and seem to have envisaged them being used to establish a profitable trade in the South Sea. To the outside eye, certainly, the agents victuallers had gained a privileged position on the expedition. So, while the Admiralty refused Anson the help of a secretary to deal with his accounts and correspondence, Tassell and Hutchinson brought on board the *Centurion* their own staff of two secretaries and two servants. As Norris confided in the pages of his diary, the whole murky business of the trade goods made him wonder whether the expedition was for private profit or to strike at the enemy.

Others coming on board the ships were to play significant parts in recording the events of the voyage. The Revd Richard Walter, a Cambridge graduate, was chaplain of the *Centurion*, and 22 years old at the beginning of the voyage. In 1748 he would appear as the author of the best-selling authorised account, *A Voyage Round the World by George Anson*. Pascoe Thomas was 'schoolmaster' on the *Centurion*, his job to instruct the midshipmen and other youngsters 'in writing, arithmetic and the study of navigation'. Keeping a journal was not part of his official duties, but his *True and Impartial Journal*, published in 1745, was based on records he kept during the voyage. His stance was that of an independent, sometimes censorious, observer of events, and his book was an effective counter to some of the more anodyne remarks of the authorised account published under Walter's name. The first of the full-length published accounts to appear was the *Authentick Journal* of 'John Philips', allegedly an officer on the *Centurion*, and although there was no officer of that name on the voyage the book was clearly based on a genuine if somewhat limited log book. Published in September 1744, it was pirated and extracted by other publishers who produced a variety of almost indistinguishable books on the voyage: *An Authentic Account*, *An Authentic and Genuine Journal*, and so on. The calamitous events on the *Wager* produced its own flurry of books, which will be looked at in their proper place.

All commissioned officers were instructed to keep logs, and many of these have survived from the voyage. A typical log book was arranged in double-page spreads (see pp. 72–3). The left-hand page showed navigational data arranged for each day in tabular form. It began with the date and went on to record wind direction, course, latitude (if possible, by estimate checked by noon-day observation) and longitude. The right-hand page contained daily entries of a more general kind, and varied in length depending on the events of the day and the inclination of the writer. Occasional one-day inconsistencies in dates between shipboard logs and books published after the voyage are explained by the twelve-hour difference between 'ship time' and 'land time'. The ship's day extended from noon to noon, not midnight to midnight. So, the entry for 10 June in a seaman's log would run from noon to midnight of 9 June (land time) and from midnight to noon of 10 June (land time). It was one sign among many to newcomers to the sea that a ship formed a separate world, with its own rules and conventions. Out of the score or more log books from the voyage that survive, those by Matthew Michell, who became captain of the *Gloucester*, and Philip Saumarez, lieutenant on the *Centurion*, are full and informative. Most of the others are sparse affairs in which the writer struggled to pen more than a line or two in an attempt to fill the daily journal entry. Free expressions of opinion were discouraged by the knowledge that all logs and journals had to be handed in to the Admiralty at the end of the voyage.

The master and other warrant officers were also expected to keep records relating to their own particular duties. Some of the most important of these for Anson's voyage, notably the surgeons' journals, no longer exist. Lawrence Millechamp, who finished the voyage as purser of the *Centurion*, wrote a journal after the event that had nothing to do with his duties as purser, but everything to do with the prize-money dispute that ran its tortuous course for three years after the expedition's return. The evidence of shipboard witnesses produced during the legal hearings into this dispute has much detail on key moments during the voyage that is not found elsewhere. Finally, a large number of letters and reports, mostly official in nature, that were written during the voyage have survived. In all, the mass of evidence is varied in nature and intimidating in size, but it lacks one element that modern commentators would regard as essential. Nowhere is there any direct record of the lower-deck point of view.

By mid-August Anson was at last ready to sail, but the delays continued. Strong westerlies penned the ships up in harbour, not only Anson's, but also a huge fleet of transports and merchant vessels bound for the West Indies, which Anson was to help escort for the first part of their voyage. Attempts by this unwieldy convoy to get to sea resulted in nothing but damage and confusion, and on Anson's ships there was panic among the invalids and marines as ships crashed into each other during the hours of darkness. It was 18 September before Anson finally got clear of St Helen's. Two days later he hoisted his commodore's broad pendant as he took up escort duties over a convoy of 152 ships, which by now included fleets bound for the American colonies, the Levant and the western Mediterranean. In the first calm weather for months the great assembly of ships made a magnificent sight, but for Anson the nit-picking tedium of convoy duty meant a further week's delay before he parted company with the slow-moving merchantmen and set course for Madeira.

An expedition whose commander and ships had been chosen in November 1739, and whose instructions were drawn up in January 1740, had taken the best part of a year to get to sea. A year later the opposition newspaper the *Craftsman* satirised such delays in its portrait of the unheroic figure of Will Wimble, 'always about to set off on an expedition, but never managed to leave Spithead'. The squadron's slowness in getting away meant that it might well be faced with a passage around Cape Horn in the southern hemisphere autumn months, when the westerly gales were at their worst.

A more immediate worry was that the expedition was no longer secret. Before Anson sailed, he knew that he had lost his most effective weapon – surprise. In June British warships stopped a Dutch vessel in the Caribbean with Spanish officials on board. Their papers showed that the Spanish government was aware of Anson's expedition and its objectives, and had drawn up instructions for its officials in Lima, Mexico City and Manila. The source of this information was a French agent, or agents, in London whose reports of Anson's expedition were transmitted from Versailles to Madrid. These reports had details of Anson's ships and possible destination, and are an impressive tribute to the efficiency of the French secret service. As early as January 1740, while Anson's instructions were still being drawn up, the French government was informing its ambassador in Madrid that 'Mons. Hanson' was under orders to take six ships round Cape Horn and into the South Sea. The only British response to the threat of espionage was the heading of correspondence relating to the voyage, 'Expedition to the West Indies' – a device that caused more confusion among Admiralty filing clerks and the London press than to the enemy. Letters in the French Foreign Office archives show that the government of Cardinal Fleury, officially neutral, was bringing pressure on Spain to intercept Anson, and in October a force of five powerful warships under the command of Admiral Don José Pizarro left Santander for Madeira, Anson's first port of call. It seemed that Anson's squadron might come to grief even before it had crossed the Atlantic.

II

The Ordeal Begins

'Methinks I still hear the humble Roaring of the Winds, and
see the Sea rising into Mountains, the Ships clambering as it
was those Hills, and then sinking into the most frightful Valley,
the Rigging torn from the Masts, and the Sails split into a
thousand Pieces shivering in the Wind; Wildness and Despair
in every Man's Countenance, as thinking each Moment would
be his last.'

Anon., *A Voyage to the South Seas . . . By Commodore Anson* (1745)

THE VOYAGE FROM the Channel ports to Madeira normally took two
weeks; it was a sign of the ill-fortune that seemed to dog Anson that
because of contrary winds it took him almost six. On the *Gloucester* two
of the invalid captains died, Arnaud and Colley, a fact that Anson reported
to the Duke of Newcastle without comment. When he arrived at Funchal
on 25 October 1740 Anson heard the unwelcome news from Portuguese
officials that ships of the line, thought to be Spanish, had been sighted
lying off the western end of the island – almost certainly Admiral Pizarro's
squadron. Although a boat sent out by Anson saw no sign of enemy
ships, watering was completed as quickly as possible. The *Gloucester*'s
captain, Richard Norris, pleaded ill health and was allowed to return
home. In the first of several promotions and replacements, he was succeeded by Matthew Michell, first lieutenant on the *Centurion*. Michell
came on board his new command with two bullocks to present to the
ship's company, but his gesture was overshadowed by the news that the
second lieutenant, mate, coxswain and a midshipman had all deserted
that day.

On 5 November the ships left Madeira, showing no lights at night,

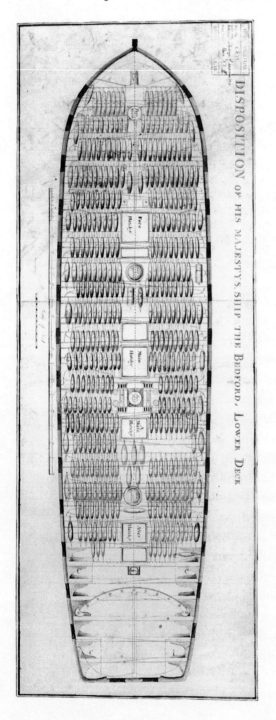

DISPOSITION OF HIS MAJESTY'S SHIP THE BEDFORD, LOWER DECK

and headed for the South Atlantic and their next port of call on the coast of Brazil. On board there was intense speculation as to why Pizarro's squadron had made so little effort to intercept them. As the writer of the authorised account pointed out, merely the sight of enemy ships would have done great, perhaps irreparable, damage to the purpose of the expedition; for the huge quantities of stores that cluttered the decks and holds of the ships would have had to be thrown overboard if the ships were to be put into fighting condition. As it was, Anson retained one of the two victuallers with the squadron, the *Anna* pink, though the master of the other insisted on keeping to the terms of his charter agreement with the Admiralty and left the squadron on 20 November. It took three days to unload the stores he carried, and during this time Anson gave orders to cut extra scuttles to let more air into the stifling areas between decks. As the ships lay to, they 'were plagued with a prodigious quantity of flies', probably from rotting provisions on board. After

The gun-deck of the *Bedford* (70 guns). This plan showing the hammock arrangement of a single watch reveals the cramped conditions below decks of a man-of-war in the mid-eighteenth century. The overcrowding would have been worse on Anson's ships because of the need to accommodate marines and invalids as well as the complement of regular crew.

little more than two months at sea typhus and dysentery had already taken a grip on the crews, and the reports to Anson from his captains at this time told a worrying story. The *Severn* had 70 sick; the *Pearl*'s crew in general were 'very sickly'; while on the *Gloucester* there were 'between Sixty and Seventy Men Sick and very ill with fevers between Decks and for want of Air'. The addition to the squadron of more than 500 invalids and marines had brought intolerable overcrowding. The *Centurion* was more than 100 over complement, the *Gloucester* almost 100, and the *Severn* and *Pearl* fifty or so each. But the most worrying situation was on the *Wager*. Her full crew complement was 120, but she sailed with only 105, and they were outnumbered by 142 marines and invalids.

On most amphibious operations the land forces were carried on transports. The ships commanded by Sir Chaloner Ogle that took troops under Lord Charles Cathcart to join Admiral Vernon in the West Indies left Spithead on 26 October, and reached Jamaica in early January 1741. Even this comparatively short passage produced a mortality rate among the troops on the transports of 8 percent, and a sickness rate of 23 percent. Anson had no transports with him, and the invalids and marines were crammed into the warships. Ships' plans from this period show how tightly packed the between-decks of a warship were with her regular complement of men. Hammocks were slung a regulation fourteen inches apart, though under normal conditions the rotating watch system allowed twice that space for the men off watch. The addition of a quarter or more to the normal crew complement was bad enough, but the problem was worsened by the fact that the extra men were landlubbers, unused to the sea and its motion. The marines and invalids were encumbrances, useless and redundant until land operations were imminent. Even those who were healthy and strong would be expected to remain below most of the time, for on deck they would be in the way of the crew. In the stinking and stifling darkness between decks, they existed on a diet of salt meat and ship's biscuit, with a ration of water of perhaps a couple of pints a day. The lot of the sick, in particular, is hardly to be contemplated. In *Roderick Random*, Tobias Smollett described his experiences as surgeon's mate on a man-of-war which sailed in 1741 to the West Indies. As a writer Smollett was not much given to understatement, but there is no reason to doubt his report on conditions in the ship's sick quarters.

> Here I saw about fifty miserable distempered wretches, suspended in rows, so huddled one upon another, that not more than fourteen inches space was allotted for each with his bed and bedding; and deprived of the light of day, as well as of fresh air; breathing nothing but a noisome atmosphere of the morbid steams exhaling from their own excrements and diseased bodies, devoured with vermin hatched in the filth that surrounded them, and destitute of every convenience necessary for people in that helpless condition.

In the pages of the authorised account the writer complained how little effort had been made by the navy to conduct proper experiments with the various devices suggested to improve the flow of air between decks. This he put down to 'a settled contempt and hatred of all kinds of innovations'. The criticism may have been a tilt at Sir Jacob Acworth, the veteran surveyor of the navy. The inventor Samuel Sutton had a sad story to tell about his experiences at Acworth's hands at this time. Armed with a supporting letter from Sir Charles Wager, Sutton asked for an appointment with Acworth to discuss the possibility of testing on shipboard one of his machines for circulating air. Having been ignored by Acworth for a week, he was finally given an appointment for 7 a.m. On the day, Sutton was kept waiting outside Acworth's office until the evening, and when the surveyor emerged he cut short Sutton's explanation of his device with the words 'that no experiment should be made, if he could hinder it'. It may not have been a coincidence that in 1753, during Anson's term as First Lord of the Admiralty, the navy adopted an improved system of ventilation by a huge bellows ('the Ship's Lungs') devised by Dr Stephen Hales, and a few years later approved Sutton's air-pump. On Anson's voyage the crews had to improvise, waving pieces of thin board backwards and forwards in an attempt to keep the air circulating.

The ships had not yet been at sea long enough for scurvy to be a

serious threat, but typhus and dysentery swept through them as they
sailed southwest across the Atlantic. Typhus, or 'ship fever' as it was often
called, was transmitted by body lice, and the hot, crowded conditions on
Anson's ships encouraged its spread. The symptoms of typhus were fever,
severe headaches, prostration, skin rash and neurological disturbance. It
carried a high mortality rate that increased with the age of the sufferer.
Especially depressing was the death in early December, probably from
typhus, of the expedition's senior surgeon, Thomas Waller of the *Centurion*. In the humid, sultry weather of equatorial latitudes 'our men grew
distempered and sickly', Lieutenant Philip Saumarez wrote, and 'a languid
fever' made its appearance. Some distraction was afforded by the ceremony
of Crossing of the Line, but Lawrence Millechamp, the *Tryal*'s purser,
describes a more brutal business than that of a jovial King Neptune and
his attendants ducking, lathering and shaving initiates in a canvas bath
on deck. On the *Tryal* at least any man who could not afford the forfeit
of brandy and sugar was hoisted to the main- or foreyard, and then
dropped a half-dozen times into the sea until he was 'as wet as a drowned
rat'.

On 21 December the squadron reached St Catherine's (Isla de Santa
Catarina), a small island off the coast of Brazil often visited in the past
by English and French ships heading for the South Sea. Eighty sick men
were sent ashore from the *Centurion* alone. There they lay in makeshift
tents made of old sails. Once the ships were cleared their below-decks
were scrubbed clean of filth and excrement, smoked to drive out rats and
other vermin, and then washed with vinegar. But the land had its own
dangers, for mosquitoes swarmed on the low-lying, marshy ground where
the hospital tents were pitched, and malaria soon appeared. The worst
casualties were on the *Centurion* and *Severn*, which between them lost
seventy-five men on the Atlantic crossing and at St Catherine's. Although
twenty-eight men from the *Centurion* died during the stay, the number
of her sick still increased from eighty to ninety-six. Anson's hopes of
getting away from the island as soon as he had watered and taken on
board fresh provisions were thwarted when the *Tryal*'s mainmast and
foremast were found to be defective, and it took almost a month to repair
them. In many ways the island, which had long been a hospitable refuge

for privateers, was a disappointment. The ships' logs show considerable quantities of fresh beef being taken on board, but how much was received in the way of other fresh provisions is uncertain. The authorised account speaks of the 'great plenty' of fruit and vegetables, and lists them in mouth-watering detail: pineapples, peaches, grapes, oranges, lemons, melons, apricots, plantains, onions, potatoes. But it went on to complain that these were for sale only at exorbitant prices, and in his account Pascoe Thomas insisted that the total amount of fresh provisions bought was only enough for a day's consumption.

Here, as elsewhere, Anson was relying for guidance on the published narratives of earlier voyages, especially those by Frézier and Shelvocke. Unlike most of his trading or privateering contemporaries, Frézier was a capable engineer and mathematician, sent to Chile and Peru in 1712–14 by the French government to survey their coasts and ports. His account of his voyage was translated into English and appeared in 1717 as *A Voyage to the South-Sea, and along the coasts of Chili and Peru*, and Anson and his officers referred to it with more approval than they did to the narratives of their own countrymen in the same region. Since the days of Frézier and Shelvocke St Catherine's had been brought more closely under the authority of the Portuguese crown. Fortifications guarded the harbour, and a new governor, Brigadier José Silva Pais, soon made it clear that he was no friend of the English. Papers later seized by Anson's men in the South Sea revealed that the governor had sent details of Anson's arrival to Buenos Aires, where Pizarro's squadron had arrived after its abortive wait for Anson off Madeira. Pizarro in the *Asia* (66), together with the *Guipuscoa* (74), *Hermiona* (54), *Esperanza* (50) and *San Estevan* (40), was waiting at the mouth of the Plate for provisions from Buenos Aires when the news of Anson's presence to the north reached him. He put to sea immediately, but sailed south in an attempt to get round the Horn before the British squadron. This decision was to have fateful consequences.

The accounts reflect the tension on board the ships as they left St Catherine's on 18 January 1741 for enemy waters and Cape Horn. Anson's instructions had given him discretion to take the Strait of Magellan route to the South Sea, but there is no discussion of this alternative among Anson's papers or in any of the accounts. In choosing the open-sea passage around the Horn, Anson was following the preferred route of most seamen of his time. First he intended to call at Port St Julian (San Julián) on the coast of Patagonia to take on salt, but the passage there was marked by dramatic incident. Only four days out from St Catherine's the repaired mainmast of the *Tryal* gave way in a storm, and the *Gloucester* had to take the sloop in tow. During the same storm the *Pearl* lost sight of the squadron, her captain Dandy Kidd died, and the first lieutenant, Sampson Salt, took command. Kidd's death so early in the voyage, following hard on Captain Norris's hasty return to England, increased apprehension that the expedition was ill-fated. If later accounts can be trusted, Dandy Kidd on his death-bed warned his officers that they would experience nothing but 'poverty, vermin, death and destruction'. Whatever the truth of this, Salt's nerve was soon to be tested to the utmost. On 9 February, on course for Port St Julian, he sighted what he took to be the five ships of the squadron, the leading vessel carrying English colours and flying the broad red pendant of the commodore. Flapping spritsails obscured much of their hulls, and it was only when the ships were within gunshot that Salt, who had already hoisted out his boat to go on board the *Centurion*, realised it was Pizarro's squadron bearing down on him. In a frantic response the *Pearl*'s crew crowded on sail, threw lumber, temporary cabins and water-casks overboard, and cut loose the longboat. In the end the luckiest of lucky chances saved the day, for the Spanish ships stood off as the *Pearl* appeared to be heading straight for a shoal. This proved to be no more than fish-spawn discolouring the surface of the water, but crossing it gave the *Pearl* a precious safety margin until darkness fell.

Despite this alarming evidence that Pizarro's ships were somewhere in the offing, Anson had no alternative but to persevere with his plan to call at Port St Julian, for the *Tryal*'s shattered masts had to be repaired before the passage round the Horn could be faced. As the ships sailed south along the Patagonian coast they saw whales, penguins, seals and albatrosses. The entrance to the harbour of St Julian was difficult to spot against the background of high ground, and in the end the *Centurion* had to send out her boats to find it. Once anchored, the crews found a bleak and inhospitable setting. There were no trees and no fresh water,

Anson's squadron off the coast of Patagonia. Engraving in *Anson's Voyage* (1748) after a
drawing by Peircy Brett. One ship (either the *Severn* or the *Pearl*) is well ahead of the
rest of the squadron, and not included in this view. The middle vessel is the *Tryal*,
shown here with only a stump of a mainmast, and being towed by the *Gloucester*.

and for those on the ships who had read their voyage narratives, the
harbour was a place of ill omen. More than two centuries earlier it
had been the scene of a mutiny on Magellan's voyage, the first ever
circumnavigation; and the gibbet on which the mutineers had been
hanged was still standing almost 60 years later when in 1578 Drake had
Thomas Doughty executed on his voyage round the world. On the *Gloucester* Captain Michell identified the place of Doughty's execution by
Drake's name, the Island of True Justice. More to the point was the
realisation that the good white salt that Narborough had reported during
his visit in 1670 – enough to fill 1,000 ships, he had claimed – no longer
existed in any quantity. Meanwhile, it took nine days to carry out the
necessary repairs to the *Tryal*. The mainmast, which had lost its top
twelve feet, was left in place, and a spare topmast was converted into a

foremast. This enforced shortening of the *Tryal*'s masts was probably the saving of the sloop in the storms to come.

The natural hazards of the passage round the Horn was not the only danger that faced Anson's ships, for an encounter with Pizarro's squadron could not be ruled out. Cannon that had been lowered into the holds in order to improve the ships' stability were remounted, and as many stores and provisions as possible moved back into the *Anna*. With the death of Captain Kidd there was a general reshuffling of officers. George Murray was made captain of the *Pearl*, and David Cheap went to the *Wager*. When he had recovered from illness, Charles Saunders was to command the *Tryal*; until then Philip Saumarez was appointed captain of the sloop. Before the voyage was properly under way, only the *Centurion* and *Severn* still had the captains they had sailed with from Spithead. This was bound to have an unsettling effect on morale given the personal nature of loyalty on shipboard. A seaman's allegiance was not to the navy as such, but to his ship and especially to his officers. The strength of the bond had been demonstrated by the wholesale transfer of the *Adventure*'s crew to the *Gloucester* when Captain Norris moved ship, but his departure was only one of several in the first months of the voyage.

The instructions Anson gave to his captains in case of separation reflected the fact that the squadron was leaving neutral waters for enemy coasts. Once around the Horn, the squadron was to rendezvous at Nuestra Señora de Socorro (today's Isla Guamblin), an island in the Chonos archipelago off the coast of southern Chile. From there it would sail to attack Valdivia, which was also appointed as the next rendezvous. The choice of Valdivia as the first objective in the South Sea was very much in line with Henry Hutchinson's recommendation of the autumn of 1739. The fortifications of the port, he reported, had been damaged by an earthquake, and hostile Indians in the interior prevented supplies and reinforcements from reaching it except by sea. Its capture would provide a base for the squadron where the ships could be careened and repaired, and its temperate climate would enable the crews to recover from the rigours of their passage round Cape Horn. Finally, Anson ordered any ship that did not find the squadron at either Socorro or Valdivia to sail to the island of Juan Fernández. For all the detail of the rendezvous

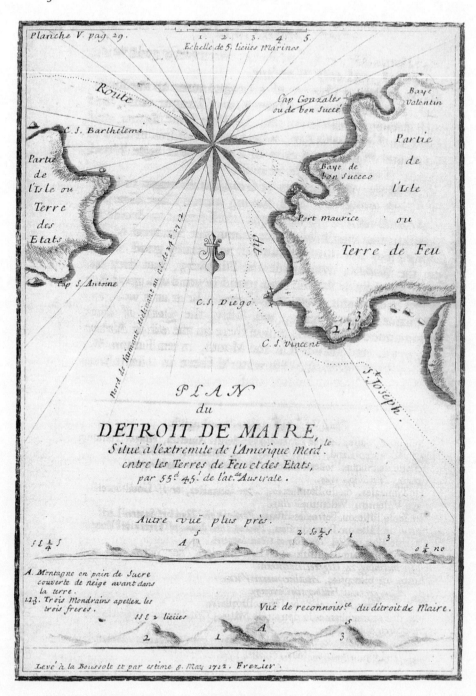

Chart of the Strait Le Maire by A. F. Frézier, 1712

instructions, Anson was adamant that the squadron must keep together, and ordered all ships to remain within two miles of the flagship. Any officer of the watch who allowed his ship to drift off station would answer for it at his peril.

On 7 March 1741 Anson's squadron reached Strait Le Maire, the gateway to the Pacific for ships attempting the open-sea passage around Cape Horn rather than threading their way through the tortuous channels of the Strait of Magellan. The weather was clear and sunny, the sea calm, and a brisk following wind took the seven vessels of the squadron through the strait in only two hours. We had 'a prodigious fine passage' through the opening, Michell wrote, with a good view of the land on either side that confirmed the accuracy of Frézier's chart. After the delays and alarms of the five-month passage across the Atlantic and down the coasts of South America, the way seemed open to the South Sea and its riches. It was a turning point on the voyage, but not in the way imagined on the ships that morning. In sombre retrospect, the authorised account recalled, it 'was the last chearful day that the greatest part of us would ever live to enjoy'.

The last two vessels of the squadron were not quite through the strait when the sky darkened and violent squalls from the south threatened to dash the entire squadron on the rocky coast of Staten Land. When the ships finally clawed their way clear they had been blown more than twenty miles east of Staten Land. It was the beginning of a three-month ordeal as the squadron tried to round Cape Horn in the teeth of continual westerly gales and huge seas. At first Anson ordered the *Tryal* ahead of the squadron to warn of icebergs, but after only two days Saumarez had to plead for relief. Carrying barely enough sail to keep clear of the ships astern, but still too much for safety, the sloop was pitching so violently that the men out on the yards were repeatedly plunged into the freezing water. Finally, Saumarez reported to Anson that the sloop was now rolling so much that in the tops his lookouts were seasick, while on deck the cannon were awash. Even if the lookouts spotted ice ahead, the sloop would not be able to fire her guns to signal danger to the rest of the squadron. At this the *Tryal* was withdrawn from her exposed position,

Anson's squadron approaching the Strait of Le Maire. Engraving in *Anson's Voyage* (1748) after a drawing by Peircy Brett. All six vessels of the squadron are sailing in close company, together with the *Anna* pink. The storm clouds are shown massing over Tierra del Fuego to the west; the lower-lying coastline of Staten Land is to the east.

and the 40-gun *Pearl* took her place, leaving Saumarez to write in his journal 'that really life is not worth pursuing at the expense of such hardships'.

Because of the delays in his sailing from England, Anson had arrived in the waters off the tip of South America in the southern hemisphere autumn, when the equinoctial gales were at their fiercest. A master mariner of recent times who has taken a square-rigged ship round the Horn has described 'the ghastly succession of tremendous storms which raced round the world' to fling themselves across the sea south of the Cape. They came always from the west, and sailing ships had to face 'a long-continued, relentless fight against violent wind and appalling seas'.

As Anson's crews braced themselves for this ordeal, they were already weakened by dysentery and typhus, and now scurvy made its terrible appearance. Long the scourge of the seas, scurvy was a mystery to the medical profession, its causes unknown and its treatment uncertain. It had been the deadly accompaniment to the long European oceanic voyages that began with Vasco da Gama (1497–8) and Ferdinand Magellan (1519–22). Their crews suffered from what was recognisably scurvy, though it had not yet been named, still less diagnosed. On da Gama's voyage it struck as his ships rounded the Cape of Good Hope into the Indian Ocean. 'Gums became swollen, teeth fell out and mouths became so foul that da Gama ordered his men to use their own urine as a mouthwash.'

The grim experiences of Samuel de Champlain and his men wintering on the icebound St Lawrence in 1535–6 were an ominous portent for many voyagers. All except ten of his crew of 110 were disabled, and Champlain's description of their symptoms is an early example of what would soon become a familiar litany of suffering at sea. 'Some lost all their strength, their legs became swollen and inflamed, while the sinews contracted and turned as black as coal . . . then the disease would mount to the hips, thighs, shoulders, arms and neck. And all had their mouths so tainted, that the gums rotted away down to the roots of the teeth, which nearly all fell out.' By the late sixteenth century English seamen, making their first long voyages to the Pacific and East Indies, had found a name for their affliction, though the eccentric spelling of the period produced a range of variants: 'scarby', 'scurbute', 'skurvie'. After his South Sea voyage of 1593 Sir Richard Hawkins suggested the use of lemons and oranges to counteract what he called 'the plague of the sea', though he also recommended two drops of oil of vitriol (sulphuric acid) diluted in water to cleanse and ease the stomach. His advice depended on having access to ports where citrus fruit could be obtained, and it was taken an important step further by the East India Company, for on many of its ships lemon juice was carried on board. Sir James Lancaster on a voyage to Sumatra in 1601 gave his crew three spoonfuls of lemon juice each day, and as far as possible kept them off salt meat. There are many references to lemon juice or 'lemon water' in the records of the East India Company in the seventeenth century, though the difficulty of procuring and preserving sufficient quantities remained a constant problem.

During the seventeenth century the navy was not much concerned with this particular aspect of health on shipboard, for it made few long voyages. In the overseas operations that began in earnest in the War of the Spanish Succession (1702–13) the main area of combat was the West Indies, where diseases of the land were more feared than those of the sea. Scurvy was as yet a peripheral problem, though as patrolling squadrons off the French and Spanish coasts began to keep the sea for months at a time it became a matter of increasing concern. For reasons that are not totally clear the experience of the East India Company, which by now was making regular voyages to China and back, seems not to have registered with those responsible for health in the navy. On board ship, surgeons were warrant officers, not commissioned officers, and although some able doctors joined their ranks much of their work consisted in doling out medicines of dubious utility to the sick, and performing crude amputations on those wounded in battle. Their views on the causes of scurvy seem not to have been sought by the physicians on shore, whose explanations ranged from a melancholic humour to exposure to sea air, from lack of ventilation below decks to an unremitting diet of salt meat. Some pernicious nonsense had clouded the issue, notably the claim in William Cockburn's third edition of *Sea Diseases*, published in 1736, that scurvy and idleness went hand in hand (a view he later modified). Another unhelpful assertion was that lemons should be avoided because they caused enteritis.

The Admiralty was not blind to the problem of scurvy as it might affect Anson's ships, and took medical advice before the expedition sailed. In June 1740 it considered Dr Cockburn's suggestion that as well as a solution of vinegar being used to wash the interior of ships' hulls, 2 oz. a day should be given to each seaman to dilute and drink. The Admiralty accepted the general usefulness of vinegar 'in preventing the Scurvey, Fluxes and Fevers', but referred the matter of its internal use to the Royal College of Physicians. The next month the college reported, again at the request of the Admiralty, on the possible merits of vitriol as a preventive against scurvy, and 'unanimously agreed it would be a very great Means to preserve them from that disorder'. Accordingly, Anson's surgeons were supplied with elixir of vitriol, in which sulphuric acid was mixed with alcohol, sugar and spices. Crab-apple juice, as recommended by the Dutch physician Hermann Boerhaave, was also listed as a possible antiscorbutic for the voyage, but then disappears from view. The Navy Board's part in all this was to supply, almost certainly without proper medical advice, a well-known patent medicine, Ward's drop and pill. This was a fearsome purgative and diuretic concocted by a quack doctor, Joshua Ward. There was a request from Anson himself for an extra supply of tamarinds, and this was approved. Tamarinds had been used by the East India Company as an antiscorbutic when no lemons were available; but there was no likelihood that the pulp of this acidic fruit would keep for any length of time. Of lemons, lemon juice, or 'rob' of lemon there is no mention in the documents of 1740; even if convinced of the effectiveness of lemons, to provide a supply for 2,000 men that would keep on a long voyage would be beyond the capacity of the Admiralty.

The first outbreaks of scurvy were described in harrowing detail by the journal-writers on the ships. As reported in the authorised account, the most common symptoms were large spots and ulcers appearing over the whole body, swollen legs, putrid gums and rotting flesh. Physical disintegration was accompanied by depression and lethargy, often mistaken by officers for laziness, and greeted with curses and beatings. Worst affected were the pensioners on board, veterans of long-distant campaigns, some of whom found their old wounds opening up again. One man who had made a complete recovery from wounds received at the Battle of the Boyne in 1690 found, 50 years later as he lay dying on the *Centurion*, that it was as if they had never healed. One of his limbs, broken in that battle and long since set, fractured again. On the *Gloucester* Captain Michell wondered at the variety of symptoms among the sufferers: 'some lost their Senses, some had their Sinews contracted in such a Manner as to draw their Limbs close up to their Thyghs, and some rotted away.' The replacement surgeon on the *Centurion*, Henry Ettrick, was wedded to the theory that scurvy was caused by poor blood circulation in cold weather. It could best be prevented by 'any food of a glutinous nature, such as salt fish, bread, and several sorts of grain'. If not quite a death sentence, such a diet would do little for anyone suffering from scurvy.

Only after Anson's voyage, and partly as a result of it, did James Lind carry out research that provided experimental evidence of the antiscorbutic properties of lemon juice, though he had no more explanation of why it should be effective than had any of his predecessors. On his celebrated Pacific voyages Cook set no particular store by lemon juice, and not until the 1790s did it become a regular navy issue. Only with the discovery of the existence of vitamins in the early twentieth century was scurvy properly diagnosed as resulting from a deficiency of vitamin C or ascorbutic acid. This was shown to be an essential element in the body tissues, and could only be obtained through the food supply. Even in men with an adequate body store of vitamin C, after a few weeks without an intake the amount of ascorbutic acid in the body would fall below measurable levels; after that scurvy might appear at any time. Greens, milk and citrus fruits all contain vitamin C in varying degrees, so a reasonably balanced diet was enough to ward off scurvy. In situations where such a diet was difficult to obtain – in prison or in an army involved in siege operations, for example – scurvy was always a danger. But it was at sea, and especially on long oceanic voyages in the days of sail, that men were most likely to go without fresh provisions for months on end.

The outbreaks of scurvy on Anson's ships were among the worst in recorded maritime history, for reasons that are not difficult to see. Many on board, particularly the elderly pensioners and the marines, were in poor health before sailing. The overcrowding on the vessels meant that there was little room for livestock – the cattle, pigs and sheep whose farmyard noises and smells were a familiar part of the scene below and above deck on ships bound for distant parts, and whose regular slaughtering provided fresh meat. With the Admiralty under strain as it fitted out great battle-fleets in the summer of 1740, Anson had to struggle to get attention. Many of his crews had been kept on board for months during the long delays at Spithead, and although they may have obtained some fresh foodstuffs from shore boats coming out to the ships, these would have been in short supply after the severe winter. The muster books of the *Centurion* show that 130 of her crew had been on board for at least a year – not an ideal preparation for the voyage ahead. Most would have left the ship on impressment or other duties during that time, but rarely for more than a day or so. When the squadron reached St Catherine's Anson had obtained supplies of fresh beef, but some of it was so 'bruised and stinking' that it had to be dumped overboard, and there is little reference to the buying of greens and fruit. By the time the squadron reached the Strait Le Maire it had passed well beyond normal safety limits. On the *Gloucester* the first cases of scurvy were reported on 11 March 1741, almost six months after the squadron had sailed from Spithead. In addition to the ravages of scurvy, modern medical commentators have identified multiple vitamin deficiencies from the journal descriptions: niacin deficiency, which produced 'idiotism, lunacy, convulsions'; thiamine deficiency, which led to beri-beri; and vitamin A deficiency, which affected the eyesight and caused night blindness.

During the weeks of continuous storms as the ships tried to beat their way around the Horn, men died in their hundreds. Account after account dwelt on the monstrous seas, and these were not just cases of timorous landlubbers aghast at their first sniff of rough weather. The experienced Captain Edward Legge of the *Pearl* wrote that in all his years at sea he had seen nothing like the mountainous waves that battered his ship. The *Centurion*, at 1,000 tons the largest vessel in the squadron, was thrown around like a toy ship by waves so high that they broke over the quarter-deck before pouring below. On the decks gratings were torn up, galleries smashed, and the heads and other structures washed away. Sails were ripped to shreds, and shrouds broken. On the *Gloucester* the mainyard broke, and the great seas pounding across the decks wrecked her barge and pinnace. The *Tryal* sloop was kept afloat only through continual use of the pumps, while the *Wager* in one jolting roll of the sea lost both her mizen-mast and main topsail yard. In freezing weather, with the gales accompanied by snow and sleet, the sea came through the leaking decks and upper works to soak everything and everyone below. Since the galley-fires could not be lit there was no hot food. Unable to wash, and with even the elementary sanitary facilities of the heads out of reach, the crews were covered with lice and other vermin. Dozens of men were injured as they were hurled about the decks; others lost their handholds aloft in the biting cold and fell overboard. Some lost toes and fingers through frost-bite, while most pitiful of all was the plight of the sick. Huddled below in wet hammocks, they received little or no attention or even food during the worst days of the passage. In a desperate attempt to keep his flagship in touch with the rest of the squadron, and unable to set any sails, Anson ordered what fit men he had aloft into the shrouds and along the yards so that their bodies gave enough resistance to the wind for the helmsman to wear ship. During this manoeuvre one of his best seamen was thrown into the sea and, to the horror of those watching helplessly from the ship, continued to swim strongly in the huge seas as he fell astern. Fifty years later, William Cowper was so moved by the pathos of this incident that he wrote a long and affecting poem about it, 'The Cast-Away'. Soon, individual deaths called for only the briefest log entry. In Michell's log of the *Gloucester* reports of deaths were removed from the main daily entry, and simply noted in the margin. On the *Centurion* the crew were so weak that dead bodies, some sown into their hammocks, others not, washed about the deck, for no man had the strength to heave them overboard.

It was a mark of the endurance of crews and ships alike that by the beginning of April the battered squadron was still afloat, and almost miraculously had kept together. Even the tiny *Tryal* was there, a tribute to her acting captain, Philip Saumarez, and his crew. To judge by the draft of a letter he wrote to Anson but perhaps never sent, Saumarez felt that this feat had gone unrecognised, and that compared with more favoured officers on the expedition he had 'a very indifferent prospect'. Any feelings of elation at getting round the Horn were short-lived, for the most disheartening moment of all was still to come. The ships' masters estimated that they had sailed ten degrees of longitude clear of the most westerly point of Tierra del Fuego. Secure with this margin of safety, the squadron was at last able to turn north towards the open waters of the Pacific. On 10 April the *Severn* and *Pearl* disappeared from sight, a cause for concern, though not undue alarm, for they would make their own way to the rendezvous at Socorro. Then, during the night of 13–14 April the incredulous lookouts on the leading vessel, the *Anna* pink, saw a lee shore only two miles away, and fired a gun and showed lights to warn the rest of the squadron. The nearby land was probably the jutting prom-ontory of Cape Noir at the western extremity of a small island (Isla Noir) off Tierra del Fuego, and it was 300 miles east of the ships' estimated position. From the *Gloucester* Mitchell could see the dark outline of ominous cliffs in the starlight, 'like two black Towers of an Extraordinary height'. One by one the ships fought to keep off the rocks, and in the end were able to make the open sea again. Providentially, it was the first clear night for more than a month.

The near disaster was a terrifying example of the perils that accom-panied the difficulty of determining longitude at sea. In the pre-chronometer age the sailing masters on Anson's ships were dependent on dead reckoning, but they had made a totally inadequate allowance for the 'drag' effects of wind and current as they struggled west in high

The squadron off Cape Horn. Engraving in Anon., *An Authentic and Genuine Journal of Commodore Anson's Expedition* (1744). This impressionistic view shows, though not to scale, the ships against the rocky coastline of Tierra del Fuego. To the far west lies Cape Noir, where the squadron almost met disaster in April 1741.

latitudes. As Saumarez admitted, they had warnings enough from earlier voyagers coming round the Horn. Frézier had been specific about ships that 'find themselves upon the Land, when they thought they weather'd the Cape [Horn], and were 40 or 50 Leagues out to sea'. The size of the error was shown by Anson's log of the *Centurion*, which gives the ship's position on 13 April as 87°51'W., an estimate changed the next day to 78°28'W. In Michell's log of the *Gloucester* the longitude before land was sighted appears as 84°12'W., a difference of three degrees from that worked out on the *Centurion*. The danger arising from these uncertainties was dramatically illustrated by the chart placed in the authorised account of the voyage: this marked the plotted track of the ships, hundreds of miles out to sea, and then the actual track, taking them nearer and nearer the rocks of Cape Noir. Ironically, it was the *Centurion* that in 1736 had been chosen for the sea trials of John Harrison's first chronometer, H-1, though it was to be nearly another quarter-century before his masterpiece, H-4, pointed the way forward to the standard chronometer and to the solving of the 'problem of longitude'. The error in location and sudden danger of Anson's situation were by no means unique. Every seamen knew the fate of Sir Clowdisley Shovell's squadron, which had lost four of its five ships on the Scilly Isles in 1707 after a miscalculation of longitude. In that instance a relatively small mistake had horrendous consequences in the cramped approaches to the English coast. Other navigators made larger errors and lived to tell the tale. On board the *Centurion* was midshipman the Hon. Augustus Keppel, a fifteen-year old at the outset of the voyage. In 1758 he was commodore of a squadron that was lucky to escape with the loss of just one of its ships when the unexpected appearance of the coast of Africa persuaded him that he was not 350 miles out to sea as had been assumed – and that was after a voyage of only seventeen days!

By luck and good seamanship Anson's ships had survived the immediate crisis, but they had no alternative but to turn back into far southerly latitudes to begin once again the task of gaining enough sea room to clear Tierra del Fuego. Still lacking the *Severn* and *Pearl*, and now with real worries that the two ships had run ashore near Cape Noir, the depleted squadron sailed beyond 60°S., only to lose sight of the *Wager*. As the remaining ships began to turn northwest another 'prodigious storm' struck them. According to the logs of the *Centurion* and *Gloucester* for 24 April, every sail on the two ships was split or blown loose, and the crews were too weak to begin to repair sails and rigging until the next day. On the *Gloucester* an angry Michell wrote that his sails and rigging were 'made of bad Canvass and rotten twine', not the first time such a complaint was to be made by captains far from home. With the ships rolling uncontrollably in great hollow seas they lost sight of each other during the night of the great storm, and when daybreak came each of the four vessels found herself on her own, though the *Tryal* and *Anna* made brief contact some days later.

The dispersal of the squadron brought both benefits and dangers. The ships could at last set a course and speed for the rendezvous best suited to their individual capabilities; no longer would they have to follow

Anson's instructions to keep within two miles of the flagship. In the legal proceedings that followed the voyage Anson blamed the *Gloucester* and her broken mainyard for the delays suffered by the squadron in rounding Cape Horn. He complained that the *Centurion*, with her sick list growing by the day, was often forced to shorten sail to wait for the *Gloucester*, but made no reference to the fact that he was carrying out his own orders. On the other hand, the ships lost the chance of help or perhaps even rescue if they ran into trouble. For all except the small crew of the *Anna*, who survived best of all in terms of health, the question was whether they would reach harbour while there were still enough men alive to work the ship. The enforced return of the squadron to latitude 60°S. had drained the human and material resources of all four men-of-war. On the *Centurion* 43 men had died during April, and almost twice that number in May as the ship edged her way north into the Pacific. By the time she arrived off the coast of Chile and on 8 May reached the first rendezvous for the squadron, the island of Socorro (Isla Guamblin), there were scarcely enough men left to work the ship.

For two weeks the *Centurion* laboured off the rocky coast, without sighting any other sail, before Anson decided to bear north. Socorro and its neighbouring islands formed part of a dangerous lee shore. The 'sandy Bay' where Sir John Narborough's *Sweepstakes* had anchored in 1670 was on Socorro's unseen eastern side, unapproachable in bad weather. For men near the end of their tether the depressing sight of the continuous surf beating on a rocky coastline was the final blow. 'Those men who had been hitherto well and in Heart ... fell down, sickened and died.' On 22 May the ship was heeled over by winds so violent that they seemed to combine 'the fury of all the storms which we had hitherto encountered ... it was a most prodigious blow, and we were thrown into the utmost consternation from the apprehension of instantly foundering'. With many of the shrouds broken, and as the ship rolled on her beam ends, the masts were expected to come by the board at any moment. All of the few available hands were needed to work on the sails and rigging, so the helm was left with only two men – one the experienced Justinian Nutt, master of the *Centurion*, the other the improbable figure of the ship's chaplain, the Revd Richard Walter, remembered

The track of the *Centurion* round Cape Horn. Engraved chart in *Anson's Voyage* (1748).
This shows the divergence between the *Centurion*'s estimated track by dead reckoning
– represented here by a dotted line – and her actual track which almost ran her and
other ships of the squadron ashore at Cape Noir. See over for an enlargement of the
southern section of the chart.

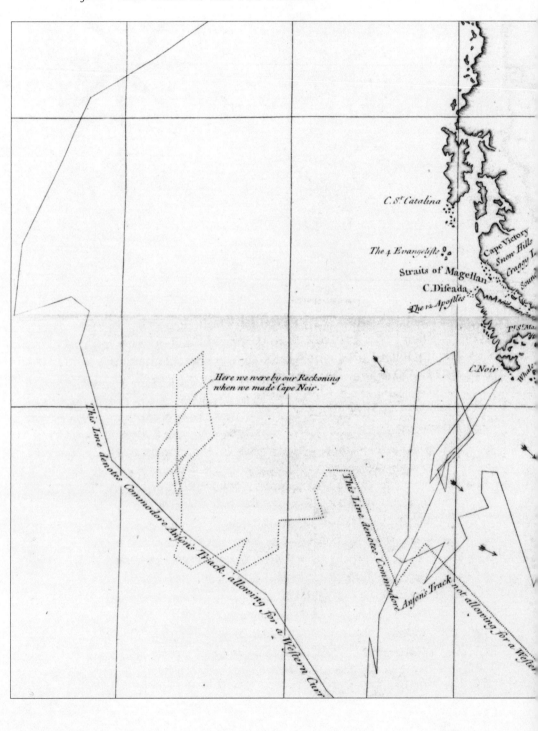

PATAGONIA

43 fa.
54 fa.
30 fa.
31 fa.
12 fa. fine black Sand.
The Port of S^t. Julian

Var. 19.^d 15.^m

42 fa. dark grey Sand

48 fa. d^o.
48 fa. d^o.
P^to de la Cru
55 fa. d^o.
40 fa. d^o.
34 fa. d^o.
58 fa. d^o.
39 fa. d^o.

Sebaeld de Werds Islands

FALKLAND ISLE

Falkland Sound

R. Gallegos
Cape Virgin Mary
B. Possession
C. Entrance
C. Gregory
Oazy Harbour
Straits of Magellan

C. Katherine's Foreland

South Ufier
C. Monmouth
R. St Sebastian
C. de Pinas
54 fa. dark grey Sand

ISLA DE TERRA DEL FUEGO

C. St Agnes
50 f.
C. St Diego
Straits le Mair
C. St John

B. of Good Success
B. de Wendon
Monagonto
Valentine B.
Vulcano

C. Gonzalvo
C. St Bartholomew
Staten Land

This Coast not well known

I. Vauverland
I. Cezambre
I. St Diago Ramores
Cape Horn
I. des Evouts
I. de St Alfonse
Hermites Isl^s

Var. 22.^d 30^m E.

Barnavelto Isles

These Arrows shew the setting of the Current.

Var. 24^d E.

Var. 23^d 15^m E.

by an acquaintance as 'a puny, weakly, and sickly man, pale and of a low stature'.

Once clear of 'this terrible coast', Anson decided to make straight for the third rendezvous, the island of Juan Fernández, on the grounds that since no other ships from the squadron had been seen at Socorro, it was unlikely that any of them would have made their way to the second rendezvous at Valdivia. Given the uncertainty about Juan Fernández's longitude, he decided to reach the island by sailing down its latitude, a common practice in the pre-chronometer era. The original rendezvous instructions now came into play with what turned out to be a deadly error that cost the lives of scores of men. The instructions stated that Juan Fernández 'is the Latitude of 33:30 South forty five Leagues west from the Coast of Chili'. The latitude is in fact 34°47'S., but what was of more significance was that the island lay much farther offshore than reported – about 120 leagues (or 360 nautical miles) west of Valparaiso, not a mere 45 leagues. We know that Anson not only had Shelvocke's *Voyage Round the World* on board, but that the book must also have been kept conveniently to hand; for its text was used as the key to the cipher for secret letters written by Anson. Shelvocke gave the location of Juan Fernández as 275 miles west of Concepción, with its latitude at 33°25'S. Whether he was following his own orders, or relying on Shelvocke, Anson was almost certainly searching too far north and too far east for the rendezvous. Clearly lacking confidence in his charts and, perhaps, in his master's navigational abilities after the near escape at Cape Noir, Anson decided that he had probably overrun the island, and turned back east. When, two days later, he saw once again the high mountains of the coast of Chile, he realised his mistake. In terms of the cost in lives it was as serious a miscalculation as the incorrect calculations of longitude on the passage round the Horn, for it took nine days of beating against the wind to get back to the original area of his search, and in that time another 70 or 80 men died. At last, to the west the peaks of Juan Fernández were sighted 30 miles distant at daybreak on 9 June.

Since the 1680s Juan Fernández had been a favourite refuge for bucca-neers and privateers in the South Sea. It also gained another kind of fame as the lonely way-station for seamen marooned or stranded there, sometimes for years on end. Most celebrated of these was Alexander Selkirk, whose solitary existence on the island was described by Woodes Rogers, and helped to inspire Defoe's *Robinson Crusoe*. The name, Juan Fernández, was that of the Spanish seaman who first sighted the island group in 1535, and it covered three islands. The largest, Más-a-Tierra, lying 360 nautical miles off Valparaiso, was the island of the buccaneers and their successors. It was this island that was now in sight, and was generally referred to as Juan Fernández (in 1966 it was to be renamed Isla Robinson Crusoe by the Chilean government). To the west was the smaller island of Más Afuera, inaccessible, and hardly known at this time. A third, tiny island, Goat Island, lay off the main island. In 1720 Shelvocke's *Speedwell* was wrecked on Juan Fernández, and it was six months before he and his crew could get away. In his published narrative Shelvocke was loud in his praises of the island and its 'savage irregular beauty': the soil was fertile, the water good and the air wholesome.

The first sighting of Juan Fernández by the *Centurion*'s crew did little to reassure them. At a distance it appeared rocky and barren, but as the ship drew nearer, the woods and grassy valleys, streams and cascades described by Shelvocke came into view. Many of the sick crawled on deck to gain strength from the sight, but relief was not yet at hand. When Lieutenant Saumarez mustered all fit hands to bring the ship into the anchorage, he found that he had only six seamen and two quartermasters. Without the help of the officers and their boy servants his task would have been impossible. It took two hours to trim the sails as the ship anchored for the night off the only safe harbour on Juan Fernández, Cumberland Bay on the island's north coast. The next morning another four hours were spent at the capstan bringing up the chain; but to free the actual anchor from the ground proved beyond the men's strength, and only the jerking of the ship in a sudden squall of wind wrenched it clear so that it dangled a few fathoms above the sea-bed. 'To so wretched a condition was a sixty gun ship reduced, which had passed Streights Le Maire but three months before, with between four and five hundred men, almost all of them in health and vigour.'

As the *Centurion* slowly worked her way into the bay it became clear that no other ship was at anchor there. As the depressing implications of this were being pondered, a sail was sighted which proved to be the *Tryal*. It was a remarkable coincidence that, more than six weeks after the dispersal of the squadron, the largest and the smallest of Anson's vessels arrived at Juan Fernández on the same day. The *Tryal*'s plight was as bad as the flagship's: 34 out of her crew of 67 dead, and 12 out of the 19 marines on board. Only the sloop's captain, Charles Saunders, his lieutenant and three seamen were able to stand the deck. As the man-of-war and sloop lay alongside each other, all attention was given to getting the sick on shore. They were dying by the dozen below deck, and it was a race against time to ferry them ashore, still in their hammocks, through the heavy surf and carry them across a rough, stony beach. All considerations of rank were set aside, as Anson and his officers worked beside the few fit men in this exhausting work.

Hanging over everything was the realisation that the death and sickness rate on the *Centurion* and *Tryal* indicated that unless the remaining ships appeared soon, it was unlikely that their crews could have survived. Macabre images presented themselves of ships still afloat, but crewed only by the dead. As the days went by hopes faded, until on 21 June a ship was seen far off, under main topsail only. This sorry sight seemed conclusive evidence that it was another ship from the squadron, and in desperate trouble. It was five days before the vessel came near enough to be identified as the *Gloucester*. Michell's journal tells the story of the ship's wavering course since her separation from the rest of the squadron. He had sighted the Chilean coast near Socorro on 16 May but, for reasons that are not explained, spent a month sailing slowly north from there towards Concepción before turning west for Juan Fernández. The repaired mainyard had been carried away again, probably in the same storm that had ripped sails and rigging off the *Centurion*; and Michell's journal reveals the problems of replacing it. On 28 May the few fit officers, seamen and boys began to set the main shrouds. It took them all morning to set six, and the afternoon and evening to get up the mainyard. At daylight the next day the work began of bending the mainsail, not completed until midday. It was a caricature of the normal shipboard operation, performed in excruciating slow motion. It was six days after the first sighting of ship from island, and island from ship, before the *Gloucester*

The east prospect of the Island of IUAN FERNANDES *in the south sea.*

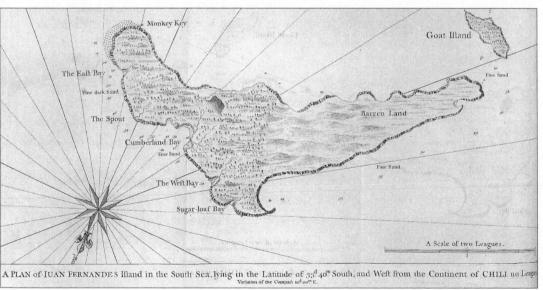

A PLAN of IUAN FERNANDES Island in the South Sea, lying in the Latitude of 33.d 40.m South, and West from the Continent of CHILI 110 League
Variation of the Compass 10.d 00.m E.

ABOVE: Juan Fernández from the east, showing the craggy profile that depressed the *Centurion*'s crew on their first sighting of the island. Engraving in *Anson's Voyage* (1748) after drawing by Peircy Brett.

BELOW: Chart of Juan Fernández (with north at bottom), showing the anchorage at Cumberland Bay. Engraving in *Anson's Voyage* (1748) after drawing by Peircy Brett.

was near enough to make out the *Centurion* at anchor in Cumberland Bay. When Anson sent out his long boat with fish, Michell kept the boat's crew to help him work the ship. He had only three officers, the master, surgeon, ten men and 'seven small boys' left on deck. He added himself to their number, though like them he was 'in a very weak condition'.

The ship's boys mentioned by Michell and in many of the other journals make up an intriguing section of the crew. We know little about them, except in general terms. Most are entered in the muster books as 'servants', attached to the commissioned officers and more senior warrant officers. No ages are given, but they could have been of any age from seven or eight upwards. Although they did a fair amount of running around at the officers' behest, they were not servants in a conventional domestic sense. They were training for life at sea, literally 'learning the ropes', and many future officers first entered the navy as young boys, sometimes in the service of fathers or other relatives. When their ship was in action the boys' agility and speed of foot were put to good use as they scurried back and forth from the magazine with powder for the great guns. On the *Centurion*, in less strenuous moments, they would have spent time under the supervision of the schoolteacher, Pascoe Thomas. Exact figures of the numbers of boys in the ships' companies on Anson's voyage, and of the proportion that survived, are difficult to establish from the muster books (where the identities of some of them are undoubtedly concealed under the heading of ordinary or able seaman). However, journal entries reinforce the impression that they survived in greater numbers and in better health then might be expected. It is striking that as the *Gloucester* struggled off Juan Fernández, seven of the 23 forlorn figures trying to bring the ship in were boys. A year later, in the ship's last days, no fewer than eleven of her 27 crew members able to keep the deck were boys. Some explanation of this comes from modern medical research, which shows that body stores of vitamin C seem to diminish with age, so the boys on Anson's ships might have escaped the worst ravages of scurvy. The journal entries, laconic though they are, also tell us something about the mental resilience of the youngsters concerned. Right up to the time of the climactic action against the galleon, the boy sailors with Anson performed a heroic part in the working and fighting of their ships.

In June 1741 the combined efforts of men and boys, officers and crew, were not enough to bring the *Gloucester* to safety at Juan Fernández. With the wind offshore, it proved impossible to work the clumsy square-rigged ship into Cumberland Bay, though the *Centurion*'s longboat with its fore-and-aft rig was able to make the trip from shore to ship and back several times. Attempts by boats to tow the *Gloucester* into soundings failed as the rowers collapsed with exhaustion at the oars. And each day men were dying below, unfed, unattended, covered in their own filth as they lay helpless in the stinking darkness of their quarters. Adding to the horror were the rats; Michell's journal refers to them time and again, swarming over living and dead, biting and scratching. On 18 July strong winds blew the ship out of sight of the island, and split the mainsail. When it was finally unbent, only Michell and a lieutenant had the strength to use a sail needle to repair the rip. The *Gloucester* was blown west as far as Más-Afuera, and by now some of the *Centurion*'s men who had come on board were showing renewed signs of scurvy. Finally, on 23 July, the ship came into Cumberland Bay; six of the worst affected among the crew had already been taken off, but two of them died in the boat before they could reach shore. In all, the *Gloucester* had lost 254 men during the passage from Port St Julian; only 92 were left, and most of them were weak from scurvy.

For weeks after the arrival of the *Gloucester* the death toll continued to mount. There seemed no explanation as to why some men died and others survived; why some made a full recovery and others were left crippled. Among those who recovered was the gunner, yet he was so ill with scurvy that he had lost the use of his legs, and when the first fresh greens and fish arrived on board he had to be held up in bed and fed. After three days of this diet he suddenly appeared 'upon deck to the great Surprize of every Body aboard'. Michell continued: 'the Scurvy had very different Effects on us; some were taken with a shortness of Breath, these were soon carried off; some quite lost their Senses. In some it got into their Brains, and they ran raving mad; others had their sinews so contracted, that they lost the Use of their Limbs.' Henry Ettrick, the *Centurion*'s

Sea lions on Juan Fernández. Engraving in *Anson's Voyage* (1748) after drawing by Piercy Brett. The male on the right was drawn from life, and was so dominant that the seamen called him 'the Bashaw' (or pasha). Lawrence Millechamp wrote in his journal that when the males 'are provoked they raise their body, flourish their tails, make a deep hollow roaring noise, and appear most noble creatures'.

surgeon, took the opportunity to dissect some of the corpses, and was greeted with a gruesome sight, 'their Blood all dried up, and their Vessels full of Water, and their Bones, after the Flesh was scraped off, appeared quite black'. Gradually fresh air and fresh provisions had an effect. As he landed Michell described the welcome sight of turnips, sorrel and watercress, and 'the greatest plenty of fish I ever saw', as well as seals and sea-lions. The huge, somnolent sea-lions provided an important source of fresh meat. They were killed with a pistol shot down the throat, and their flesh cut into steaks and broiled. As some of the men recovered their energy they found a more diverting way of killing them, 'which we call'd Lion bating, each of us took a Half-pike in his Hand, and so prick'd them to death, which commonly was Sport for three or four Hours before we kill'd them'. The goats that had played so prominent a part in Selkirk's story were less in evidence, for the Spaniards had belatedly realised their food potential for buccaneers and other unwelcome visitors, and had put dogs on the island. These had killed many of the goats, and driven the survivors to the highest peaks. Among these were animals 'of extreme age' whose ears had been slit, and several of the journal-keepers speculated that these were the same goats caught as kids by Selkirk and marked on the ear.

For the crews of all three vessels the first weeks on the island were a time of convalescence, of a painfully slow return to health. All who could stand were put to work: wooding, watering, salting down the huge quantities of cod that had been caught, repairing the rigging and mending the sails. But a bird's-eye view of the beach would have revealed a scene far removed from the usual bustle and animation that marked ships in harbour. Many of the crew could walk only with crutches, and those employed in fetching wood carried a single piece at a time. Everything was done with agonising slowness. Yet time was not on Anson's side. Soon after landing, the *Centurion*'s crew had found pieces of pottery, ashes and remains of food on the shore. It was clear that Spanish ships had recently been in the harbour, a sobering thought given the weakness of the crews. As one officer noted, although the *Centurion* was a 60-gun ship, almost any privateer afloat would be able to take her. Whether the Spaniards were from Pizarro's squadron, or from ships sent out from Callao, Anson had no way of telling. So when on 16 August a sail was reported to the north of the island, the odds were that it was Spanish, perhaps the outrunner of a powerful squadron. The more optimistic hoped that it might be one of the missing ships, the *Severn*, *Pearl* or *Wager*. To everyone's surprise, as the ship drew nearer, it became clear that she was the *Anna* pink. Even more surprising, the victualler appeared to be in no difficulty, and by late afternoon was moored in the bay.

That a small merchant vessel had survived, and had reached the rendezvous with her crew of sixteen in reasonable health, seemed at first sight an unlikely proposition. Like the rest of the squadron, the *Anna* had suffered damage and sickness among the crew in the passage round the Horn; but at no stage does the master, Gerard, seem to have contemplated turning back. After the great storm that dispersed the squadron on 24 April the pink made every effort to reach the rendezvous at Socorro. As she came into the latitude of the rendezvous in mid-May a strong westerly wind blew the ship towards a high and rocky coastline, and by 18 May, with the anchors not holding, the crew gave themselves up for lost as the ship was driven towards the cliff. At the last moment a small opening appeared in the rocks, and with her anchors cut away the ship was steered through a narrow cleft and into a fine harbour. There the *Anna* stayed for two months, while the crew recovered their health. Water was so close at hand that it could be run into the longboat through a hose; wild greens were abundant; while for food there were shellfish, geese and penguins. Except for one Indian family of a man, woman and two children the area appeared uninhabited, though fears that Spaniards might be close at hand prompted the master to give up his practice of firing an evening gun. With some rough-and-ready repairs carried out to the ship, and with the crew recovered, the *Anna* left her secluded refuge (still called today Bahía Anna Pink), and arrived at Juan Fernández as though complying with the terms of her charter in this way was the most normal thing in the world.

The contrast with the dreadful state of affairs on the men-of-war is striking, and cannot be explained away – as the writer of the authorised account attempted to do – by the fact that the pink spent two months in harbour from mid-May onwards. By then the death toll on both the *Centurion* and *Gloucester* was already high. We know little about the crew of the *Anna*, but it was likely that she had more experienced seamen than the men-of-war. What we do know is that she was not encumbered with huge numbers of men to work the guns, nor did she carry dozens of pathetic passengers in the shape of elderly invalids and raw marines. Her more useful cargo was of provisions, and there was no shortage of food for the small crew. Indeed, Anson's first action once the pink arrived at Juan Fernández was to put all his men on full rations of bread once again. This is not to say that the vessel escaped unscathed. So damaged had she been by the heavy seas that a survey at Juan Fernández reported that not all the spare plank and iron available on the other ships would be enough to repair her. She was therefore broken up, and her master and crew sent on board the *Gloucester*. Even so, this humblest of Anson's

The Commodore at Juan Fernandez.

Scene at Cumberland Bay, Juan Fernández. Engraving in Anon., *An Authentic and Genuine Journal of Commodore Anson's Expedition* (1744). Almost certainly not based on a first-hand drawing, this illustration nevertheless gives a vivid impression of the first days at Juan Fernández: the *Centurion* at anchor in the bay, the men unloading stores and felling trees watched by Anson and a group of officers, the sick being tended, sea lions and goats.

vessels had done enough to leave a lasting impression on the mind of the Earl of Sandwich, appointed First Lord of the Admiralty in 1748. He clearly read carefully the chapter on the *Anna* in the authorised account of Anson's voyage published that year, and remembered it. In 1772, when Sandwich was once again First Lord of the Admiralty, the preparations for Captain Cook's second Pacific voyage were disrupted by arguments over the type of ship or ships to be taken. Joseph Banks was dismayed that Cook intended to sail in a small, cat-built collier, the *Resolution*, the same type (and indeed, from the same yard) as the *Endeavour* of his first Pacific voyage. Banks, with his entourage of naturalists, artists and musicians, wished for something altogether more splendid and commodious than a converted collier; but Sandwich intervened decisively in favour of the *Resolution*. Among his arguments was the contrast between the performance of the *Anna* on Anson's voyage and that of the conventional men-of-war such as the *Pearl* and *Severn* or the large ships of Pizarro's squadron. The *Anna*, 'a collier like the Resolution', he reminded Banks, 'did get round [Cape Horn] & made her way thro these stormy seas, which were so difficult to resist'. Before we hail the *Anna*'s master, Mr Gerard, as the unsung hero of the Anson expedition, it is perhaps worth noting that some of the pink's crew petitioned to be transferred from the *Gloucester* to the *Centurion* because of the treatment they had received from the master while on the *Anna* – and that Anson allowed the petition.

After the weeks of slow recovery Anson prepared to sail in September 1741. Juan Fernández had been a haven for his scurvy-stricken crews, and earlier praise by buccaneers and privateers was pushed to new heights. While the journals of the officers concentrated on the practicalities of the island – 'it seems providentially calculated for the relief of distressed adventurers,' Saumarez wrote – the writer of the authorised account indulged in flights of poetic fancy as he described a landscape that gave satisfaction to both body and mind, a place where life-giving greenstuffs were set among lush valleys and cascading streams. As for the gentle, park-like declivity where Anson pitched his tent, 'I despair', the writer remarked, 'of conveying an adequate idea of its beauty'; and he was glad to have Lieutenant Peircy Brett's drawing to illustrate the location. Pascoe Thomas was even more effusive, concluding with words from Milton's *Paradise Lost* and the thought that 'there can scarce anywhere be found a more happy Seat for the Muses, and the Flights of Fancy, or Pleasures of the Imagination'.

Much of this, one suspects, was composed later, a retrospective written in comfort and safety. During the actual stay on the island the memory of mass deaths and the premonition of continuing danger dominated the minds of officers and men alike. Before the ships sailed, the dreadful

A View of the COMMODORES TENT *at the Island of* JUAN FERNANDES.

The Commodore's tent on Juan Fernández. Engraving in *Anson's Voyage* (1748) after a drawing by Peircy Brett. The accompanying text described the idyllic scene: 'a small lawn, that lay on a little ascent, at the distance of about half a mile from the sea. In the front of his tent was a large avenue cut through the woods to the sea-side, which sloping to the water with a gentle descent, opened a prospect of the bay and myrtle sweeping round it, in the form of a theatre . . .'

roll-call of the expedition's losses was drawn up. Two-thirds of the combined crews and supernumeraries of the three vessels were dead, 626 out of the 961 who had left England. The survivors, 335 in all, were fewer in number than the normal complement of the *Centurion*. The problem was not that there were not enough men to sail the ships, but that there were not enough to sail and fight them. The complement of a 1,000-ton, 60-gun ship such as the *Centurion* was determined by the number of her guns. Her complement of 400 men gave her a ratio of one crew member to every 2.5 tons. A merchantman, by contrast, would manage with a ratio of one crew member to every fifteen tons. In one other way the casualties were not quite as crippling as might appear, for a large proportion of the losses had been among the invalids and marines, almost all of whom had died. Even so, the fighting strength of the expedition in relation to the task it had been set was now totally inadequate, and the 600 dead from the ships still with Anson were only the known losses. The unspoken probability was that there were more to come, for it seemed unlikely that any of the three missing ships, the *Severn*, *Pearl* and *Wager*, had survived.

III

The Missing Ships

'You are no doubt already informed of some of our misfortunes, because I have been told that some of the Officers and Men are got home, but they know only a few of them and probably have not told the Truth, for what can be expected from such Poltroons . . .'

Captain Cheap to Anson, December 1745

THE *SEVERN* AND *PEARL* had lost company with the rest of the squadron during the night of 10 April as it sailed north, almost to its doom three days later on the rocks of Cape Noir. Whether the two ships also lost sight of each other during the storms of that night is not quite clear. The point is an important one given a later accusation that their captains, Edward Legge of the *Severn* and George Murray of the *Pearl*, were acting in concert with each other during these terrible days. The evidence of the ships' logs is, on the face of it, contradictory. The entry in the log of the *Severn*, signed by Legge, was brief but unambiguous. At 10 p.m. he 'lost sight of all the Squadron save the *Pearle*', wording he later repeated in a letter to the Admiralty. Murray's log of the *Pearl* recorded that he lost touch with all ships in the squadron at 1 a.m., but that when daylight came at 6 a.m. he saw the *Severn*. It is not out of the question, of course, that one ship might have glimpsed the other, while remaining invisible herself. Since we know nothing about the specific visibility conditions that night, what lights were carried on the ships, and how alert their lookouts were, that remains a possibility.

What is beyond doubt is that the two ships and their crews were in a wretched condition by this time. On the *Severn* Legge reported that

DEATHS October 1740–July 1741

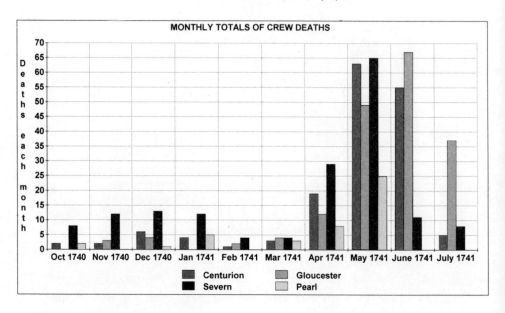

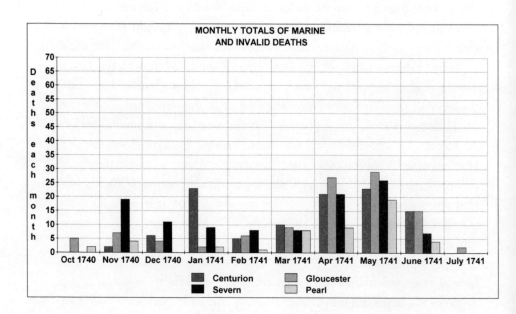

most of his men were 'sick and so numbed as to be of no service', and the rest were so disheartened that it was impossible 'to encourage them or to drive them to their duty'. On the night of 10 April he had scarcely enough men to lower the mainyard. Murray had a similar tale of woe to tell on the smaller *Pearl*: 80 or 90 men sick, two or three dying each day, rigging knotted and broken, and his only sails those bent to the yards. Anson's response to Murray's dismal report to this effect on 8 April was tart and to the point: 'every other ship had had the misfortune to have their sails blown out of the bolt ropes, and concluded after his most obliging manner with making me a compliment'. For three days the two ships kept company with each other on a north-northeasterly course as they tried to come up with the rest of the squadron. On 13 April they experienced the same fearful shock of sighting a lee shore when they assumed that they were hundreds of miles out to sea, though their situation was not quite as perilous as that of the other ships since they sighted land at 8 a.m. in the morning, when it was visible some distance off (five or six leagues). As fog closed in, the two ships slowly wore round (it took the *Severn* an hour to do this) and held off to the west. Consultations involving all the commissioned officers agreed that unless a favourable wind set in they should retrace their route around the Horn. On 17 April northwesterly gales blew the ships back towards the lee shore, and the lookouts thought that they saw land again. It was a decisive moment: to save ships and crews a new course was ordered – south and then southeast, to take them back round the Horn.

Both captains recognised the implication of what they had done. A later authority on the voyage, Vice-Admiral Boyle Somerville, wrote: 'Not to put too fine a point upon it, they deserted his [Anson's] flag in war-time and on active service.' In long reports to the Admiralty Legge and Murray set out their case: it was a question of survival as against the almost certain loss of their ships. And, as events were to show, for Murray it was a question of survival so as to be able to fight another day. Their reports illustrate the conditions experienced on the two ships as they fought their way round the Horn. Whether they were any worse than those on the other ships is difficult to judge. Anson's rejoinder to Murray's complaint on 8 April about his lack of sails was a telling one; and there is evidence that in his later report Murray made a grim situation blacker than it actually was. His letter to the Admiralty from Rio de Janeiro described how, as he struggled to round the Horn in the gales of March and April, he 'generally buried two or three a day', rising to five or six on occasion. The muster book of the *Pearl* does not confirm these figures. The ship's nominal complement was 250 crew. Among the crew there were three deaths in March and eight in April. The worst monthly figures – 25 deaths – were in May as the ship was returning to Rio. Even if the fifteen deaths in March and April among the marines and invalids are included (and however sad these deaths they had little bearing on the working of the ship), the total number of deaths in March and April on the *Pearl* was 25. These were lower proportionate figures than those on the *Centurion* and *Gloucester* for the same period.

The *Severn* (complement 300) was a different case altogether. For reasons that are not at all clear, the death rate on Legge's 50-gun ship was the worst in the squadron. The deaths among the crew began early: 33 by the end of December 1740 (compared with twelve on the *Centurion*, seven on the *Gloucester*, and four on the *Pearl*). Most of these would have been deaths from typhus, from which many of the *Severn*'s crew seem to have been suffering before they left England. In April, the month when Legge and Murray decided to turn back, 29 crew members died on the *Severn*, followed by 65 deaths in May. If one awful month stood out among the others on all the ships it was May, with 300 deaths among crew, marines and invalids on the *Centurion*, *Gloucester*, *Severn* and *Pearl*. Most of these were deaths from scurvy, though the typhus and dysentery outbreaks of the Atlantic crossing played their part in this death toll, for they would have lowered the resistance to illness and reduced body stores of vitamin C. By the time the *Severn* reached Rio de Janeiro in early June, more than half her crew (158) were dead. Of the survivors, 114 were 'sick and absolutely unable to stir', leaving only 30 men and boys fit for duty. In addition, almost all the invalids and marines were dead, including the 35 taken on board from the *Wager* at Port St Julian. In terms of deaths per month at sea the *Severn* suffered more than any other ship in the squadron. The higher totals of deaths numbers on the *Centurion* and *Gloucester* are explained not only by the larger complement of the *Cen-*

turion, but by the fact that both ships were still at sea throughout June, and the *Gloucester* throughout July as well. The *Severn* by contrast reached Rio de Janeiro on 6 June, but had lost almost a quarter of her crew the previous month.

Some evidence exists – not conclusive but certainly suggestive – that after the event at least one log on the *Severn* received additional entries to stress the ship's perilous situation. The log book of Lieutenant Alexander Innes is conventional in form and substance until it comes to the events of 10 April and later. On three days, 10, 13 and 25 April, entries have been added, in the same handwriting. There was no room for them on the right-hand or journal page of the log book, where entries in continuous prose were normally to be found. The left-hand page was laid out in the usual columnar form, with details of wind, courses and so on. Starting in the gaps between the columns, but then running over the original entries, are three additions: 10 April: 'The ships upper works and decks very leaky, the seamen never dry in their hammocks the rigging verry bad several of the lower shrouds broke and stranded and the seamen mostly sick, and those that come upon deck are lame and very weak'; 13 April: 'I don't think thers 50 Men in the Ship able to come on Deck and they much fatigued and weak'; 25 April: 'Its so excessive cold with snow and hard gales that all the seamen in the ship cannot furl the maintopsail, they are nummed before they gett upon the Yard.' There is no reason to doubt the truth of these entries, but their belated appearance raises the suspicion that they were added to an otherwise rather sparse document in an attempt to provide support for the decision to turn back.

The death rate on the *Pearl* was well below that of the other main fighting ships in the squadron, and calls into question Murray's decision to give up. In a recent analysis of the medical aspects of the voyage Sir James Watt has suggested that 'vitamin deficiencies, particularly niacin, had affected the judgement of the two captains'. Murray later wrote at length and with some emotion about the state of affairs on the *Pearl* after her narrow escape from the lee shore on 13 April, but his last lines hint at a significant breakdown of discipline:

Double Page of the log book of Lieutenant Alexander Innes of the *Severn*. This follows the conventional arrangement, with navigational data arranged in tabular form on the left, and daily journal entries on the right. It seems evident that both pages had

Remarks on Board His Majesties Ship Severn 1741

Verry hard gales & Squalls Blustering Wr wth rain & Sleet & Verry hazy Wr At 6 pm up Mn Sail at 7 In Mn topsl Ag Sett Mn Sl At 2 AM Lowrd down Our Mn yard and lay too Undr Forsl all the Parrell of the Mn topsl yard Broke Lost sight of the Commodr & all the Squadn Except the Pearle At 6 AM up Forsl and lay too Undr Rn & Ballanced Mizon At 10 made Sail and Bore away to the Eastward 10 or 12 Miles

Do Do wth rain Sway'd up the Fore yard & Sett Do Sail At Midnight made sail At 5 AM Sett fore topsl At 9 Up Mn yard At 10 Sett Do Sail Mn fore topsl

Hard gales & Squalls Wr w haile At 7 AM Wore & lay by

Hard gales & hazy Wr w rain & Sleet & Exceeding Cold Wr Made Sail Sett the Fore & Mn sail Discover'd the Mn top yard Broke In the Slings Unbent the Sail & gott down the yard At 7 AM Saw the Land bearing from NW to NNE Do abt 5 Leags Do Wore Ship Lowrd down the Mn yard and Shifted the Mn sail upon the Accn one of the Yard Arms of the top yard Runn through it

The 1st latt parts Little Wr & rain the Middle fresh gales & Cloudy At 11 AM Lay too for the Pearle Departed this life Jno Turpin & Richd Allerton Seamen

For the Most part Fresh gales & hazy At 4 PM made Sail At 7 AM Wore f Sigt Departd this life Owen Davis & Robert Pratt Seamen

Mod & Cloudy wth rain At 5 PM Bore Ship At 8 AM Sett Mn top Began to fill Salt Watter in the Hold Departd Reed and Smith Soldrs Jno George and James Ferguson Seamen

For the Most part Mod & Cloudy wth rain At 2 PM Ho Mn topsl Left Off Servg Pease & Oatemeal apart 8 AM Bore away In Order to Return Back to the first Port as wee are not Able to beate any Longer Depd James Daugherty

Hard gales & Squally gott down Mizn topmt Do yard & Crossjack yard At 9 AM Sett Mn top Shortd sail for the Pearle Depd Wm Oram Thos Forester & Wm White

For the Most part Mod & hazy wth haile rain & Sleet & Snow Exceeding Cold Wr 2 pas 2 PM Lay too for the Pearle Depd Neile Macannon Soldier

Mod & Cloudy wth Snow & Sleet Departd his life Thos Binham and Do Condy Macdugal Ships Cook

The 1st Middle parts Little wd & Cloudy Wr the latter hard gales & Squally At 4 PM Ho fore topsl At 4 AM Ho Mn topst Broke the Mn Sheet Depd Wm Sing

Mod & Cloudy At 5 AM found 4 of y Larbd Mn Shrouds Do broakten Departed this life Adam Jourdon

Do & hazy At 8 PM made a Sign for Warring Departd his life Thos Thwait Edward Cooke Thos Grimes

Mod & Cloudy Frosty Wr w Snow At 7 AM Ho Do & Ho Depd his life Jos Parker George Forbes Jonathan Johnson & Jno Alderman

Fresh gales & hazy Wr wth Snow & Sleet Cold Wr At 4 PM In fs Mn topsl At 8 Do made a Sign to tack At 6 AM Lost sight of the Pearle Ho Mn top At 9 up Sl & Lay too Undr Rn Mn Sl At 11 up Mn Sl & Lay too Undr Rn & Ballanced Mizon

been completed up to 25 April 1741 before the three extra entries were added (see p. 71) (see p. 71) for their wording), and that the only space left for them was among the columns of data on the left-hand page.

Those poor men who had stood the deck with a resolution not to be met with in any but English seamen, though they were very thinly clad, having sold their clothes at St. Catherines, and when chased by the Spaniards [Pizarro's ships] had thrown half ports, bulkheads and tarpaulins overboard, for want of which they were continually wet in their hammocks, the tarpaulins I made being of little service for want of sun to dry them. Yet under all these difficulties and discouragements they behaved beyond expectation hitherto, but being now quite jaded and fatigued with continual labour and watching, and pinched with the cold and want of water, on discovering how far we were out in our computation they became so dejected as to lay themselves down in despair, bewailing their misfortunes, wishing for death as the only relief to their miseries, and could not be induced by threats or entreaties to go aloft.

It took the *Severn* and *Pearl* seven weeks to get back round the Horn to Rio de Janeiro. Only help from French and Portuguese men-of-war enabled the *Severn* to make harbour as she lay off the bar, for her crew were too weak to furl the sails or to weigh the anchor. On the *Pearl* the hundred deaths among crew and supernumeraries proved in a way to have been providential, for there were only three casks of water left when the ship reached Rio, and with a full complement water would have long since run out. Within a month Murray was eager to 'have another touch at Cape Horn', and rejoin Anson. As senior officer, it was Legge who would make such decisions, and he flatly refused Murray's request. Both ships were far short of their complement, and many of those who had survived were not fit for duty. All his advice was that 'to put our men on board and to give them salt provisions before they are thoroughly recovered, would be to murder them'. Even if the *Pearl* managed to get into the South Sea, the odds were that Anson, if still alive, would be on his way home. Murray accepted his superior's orders, but only under protest – 'I can look on the loss of my passage in no other light than a disgrace' – and in December 1741 the two ships left Rio for the West Indies and, eventually, England.

They arrived home to less than a heroes' welcome. There was no formal investigation by the Admiralty into the concerted separation of the two ships, but this did not stop comment. In April 1742 the *London Magazine* reported that Anson had arrived in the South Sea, despite 'the dismal accounts' brought by the *Severn* and *Pearl*, which seem 'to have suffered more by returning than he did by proceeding'. A letter from Anson's brother, Thomas, referred with understandable resentment to Captain Legge's insistence that Anson must be dead. But despite these hints of criticism about Legge's pessimism, no open attack on the conduct of the two officers appears to have been made until Pascoe Thomas, the schoolmaster on board the *Centurion*, wrote of the *Severn* and *Pearl* in his account of the voyage published in 1745 that on the day of their disappearance they 'seemed to me to lag designedly', and that as the rest of the squadron continued under easy sail, and then lay to during the night, the two ships made no attempt to regain their position. Confirmation of part of this comes from Saumarez, who entered in his log that the *Severn* and *Pearl* 'probably fell astern by not carrying so much sail as the rest of the squadron'; but it is impossible to tell whether this was simply a factual observation or intended as a criticism. The log of the *Tryal*, where Saunders had resumed command, shows that the sloop was sent by Anson to search for the missing ships on 11 April, but without success.

The implication of desertion was not repeated in the authorised account of the voyage published in 1748. Instead, it mentioned the 'great joy' with which the news of the survival of the two ships was received by the *Centurion*'s crew at Canton, and noted how well Legge had kept station until his crew was afflicted by 'extraordinary sickness'. By this time Legge was dead, but his brother wrote to Anson after the book's publication thanking him for protecting Edward's memory 'against coffee-house censurers, and the cavils of those children of ease who sit at home and, without risking themselves, blame every man's conduct they do not and cannot understand'. And a tradition in Murray's family that Anson presented him with a gold watch when they met again in England may be further proof that Anson was not disposed to blame Legge and Murray for the decision to turn back

In his account of Anson's voyage published in 1934 Vice-Admiral Somerville resurrected Pascoe Thomas's strictures. He accused Legge and Murray of lagging behind 'deliberately and concertedly' before deciding to desert the expedition, and pointed out that the smaller ships, *Wager*, *Tryal* and *Anna*, had persevered despite the appalling conditions. These assertions were indignantly denied by one of Murray's descendants, Lt.-Col. Arthur C. Murray (Viscount Elibank), who used the logs of the *Severn* and *Pearl* to good effect to show the desperate state of the two ships. Although he had the better of the argument, Murray was unable to produce evidence to answer Somerville's contention that the two captains had decided at some stage on the gruelling haul round Cape Horn to desert the squadron. Neither Somerville nor Murray saw the letters exchanged by Legge and Murray after the separation, or their reports home to the Admiralty. Their revelation of a dispute between Legge and Murray about whether they should try to rejoin Anson argues against any prior arrangement by the two captains to desert the squadron. The gloomy Legge does not emerge as the ideal captain for the testing circumstances in which he found himself, but it was Murray who on 14 April 1741 had taken the initiative with his forthright declaration that without a change of wind 'our passage is lost, and that we must bear away round the Cape'.

The *Wager*, with only a stump where the mizen-mast had been, was in even worse condition than the other ships of the squadron as she clawed her way north along the coast of Chile. An East Indiaman, the *Wager* had been bought by the Admiralty on the outbreak of war and refitted as a sixth rate carrying 28 guns. Apart from the *Tryal* sloop she was the smallest of the naval ships in the squadron. Despite this, she had the largest number of invalids and marines on board, while her crew was below complement even before sailing. The last entry in the *Wager*'s surviving muster book is for 2 November 1740, at which time she carried 106 crew and 142 invalids and marines. At Port St Julian the ship's plight was recognised when 35 invalids were transferred to the *Severn*, and another ten to the *Centurion*. The *Wager*'s function was as a support vessel, an armed transport, rather than as one of Anson's frontline fighting ships. She carried the field guns and ammunition for land actions, and twenty tons of merchandise to open up trade. Years later, a seventeen-year-old midshipman at the time of sailing remembered how the *Wager*, 'an old Indiaman ... was deeply laden with all sorts of careening gear, military and other stores, for the use of the other ships: and, what is more, crowded with bale goods, and encumbered with merchandize'. Her captain, David Cheap, was her third since leaving Spithead, and it was his first experience of command, for he had sailed as lieutenant on the *Tryal*. He had been in poor health since the beginning of the voyage, suffering (he wrote later) from rheumatism and asthma. The ship's only other commissioned officer was the lieutenant, Robert Baynes. Neither he nor the master, Thomas Clark, was to impress in the days that lay ahead. Stronger personalities were to be found among the lesser warrant officers: the gunner, John Bulkeley, who had been in the navy since 1728, and had charge of a watch throughout the voyage; the carpenter, John Cummins; the boatswain, John King; and the surgeon, William Elliot. There were also four midshipmen on board who were to play distinctive roles, and all of whom except the first-named wrote narratives of their misadventures: Henry Cozens, Alexander Campbell, Isaac Morris and the Honourable John Byron (a future admiral, and grandfather of the poet).

Five days after the near escape from the rocks of Cape Noir the *Wager*, crippled and lagging behind, lost sight of the other ships of the squadron. There were mutual recriminations about how this had happened, and matters were not helped by the fact that Cheap was ill in his cabin. His main reaction to the disputes going on above him was to issue the officers with pistols. When the ship seemed to have made enough westing to be able to turn back north into the Pacific, he was adamant that they should head for the first rendezvous set by Anson, the island of Socorro, just off the Chilean mainland in latitude 45°S. Baynes and Bulkeley, worried about the dangers of once more sailing towards a lee shore with a disabled ship and only a dozen men fit for duty, argued in vain that the *Wager* should make for the second rendezvous, the island of Juan Fernández, well out to sea. The only chart available was an old one published with the account of Narborough's voyage 70 years earlier,

Loſs of the Wager, Man of War, o...

ger Island, near Mount Misery .

The wreck of the *Wager*. Anon. The engraving offers a dramatic reconstruction of the shipwreck of 14 May 1741. Artistic licence has led to some telescoping of events, with survivors huddled beneath an upturned boat, in Indian huts and in a rudimentary tent, while others are struggling with wreckage on the beach or are still stranded on the ship.

and it gave no indication of the complexity of the jagged coast ahead. On 13 May 1741, as gales blew the ship steadily northeastward towards the feared but still unseen lee shore, Cummins thought he caught a glimpse of land to port – in other words on the seaward side of the vessel. His tentative report was ignored by Baynes, in charge of the deck, but that afternoon, to the consternation of all on board, the unmistakable outline of a high coast was seen stretching along the northwest horizon. The *Wager* had driven inside the jaws of the Gulf of Penas (aptly named – the Gulf of Sorrows or Troubles). It took three hours for the few fit hands and officers to wear the ship round so that she was pointing south in an attempt to retrace her course out of the trap. Hardly had the vessel come round than Cheap was thrown down the quarterdeck ladder by a great wave, and dislocated his shoulder. One of the men carrying him below remembered that the dislocation was so severe that the shoulder-bone stuck out below the armpit. At this time of crisis, or so Cheap was told later, his second in command, Baynes, disappeared below, bottle in hand.

Drugged with opium by the surgeon to ease the pain, Cheap lay unconscious below as in driving rain and gale-force winds the *Wager* careered blindly on in visibility so poor that the bow of the ship could not be seen from the main part of the deck. Shortly after 4 a.m. the ship hit rocks, and for the next two hours lurched forward in the darkness through a wild expanse of breakers. As she crashed from one rock to another the rudder broke, and water rushed through the shattered hull up to the level of the hatches. At daybreak the ship was on the point of sinking when she drove forward one last time, grounded, and juddered to a halt. She had wedged between two large rocks.

As the ship finally came to rest all semblance of authority disappeared. Some of the crew smashed open wine casks and arms chests, while those sober and fit enough to take to the boats managed to get ashore to a rocky beach about a musket shot away. As the ship began to break up one of the midshipmen, Alexander Campbell, went back on board to persuade those still on the wreck to leave it. He found a scene of total disorder – 'Some were singing Psalms, others fighting, others swearing, and some lay drunk on the Deck'. He gave up his efforts when one of the men threw a bayonet at him. On shore matters were not much better among the 140 officers, crew and supernumeraries who shivered without shelter in teeming rain, many of them sick. Cheap was carried into a hut in which lances lying on the floor showed that Indians visited the spot, while some of the men propped the upturned hull of the cutter off the ground and crawled underneath. Apart from a few stunted trees and bushes the bay was barren, with a rocky stretch running down to the water, and marshy ground farther inland.

As the last of the men came ashore from the wreck, leaving behind them the corpses of those who, ill or drunk, had drowned in the water-logged hulk, they added to Cheap's problems. Still suffering from his injury, but at least on his feet, he managed to get some tents put up, and the food placed under guard, but he met abuse at every turn. His insistence on heading for Socorro rather than for the open sea and Juan Fernández was blamed for the loss of the ship. The boatswain, John King, had shown his animosity towards Cheap by firing a four-pounder cannon in his direction from the wreck, while on shore Henry Cozens was among the more troublesome of the malcontents. He had read his South Sea narratives, and infuriated Cheap with references to previous shipwrecks that had been followed by mutinies. Matters reached a head on 10 June, and as Cozens, truculent but unarmed, rampaged drunkenly around the beach, the captain shot him in the head. It was less the shooting, 'rash and hasty' though Byron later judged it, than Cheap's refusal to allow the surgeon to attend to Cozens's wound that antagonised many of those who had previously supported the captain, the more so when the young midshipman died after lingering in agony for two weeks. His death brought the total of fatalities to 45 since the ship struck. This left about a hundred men still alive, with limited supplies of food and other stores, and no prospect whatever of rescue from a desolate spot rarely, if ever, visited by Europeans.

As the *Wager* settled deeper in the water, boats went out each day to rummage around in the submerged hull for anything of value. Bulkeley had kept a journal, but he could not find it in his quarters on the ship, nor any other journals. Torn-up pages from the master's log that were washed ashore indicated that someone on the wreck had deliberately destroyed logs and journals. This was not the only sinister aspect of the final days of the *Wager* that came to light, for the search parties also found on the wreck the body of a man who had been murdered. As they returned with provisions and stores, hooked out of the hold with long poles, armed officers guarded the landing of the water-soaked goods. Cheap was never without his pistols, and was usually accompanied by

The shooting of midshipman Cozens on Wager Island. Anon. Engraving in *A Voyage to the South Seas . . . by Commodore Anson* (1745). Another drawing done after the event, this engraving offers a rather too energetic scene of crew activity as a backcloth to the action of Captain Cheap in pistolling Cozens. The most damning aspect of the reconstruction of the incident is that Cozens is clearly unarmed, holding his hands up in a gesture either of self-defence or surrender.

A Representation of Cap.t Cheap, Commander of the Wager, Shooting M.r Cozens his Midshipman; with the Crew building their Tents, after the Ship was Cast away on a desolate Island on the Coast of PATAGONIA.

Elliot the surgeon, Harvey the purser, and Lieutenant Hamilton of the marines. The food was put in a store tent guarded by armed marines, though thefts still occurred, and were punished by savage floggings of up to 400 lashes and banishment from the camp. The daily ration was a half-pound of flour and a piece of salt pork, supplemented by shellfish, boiled seaweed, wild celery and the occasional wildfowl. These additions to the ration were essential if the men were to stay alive, but in the driving rain and freezing winds, Bulkeley wrote, 'a Man will pause some Time whether he shall stay in his Tent and starve, or go out in Quest of Food'. Many remained under cover, getting weaker by the day. Two dogs presented by a group of Indians who visited the camp were immediately killed and eaten. A ship's boy had to be forcibly restrained from eating the liver of one of the bodies washed up on the beach. Only alcohol was plentiful, for the *Wager* had carried on board much of the squadron's allowance of wine and spirits.

A week after the shipwreck the longboat was dragged clear of the tangle of debris on deck and brought ashore. It was about 38 feet long, and together with the 30-foot cutter and two smaller boats offered a glimmer of hope that the bedraggled survivors might yet escape. The carpenter, John Cummins, immediately started work. With tools salvaged from the wreck he sawed the longboat in half, inserted an extra twelve feet of hull, and added a deck. When completed it would be 50 foot in length and able to squeeze in many, though not all, of those on shore. As Cummins and his helpers continued their work, the question of possible destinations became a subject of heated discussion. By now it was clear that the ship had been wrecked on an island (called Wager Island by the crew and still known as Isla Wager) somewhere off the Chilean coast between latitude 47° and 48°S. The bay where the crew had set up camp was hemmed in by hills, and a scrambled ascent of the highest, Mount Misery, up steps hacked in its steep sides, gave only a view of yet higher hills on all sides except to seaward. There the prospect was equally depressing: a rugged coast and huge breakers. In the absence of any reliable chart, planning an escape route was a matter of guesswork and argument. The nearest European settlement anyone could put a name to was Valdivia, about 600 miles to the north; but even if a small-boat voyage over that distance along an unknown coast was feasible, those who made it would at the end find themselves inside a Spanish gaol. Four hundred miles or so to the south lay the western entrance of the Strait of Magellan, on the face of it an even more daunting prospect, since arrival there would mark the beginning rather than the end of a fearsome journey. Even so Bulkeley became convinced that it offered the better option. He borrowed Cheap's copy of Narborough's narrative of his passage through the strait in 1670, and thought that it was enough of a guide for them to make the passage. Once through the strait they would sail north along the oceanic coast to Brazil and safety.

Cheap had other ideas, insisting that whatever their destination it must be to the north. He still clung to his instructions to rendezvous with Anson at Socorro. If the commodore were not there then perhaps he would be found at Valdivia; or, if all else failed, they might capture a Spanish trading vessel somewhere along the coast to the north. There could be no compromise between the two plans; the arguments that took place confirmed that Cheap had lost most, if not all, of his authority as captain. Under a more trusted officer, the plan to take the boats north into warmer waters and there seize a Spanish ship might have appealed to the crew. It was a stratagem followed almost as a matter of course by English buccaneers crossing overland into the South Sea in the days of Morgan and Dampier. Tired of the incessant disputes, the young midshipman John Byron built a little hut away from the main encampment, and lived there with an Indian dog for company. It was not long before hungry seamen seized and killed the dog, and after his protests were ignored Byron joined in the meal. Three weeks later, in the extremes of hunger, Byron returned to the spot to look for the dog's skin and paws, thrown away at the time, but which he now retrieved and ate. Among the deaths one was especially poignant, for on 30 July the last private soldier among the invalids died, leaving only one officer and a surgeon alive from the company of pensioners. The sequence of hunger, starvation and death further weakened Cheap's authority. For many among the crew, and not only the habitual trouble-makers, that authority had vanished when the *Wager* ran onto the rocks and – in accordance with Admiralty regulations – their wages ceased.

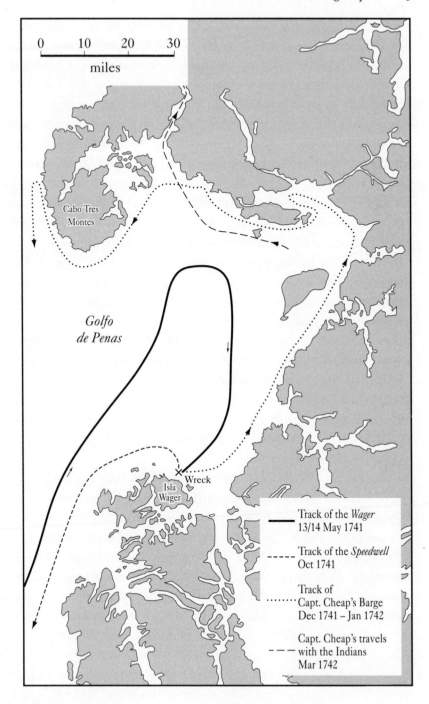

The wreck of the *Wager*

Bulkeley, who seems never to have wavered in his belief that one day he would return home, and there be held accountable for his actions, put his rescue scheme on paper. It was dated 2 August 1741, and consisted of the simple statement that the surest way to save the crew was to sail through the Strait of Magellan 'for England'. The 46 signatures on the paper were not arranged in 'Round Robin' form, but were boldly headed by the names of Bulkeley and Cummins, followed by those of the other warrant officers, the three midshipmen and 25 seamen. Finally came the names of the three marine officers, headed by Captain Pemberton. The names of Cheap and his 'party' (Elliot, Harvey and Hamilton) were missing, as was that of Lieutenant Baynes. The following days were taken up with long and often acrimonious discussions between Cheap and the adherents of the southern route. Matters were not helped when Bulkeley told Cheap that if he agreed to sail with the main party his command would be conditional, that all decisions of importance were to be subject to consultation. Cheap, although seeming to agree with all that was put before him, now rarely ventured from his tent. Working through the purser, Thomas Harvey, he tried to persuade selected crew members to join his cause through gifts of liquor. Such methods reminded an indignant Bulkeley of how things were done at home. He accused Cheap of fomenting 'a Sort of party rage' by bribery, and was persuaded by Lieutenant Baynes that if the captain persisted in his stand he should be arrested for the murder of Henry Cozens.

Once again Cheap backed away, but on both sides the intrigues, the quarrels, the reconciliations continued. The men of straw, waverers such as Baynes and the master Thomas Clark, were tempted first by one side then the other. While Cheap insisted that he would act as captain, bound only by the rules of the navy, Bulkeley took his inspiration, or at least his rhetoric, from the distant but not forgotten political struggles of Stuart England. The gunner remarked of Cheap that although he would be allowed a limited command he was 'too dangerous a person to be trusted with an absolute one'. However expressed, such sentiments ran counter to every rule and regulation of a navy that vested sole command in the captain. They were, in essence, incitements to mutiny, and on 9 October 1741 the confrontation came. The longboat was at last ready for sea, but

Cheap's own attitude was still not clear. Tired of the captain's procrastinations and evasions, Bulkeley and his associates sent armed sailors to arrest him on a charge of murder, together with Lieutenant Hamilton. The initiative, Bulkeley wrote, came from Pemberton, captain of marines. Cheap was disarmed, and his hands bound behind him.

Four days later the longboat, christened the *Speedwell*, sailed south with 59 men on board. With her went the cutter, with twelve men, and the small barge, with ten. Cheap, accompanied only by Lieutenant Hamilton of the marines and the surgeon, was left with the yawl together with provisions, weapons, navigational instruments and a Bible. The list is Bulkeley's, and must be set against the later statement by Cheap that he had been left only a small amount of bad flour and a few pieces of salt meat. Also on Wager Island were a dozen or so deserters, who had set up camp a few miles off, and whose intentions were uncertain. The crew of the *Wager*, once held together by the uncompromising clauses of the Articles of War, had split into three groups: those loyal to Cheap, whose numbers were about to be swollen; the deserters, mostly men who had fled the camp to avoid punishment; and the main party made up of those who in Cheap's eyes at least were mutineers. Before the *Speedwell* sailed off under the nominal command of Lieutenant Baynes, Bulkeley drew up a paper that laid down guidelines for the voyage ahead, and also justified Cheap's arrest. There was no reference to a possible charge of murder; the action taken against the captain was explained by the accusation that he 'hath rejected every thing propos'd for the publick good'.

As on so many other occasions during the previous five months, action was followed by indecision and second thoughts. Cheap and Bulkeley embraced in a 'tender and affectionate' farewell, each presumably happy to do this on the assumption that the other was facing certain death. Bulkeley drew up yet another paper justifying the action taken against Cheap, this time stressing that if the captain had agreed to go with the main party it would have been as a prisoner following his arrest for murder. The paper continued that the awkwardness this would have presented did not arise because Cheap had refused to leave the island. This was only half the truth; for although Cheap had refused to sail south he was as eager as anyone to get away, but in a different direction. When

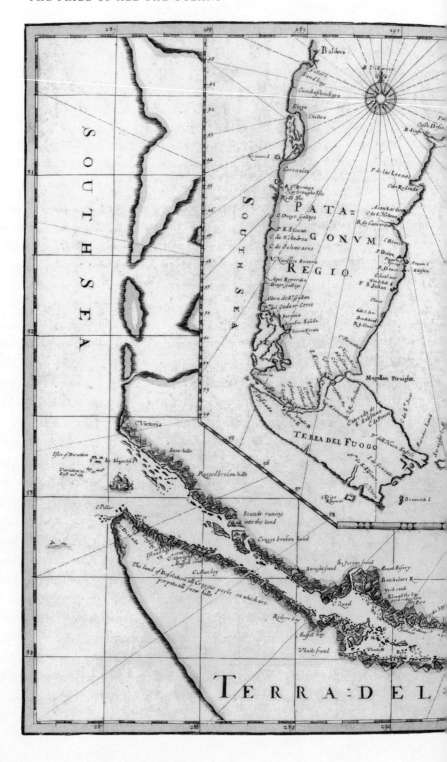

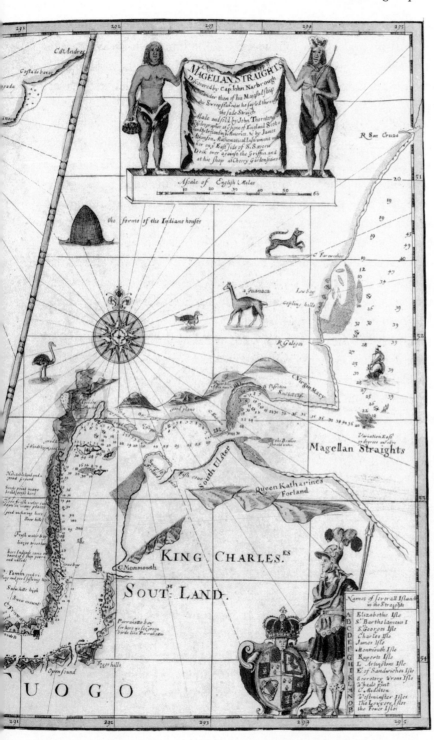

John Thornton.
'A New Mapp of
Magellans Straights'
(1673). Engraved from
a manuscript original
by John Narborough,
who sailed both ways
through the Strait of
Magellan in 1670–71,
this represents the
best depiction of the
region at the time of
Anson's voyage.

Bulkeley eventually reached safety at the Rio Grande, his report to the nearest British naval officer followed the same line, with its explanation – inexplicable to anyone not in possession of the full facts about the situation on the island – that Captain Cheap 'at his own request, tarried behind'.

Two days after leaving Wager Island the three boats had still sailed only a few miles, and when the schooner's topsail split the barge was sent ashore to fetch some more canvas. In what seems to have been a premeditated move, the nine men on board, who included midshipmen Campbell and Byron, decided to return to Captain Cheap's little group. The loss of the barge was a serious blow to the escape party, for as the smallest of their three boats it would have gone inshore to look for food in places inaccessible to the two heavier boats. Even more catastrophic was the loss of the cutter in a gale at the beginning of November, which left more than 70 men without any boat to act as tender to the *Speedwell*. On the 50-foot schooner the overcrowding now became intolerable – whether above deck in the wet and cold, or below in the stench of a hold where there was not enough head-room to stand or even sit. In a mysterious episode ten of the men volunteered to leave the boat and go ashore, where they thought that they might find the cutter, or build a canoe. Whether this death sentence was really self-inflicted is impossible to say. Bulkeley, as was his wont, drew up a paper in which the ten men declared that their action was of their own free will and choice. They went ashore two days before the schooner entered the Strait of Magellan, and vanished from view. The 21 deaths and disappearances on the voyage so far had brought the number of men on board down to 60, so there was some little relief from the overcrowding.

The passage of the 350 miles of the strait was as difficult as Cheap had predicted. Narborough's description was of only limited use among swirling currents and along rocky channels that turned back on themselves, split and then joined again, or ran into dead ends. On the low deck of the *Speedwell* the improvised tiller could only be held by a helmsman sitting down with his feet braced against a block, and there were many occasions when the schooner became unmanageable. At one time tremendous gales blew the little craft at frightening speed past rocks 'so near that a Man might toss a Biskit on them'. Disputes continued, and ten days were wasted as the schooner retraced its track to Cape Pilar at the western entrance of the strait after an argument between Baynes and Bulkeley about whether they had actually got inside the strait. Rain, mist and fog added to the difficulties of navigation, accomplished against a backdrop of continual bickering and constant hunger. The story of the ordeal as told in Bulkeley's journal makes ugly reading, as men sold flour at a guinea a pound, only to starve to death later, their pockets heavy with coin. Without a small boat, often the only way to find food was to swim ashore through the icy waters. Those who could not swim, or were too weak to do so, died; for in a situation where to give a morsel of food to a companion would shorten your own life it was every man for himself. On 6 January 1742 the purser, Thomas Harvey, 'died a skeleton for want of food'. He was probably the first purser in the navy who had ever died from hunger, Bulkeley wrote in a joking aside that indicates something of the callousness that now reigned. In the end it took more than a month to get through the strait, and there was still the long haul north along the mainland coast to Brazil to come.

From now on the *Speedwell* was well offshore much of the time, and even when the coast was within sight breakers made landing difficult. On one occasion those who could swim got ashore in a bay in latitude 37°25'S. and found water and plenty of seals. On the boat the non-swimmers were reduced to stripping the seal-skin covers from the hatches, burning off the hair, and chewing the skin. It was at this same spot, named Freshwater Bay by Bulkeley, that eight men who had swum ashore to search for food and water were stranded. Their story was to be told by one of their number, midshipman Isaac Morris, who accused the men in the *Speedwell* of deliberately abandoning the shore party in order to save provisions. Certainly the situation on the boat was desperate: Bulkeley was reckoned to be one of the strongest men in the boat, but even he could not stand on deck unsupported for more than ten minutes. His own explanation was that a gale blew the little schooner away from the bay, and that he did all that he could for the men left behind by floating ashore a cask holding clothes, muskets, ammunition, flints and candles. Bulkeley being Bulkeley, the cask also contained a letter of explanation, while on the boat he drafted a long memorandum justifying his action. It concluded with the observation that on last sight the men on the beach were making signals 'wishing us well'. If Morris's account of the castaways' indignation at their 'inhuman Treatment' is to be believed, the signals were of a different kind.

The eight men stayed at Freshwater Bay for a month, sleeping in a hole in the ground and living on seal-meat, until they decided to trek along the coast to Buenos Aires, 300 miles to the north. By now a Spanish prison seemed preferable to slow starvation. Two attempts failed as they ran out of food and water, and were forced back to the bay. To gather seal-meat for a third attempt, the men split into two parties, one to stay guarding the fire and the weapons, the other to go hunting for seals. After following this routine for some time, Isaac Morris and three of the men returned one evening from hunting to find two of their companions stabbed to death, and the other two missing. The camp site had been cleared of guns, ammunition, flints and other oddments, and the fire had been stamped out. What happened that day remains a mystery. There was no sign that the camp party, although armed, had put up any resistance, and no trace was found of the two missing men. For the four survivors the situation was desperate. There was no telling whether their companions' killers might not return, and meanwhile they were without weapons, food, or even any means of making a fire. For the third time they determined to reach Buenos Aires, but once again were forced back to Freshwater Bay, where they survived on raw meat, shellfish and roots. There they were found by a large party of mounted Indians, and although they had been captured rather than rescued, that night they feasted on roast horsemeat, their first hot food for three months.

As slaves they were passed from one Indian group to another in return for trinkets or, on one occasion, to pay a gambling debt. Footweary but reasonably treated, they wandered for a thousand miles in the interior of Patagonia. In late 1743 three of them were ransomed by an English merchant living in Buenos Aires; the fourth, John Duck, a mulatto, was kept behind by the Indians. The ransom extricated Morris and his two companions from the grasp of the Indians, only to deliver them into the harsher captivity of the Spanish garrison at Buenos Aires. When they refused to convert to Catholicism they were sent in early 1745 as prisoners of war on board the *Asia*, once the proud flagship of Admiral Pizarro's squadron, which had left Spain in search of Anson, but was now laid up in Montevideo harbour. Almost four years had passed since the wreck of the *Wager*.

Morris and his party had been stranded on 14 January 1742. Their abandonment, whether deliberately planned or not, meant that as the *Speedwell* sailed on only 33 men were left on board. All were now in a wretched condition, but the worst was over, for on 28 January 1742, after sailing unmolested across the La Plata estuary, the schooner reached the Portuguese waters of the Rio Grande after a voyage of more than 2,500 miles. In the days before landing the master, Thomas Clark, and his son both died, to be followed by Thomas Maclean, the cook. Aged 82, this tough old man had survived the rigours of the previous fifteen weeks, only to die almost within sight of port. To the Portuguese officials who came on board the 30 starving survivors were apparitions regarded with horror and their story with disbelief. Though marked by selfishness and brutality, the voyage had been one of the most remarkable small-boat endeavours of all time. John Bulkeley was the driving force; but the vessel itself, rebuilt under the most adverse conditions by John Cummins, had performed beyond all expectation.

The return to England of the survivors was not as straightforward as they had hoped; their lot was that of stranded seamen the world over. Quarrelling with each other, they broke up into small groups that made their own way home. Bulkeley, Cummins and the cooper, Young, reached Bahia, and eventually boarded a ship bound for Lisbon, where they took passage for England in a warship. Their arrival at Spithead on 1 January 1743 was not quite the joyous occasion they might have anticipated, for Lieutenant Baynes had returned before them, and had given the Admiralty his own version of events. The last extant muster book from the *Wager* stops on 2 November 1740, when it was sent back to England from Madeira. A new one was then started, only to be lost in the shipwreck. On Baynes' return to England in late 1742 the Admiralty put the original muster book before him in the hope that he could bring it up-to-date. The attempt was not totally successful, although the book is dotted with the lieutenant's notes on those members of the crew whose fate he could remember: 'left behind in the South Seas'; 'coming home'; 'drowned but the time not known'; and a damning entry opposite Cozens' name – 'shot by the Captain about the End of June 1741'. With Baynes having given at least some indication of their role in events, Bulkeley, Cummins and Young were detained on board ship for two weeks. At that point the Admiralty decided that no full enquiry could be made until Cheap got back, although to most it seemed improbable that either he or any other member of the *Wager*'s crew would ever return. Meanwhile, the survivors were not to be taken back into the navy, nor were they to receive arrears of wages, until the enquiry was held. Bulkeley had sent a copy of his journal to the First Lord of the Admiralty, the Earl of Winchilsea, but it was returned unread on the grounds that it was 'too large ever to be perused'. More probably, the Lords of the Admiralty had no wish to commit themselves to an opinion on the strength of a gunner's journal about what rumour had was 'a dark and intricate business'. At least they made no effort to prevent its publication later that year by Bulkeley and Cummins under the rather anodyne title of *A Voyage to the South-Seas, In the Years 1740–1. Containing, a Faithful Narrative of the Loss of His Majesty's Ship the Wager*.

For Cheap the shipwreck had deprived him not only of his first command, in circumstances that cast doubt on his competence, but had brought humiliation and violence. A naval captain, hands tied behind his back, arguing with his crew, was a contradiction in terms. When the majority of the *Wager*'s survivors sailed off in their three boats they were effectively leaving Cheap, the surgeon Elliot and Lieutenant Hamilton to their deaths. The decision by the two midshipmen, Byron and Campbell, to return with the barge and seven men to Wager Island gave Cheap at least the semblance of a command once more. When the deserters also returned to the main camp, Cheap's party numbered nineteen men with two boats, the barge and the yawl. The captain himself became 'very brisk' again, and determined to put into effect his favoured scheme to sail north to the island of Chiloé. It was 300 miles distant, along a rockbound coast that had never been properly charted. The first day's

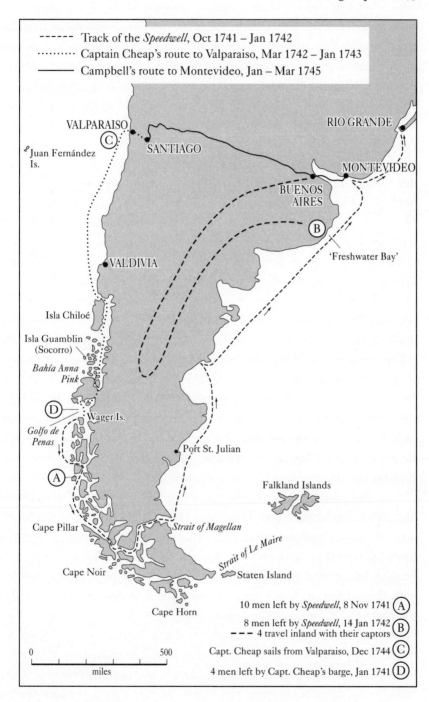

The escape from Wager Island

rowing showed the problem as huge waves threatened to swamp the boats, and to lighten them most of the carefully hoarded provisions had to be thrown overboard. Continuous rain, heavy seas and contrary winds marked their painfully slow course along the coast. Sometimes they were able to spend the night ashore, but often they had to lie on their oars, taking it turn and turn about to prevent the boats drifting onto the rocks. Apart from the occasional wildfowl or seabird shot by Elliot or Hamilton they existed on shellfish. For most of the time they had no fire and no dry clothes. Disaster struck one night when the yawl's anchor failed to hold in the heavy breakers, and it capsized. As the yawl was swept out to sea, one of the two boatkeepers left on board was thrown into the surf and survived; but the other was drowned as the upturned hull disappeared from the sight of the horrified watchers on shore. Their situation was now desperate, for the barge was not large enough to take all eighteen of them. In a mirror image of events on the southern voyage of the *Speedwell* four marines were left on shore with muskets and ammunition. Their abandonment was a sacrifice in vain, for the northerly winds made it impossible to get the barge round the headlands of the great promontory (Cabo Tres Montes) that guarded the northern exit of the Golfo de Penas. Battered and dejected, her crew returned to the bay to pick up the marines, but they had disappeared. Only a musket lying on the beach indicated that this was the place where they had been marooned. By early February 1742 the barge was back at Wager Island. Another man had died on the return voyage, leaving thirteen in all.

On the island divisions and arguments surfaced once more. Cheap and Elliot lived in one hut; Hamilton, Byron and Campbell in another; and the remaining men where they could find shelter. Help came in the form of a party of Indians whose chief, bearing the Spanish name of Martín, had visited the camp site soon after the shipwreck. Negotiating with the surgeon in pidgin Spanish, he agreed to guide the barge along the coast to Chiloé on the assurance that he would be given the boat on arrival. Sick, starving and exhausted, the thirteen survivors once more put to sea. Two men died, amid complaints that Cheap had secreted what food there was for himself. These deaths precipitated the breakup of the little group, for after burying the bodies of their two comrades the six remaining seamen took advantage of the absence of Cheap and the other officers, who had gone along the shore looking for shellfish and seaweed, to seize the barge and its contents. They rowed away, watched by Elliot the surgeon, who lay sick and helpless on the ground, and were never seen again. Although Cheap, Hamilton, Byron and Campbell were in slightly better condition than the surgeon their situation seemed hopeless. They had one musket, but no ammunition, and what powder was left would be needed to light a fire. 'I wish I could forget the rest of our Story,' Cheap wrote later as he railed against 'the Barbarity of these six Villains' who had abandoned their officers. Once again Martín came to the rescue. With the single gun his only promised reward, he agreed to take the Englishmen by canoe to Chiloé. Elliot's death at this moment was especially poignant, for his skill in hunting and shooting had helped to keep the others alive. But as his exertions weakened him so that he could no longer stand, there is no indication that Cheap, who because of his rank was the only one of the party to be given food by the Indians, made any attempt to share it on any regular basis. Byron records one occasion when the captain handed a piece of seal-meat to Elliot, 'who was the only man in favour at this time', but this seems to have been the exception rather than the rule. Not for the first time, Cheap emerges as a deeply unsympathetic character. At no time did he provide a detailed account of events to match Bulkeley's, so we see him mainly through the eyes of his companions. They had little good to say of an officer who seemed to put self-preservation before any concern for his men.

The canoe journey north was the worst ordeal yet. Byron and Campbell were forced to paddle the canoes, often without food for days on end. They had no footwear, their clothes were in tatters, and they were covered with lice. Berries, shellfish and the occasional piece of seal-meat kept them alive. Cheap was better treated but, according to Byron's later account, had disintegrated mentally and physically. His legs were as 'big as mill posts, though his body appeared to be nothing but skin and bone'. Covered with ants and lice, his beard as long as a hermit's and his face filthy with train-oil, in the end he could not remember his own name. At the bay where the *Anna* had found shelter the previous year, Hamilton refused to go any further, and was left behind. At last the three survivors, after a hazardous open-water crossing, reached the island of Chiloé. They were taken by stages under armed guard to the town of Chaco in the north of the island, where the governor resided. There they were joined by Hamilton, escorted in by a Spanish party sent to find him. Kind treatment, and a relaxed form of imprisonment that allowed Byron, an inveterate ladies' man, some social life, brought a slow recovery. Although at the beginning of 1743 the four men were sent under guard to Valparaiso on the mainland, and there held for a while in the condemned cell of the local prison, a move inland to the capital at Santiago improved their lot immeasurably. Released on parole, they were entertained by local dignitaries, swapped stories of danger at sea with Admiral Pizarro's officers, who had just reached Chile in the *Esperanza*, and discovered that Anson's generous treatment of prisoners he had taken off the coasts of Chile and Peru had convinced people that these Englishmen had nothing in common with the buccaneers of fearful memory.

While in Santiago, Cheap had the first opportunity to put his own version of events on paper. In a long letter of February 1744 to Richard Lingley, an English merchant in Buenos Aires who had used his contacts in Santiago to help Cheap and his companions, he described the shipwreck in some detail; but passed over the events of the next five months in a few lines. In his relation of events Cheap accepted no responsibility for his misfortunes. On the night of the shipwreck the surgeon had drugged him without his consent, so he was not to know that the lieutenant and gunner had disobeyed his orders and let the ship run onto the rocks. The blame for the behaviour of his 'mutinous and disobedient men' Cheap placed on the officers, and above all on Captain Pemberton of the marines. He made no mention of the shooting of Cozens, though in one place he admitted that he 'even proceeded to Extremities'. There was no acknowledgement of Elliot's loyal services, merely a reference to his death through hunger. Cheap's only words of praise were for Lieutenant Hamilton.

Cheap and his three companions stayed in Santiago until in late 1744 they were offered a passage from Valparaiso on a French frigate bound for Spain. Campbell refused the offer, for a rift had developed between him and the others, and particularly Cheap, over reports that the midshipman intended to marry a local woman, convert to Roman Catholicism, and join the Spanish navy. The truth of this is difficult to determine, and in the end it may have been nothing more than that Campbell preferred the company of Spanish naval officers, and decided to travel with several of them to Buenos Aires and then back to Europe rather than accompany Cheap. Whatever his reasons, he was to have by far the more eventful journey home. After crossing the Andes by mule, Campbell joined Admiral Pizarro to return to Europe on board the refitted *Asia* (whose fortunes until this time are followed in the next chapter). On the ship he found the three other survivors from the *Wager*, fellow midshipman Isaac Morris and the two seamen who had survived their marooning at Freshwater Bay and subsequent wanderings. It was a moot point which of the two midshipman, Campbell or Morris, had wandered farthest and suffered most since leaving Wager Island.

When the *Asia* was only three days out from Montevideo, eleven Indians taken prisoner in fighting against the Spaniards, and now bound for the galleys, rose in revolt. They killed about a score of the crew, and cleared the quarterdeck. At first the Spaniards below suspected that the Englishmen had joined in the rising, but on finding that only the Indians were involved they used their superior numbers to recover the ship. On the death of their chief the remaining Indians jumped overboard and were drowned. The scenes of melodramatic horror seemed a fitting climax to the experiences of the men from the *Wager*. After further spells in prison after reaching Spain Isaac Morris and his two companions finally reached England in July 1746, two months after Campbell. Much to Campbell's discomfort, Cheap was also back, together with Hamilton and Byron, after experiencing further delays as prisoners of the French. As far as the Admiralty was concerned Campbell was now an untouchable. He was accused not only of becoming a Roman Catholic, but also of taking a commission in the Spanish navy, a charge levelled at him by Cheap, but which Campbell always denied.

1746 was a year of reunion for the *Wager* survivors, but it was a forced reunion that reflected the disputes and the bitterness of the voyage. As soon as Cheap got back the Admiralty set court-martial proceedings on foot. It was not quite the enquiry that many had anticipated, and Bulkeley had feared, for it took the form of the customary investigation into the loss of a naval vessel. The hearing, despite the threatening noises made by minor officials in the direction of Bulkeley and Cummins to the effect that mutiny was a hanging offence, confined itself to the circumstances of the shipwreck on 14 May 1741; and the gunner and carpenter were called only as witnesses to the events of that day. The run-up to the court martial had been ominous for the longboat survivors. Admiralty messengers found and took into custody Lieutenant Baynes, the boatswain John King and the carpenter John Cummins. The first that Bulkeley, who during 1745 had commanded a privateer, knew of Cheap's return and of the decision to hold a court martial was when he read a newspaper notice that all crew members from the *Wager* were to report to Spithead. After doing so, he too was taken into custody and sent on board the *St George* at Spithead. Although he was allowed pen and paper he was warned that 'no Man after Sentence of Death shall be indulged with it on any Account'.

For all except Baynes the actual court martial on 14 April 1746 was a reassuring anticlimax, for it dealt only with the wreck of the *Wager*, and the sole charge brought by Cheap was against the lieutenant, whose negligence he held responsible for the loss of the ship. In all, eight witnesses were called. They agreed on the severity of Cheap's injury, but their recollections of that awful night five years earlier were blurred and confused. The findings of the court martial were also far from clear-cut. Baynes was blamed for not informing the captain that the carpenter had thought that he saw land to the northwest, and for failing to use the lead or to anchor. On the other hand, the court recognised that the carpenter's sighting of land had been momentary, that the anchor cable was jammed, and that there were only thirteen 'sickly' men to clear it and to work the ship. Accordingly, Baynes was acquitted of blame for the loss of the *Wager*, but at the same time reprimanded for omissions of duty.

Neither during the court martial nor at any other time was there any formal investigation into the events that followed the shipwreck, despite the violence used against the captain. Only a few months before the court martial Cheap on his way home had written to Anson with a vehement denunciation of his crew – 'poltroons' who refused to face the enemy, and instead had fled south 'after most inhumanly abandoning us & distroying at their Departure every thing they thought could be of any use to us'. Remarkably, in a navy that prided itself on its discipline and adherence to the letter of the law, this was the mutiny that never was. Not only were wages paid to the survivors, up to the time the *Wager* was lost, but Bulkeley was even offered command of a small cutter (which he declined). The entire episode, known to the public at this time only through the exculpatory book published under the names of Bulkeley and Cummins in 1743, was clearly an embarrassment to the Admiralty. To bring charges of mutiny against Bulkeley and other members of the crew would have raised the whole question of Cheap's conduct, and particularly his shooting of Cozens. In addition, there was a legal grey area. Since entitlement to wages in the navy ceased when a ship was lost, it was a matter of some uncertainty whether a crew's duty to observe naval discipline continued after that point. The authorised account of Anson's voyage, published two years later at a time when Anson was one of the Lords of the Admiralty, is revealing here. Although in the chapter on the wreck of the *Wager* the words 'mutiny' and 'mutineers' are used, there is also what appears to be an escape clause which noted that the crew 'conceived' that once the ship was lost the officers' authority ceased. That a loophole did exist was shown by the passing in 1747 of an Act which extended naval discipline to the crews of ships wrecked or captured, and also allowed for their wages to continue after that point.

The wreck of the *Wager* gave rise to a flurry of books. Not only was the drama a subject of continuing interest to publishers but several of the survivors had their own stories to tell and their own cases to plead. The Bulkeley and Cummins *Voyage to the South-Seas* of 1743 was the first published account, and long extracts from it were printed in the *London Magazine* each month from July 1743 to February 1744. It was also reprinted in one form or another in four of the general accounts of Anson's voyage that appeared in 1744 and 1745. It was followed in 1747 by *The Sequel to Bulkeley and Cummins' Voyage*, written by Alexander Campbell. He pronounced himself angry at what he saw as his unfair rejection by the navy, but in that same year we catch a rather damning glimpse of him, now in the service of the King of Portugal. Edward Legge, captain of the *Severn* on Anson's voyage, and at this time commodore of a squadron in Portuguese waters, wrote that Campbell was busy enlisting English seamen, and sending them overland to Cadiz to join the Spanish navy. 1751 saw two books: *A Narrative of the Dangers and Distresses of the Voyage* by Isaac Morris, which described the fortunes and misfortunes of the group abandoned at Freshwater Bay; and *An Affecting Narrative* published under the name of the cooper, John Young, but based on the Bulkeley and Cummins book with elaborations by a hack writer. Bulkeley's book was reissued in 1757, with additional material, including a brief account of Cheap's adventures after he left Wager Island. Finally, in 1768, came the only account that put forward any defence for Cheap (who had died in 1752), and in doing so attacked what the author, John Byron, saw as the tendentious version of events published by Bulkeley and Cummins. There is no explanation why Byron's *Narrative* appeared so long after the events it described, but a factor in its publication may have been that Byron by this time was a celebrated figure. He had commanded a naval discovery expedition to the Pacific in 1764–6 which, among much else, claimed to have seen giants in Patagonia. The voyage also held a more chilling reminder of Byron's youthful experiences, for his sailing orders included an instruction to search along the Patagonian coast for survivors of the *Wager*, and to bring them home. It was 23 years since the shipwreck.

All these survival narratives had in common a revelation of the behaviour of men thrown into circumstances of extreme danger and deprivation. The disciplined environment in which they lived and worked disappeared with the wreck of the ship and Cheap's failure to maintain his authority. It was not a question of all now being equal, but of a few determined men reconstructing a system of rules that would enable the crew, or at least some of them, to survive. As Bulkeley explained, 'Persons of our Station' would never normally take the lead. Cheap's refusal to contemplate any course of action other than a blind obedience to orders that most felt no longer had relevance to their plight, brought others to the fore. Among them Bulkeley stands out, a reminder of the ability that might be found among seamen who did not hold a commission. His mortification at the loss of his journal when the *Wager* struck, and his determination to start another, already marked him out as something unusual among men who did not take readily to pen and paper. So did his claim, whether true or not, that he carried a copy of Thomas à Kempis's *Imitation of Christ* with him throughout his adventures. Bulkeley's mental toughness was matched by physical strength. Unafraid of confrontation with his captain, ruthless in dealing with opposition from his companions, unscrupulous in abandoning men whose presence threatened the survival of the rest, the gunner becomes the key figure in the story of the *Wager*. On the last desperate stages of the voyage of the *Speedwell* it was somehow inevitable that with the men on board too weak to manage the boat it was Bulkeley who was still on his feet, if only for a few minutes at a time; and that it was Bulkeley who at the end piloted the ramshackle little craft into safe anchorage at the Rio Grande. The story of course lost nothing in the telling, and the telling was Bulkeley's; but the issue of his personal dominance, whether for better or for worse, was not challenged in the other accounts.

The story of the *Wager* exposed extremes of human behaviour in adversity – from callous disregard of the sufferings of others to almost unbelievable feats of endurance. After all the divisions and quarrels, the deaths and disappearances, only 29 of the regular crew of the *Wager*, together with seven marines, eventually got back to England. It took some of these men five years, during which time they were rarely out of danger. On the map the routes of their escape from Wager Island form a spider's web stretching across a vast area of present-day Chile and Argentina. Those tracks might give an impression of purpose and direction, but they had been drawn in blood.

IV

'To Distress and Annoy the King of Spain'

'When you shall arrive on the Spanish coast of the South Sea, you are to do your best to annoy and distress the Spaniards . . . by taking, sinking, burning, or otherwise destroying all their ships and vessels that you shall meet with; and in case you shall find it practicable to seize, surprise, or take any of the towns or places belonging to Spaniards on the coast, you are to attempt it.'

Instructions to Commodore Anson, January 1740

BY THE BEGINNING OF September 1741 Anson was preparing to sail from Juan Fernández with what was left of his squadron. The weakest among the men who had reached the island had either died soon after arrival or were on the way to some sort of recovery. To help the sick back to health discipline was relaxed to the extent that those able to look after themselves were allowed to build huts away from the beach and the festering hospital tents. August had been the turning point, with only nine deaths, most from the *Gloucester*. During the weeks of convalescence much-needed work was carried out on the ships lying at anchor in the bay. Hulls and masts were repaired, sails and rigging overhauled, and as much scraping, caulking and painting done as the crews' strength allowed. Everything was in short supply – from 'junk' for new ropes to spare masts and anchors – and there was much improvisation. So before she was scuttled the *Anna*'s foremast was taken out to replace the rotting mainmast of the *Tryal*.

The squadron's objectives once it left its island refuge were still

unclear. Everything had changed since Anson had received his instructions to rampage through the South Sea, attacking the main ports and
rousing local populations to rebellion. The expedition had received no
news from the outside world since its call at St Catherine's the previous
December. Peace might have been declared between Britain and Spain;
more likely, France might have joined the war. If a sail came in sight, it
might be friend or foe, man-of-war or merchant vessel. Anson and his
men could only guess at the course of the war in the Caribbean, the
whereabouts of the Spanish squadron sent to intercept them, defensive
measures taken by the authorities in Peru and Chile, and the fate of the
Severn, *Pearl* and *Wager*. The loss of these vessels was a devastating blow.
The *Severn* and *Pearl* were powerful men-of-war, while the smaller *Wager*
carried the field guns, mortars and ammunition for land operations. This
weakening of the squadron made the full execution of Anson's orders
impossible. Together with the death rate on the surviving ships it not
only wrecked any hopes of aggressive operations against the major ports
of Spanish America, but put the safety of those ships at risk if they met
Pizarro's squadron. The assumption was that the Spanish ships would
certainly have suffered, as Anson's had done, in getting round the Horn,
but that with the port facilities of Chile and Peru at their disposal they
might well have refitted and put to sea again.

Despite his losses, Anson was determined to follow as much of his
original instructions 'to distress and annoy the King of Spain' as possible.
He decided to sail north from Juan Fernández, in the first instance to
the Isthmus of Panama. If Vernon's forces in the Caribbean had succeeded
in following up the capture of Portobelo with further successes, Anson's
few ships could yet play a crucial role in operations across the isthmus.
There might even be a combined assault on Panama. Such thoughts were
pushed into the background when on 8 September a sail was sighted
creeping over the northeast horizon. Signal guns brought the men from
their huts back to the beach, where hopes ran high that yet another of
the missing ships was making her rendezvous. As the distant sail kept
steadily on a course that took it well to the east of the island those hopes
faded. The ship could only be Spanish, and her lookouts might have
spotted the masts of the anchored ships in the bay. Although a crew was

hastily assembled and sent on board the *Centurion*, including the only ten fit men from the *Gloucester*, she was not ready for sea until late afternoon. As the light faded Anson's ship was towed out of the bay in pursuit, but when morning came there was no sign of the strange sail. For the next two days the *Centurion* held to a southeast course in an attempt to come up with it. On 12 September, as Anson decided to abandon the chase, a sail was sighted four or five leagues distant. Its behaviour as it kept steadily on course towards the *Centurion*, fired a gun, and hoisted Spanish colours, aroused fears that it might be one of Pizarro's squadron, and the *Centurion* was quickly cleared for action. The flimsy walls of the officers' cabins were knocked down, and stores and other baggage that might hamper the working of the guns were thrown overboard. As the Spaniard loomed out of a rain squall it was clear to all that she was a merchantman, and when the *Centurion* fired four shots into her rigging she surrendered. They were the first shots fired in anger by any of Anson's ships since their departure from Spithead a year earlier.

Lieutenant Philip Saumarez went on board and soon sent back 25 passengers, and details of the prize. She was a 450-ton merchant vessel, the *Nuestra Señora del Monte Carmelo*, sailing from Callao to Valparaiso with a cargo of sugar and cloth. For her captors this was uninteresting and unsaleable booty, but the passengers on board carried coin and silver worth £18,000. The fact that the ship carried only three four-pounder guns, and no small arms, was testimony to the normal security of the sailing route between Peru and Chile. No foreign marauder had been seen in 'the Spanish lake' since Shelvocke's privateers twenty years earlier. The *Carmelo*'s master, Manuel Zamorra, had mistaken the *Centurion* for a Spanish ship, and by the time he realised his mistake it was too late to escape. Of more immediate interest even than the treasure were the official letters on board, and the news they contained. The war was still in progress, but in the Caribbean Vernon's attack on Cartagena had failed, and the British had withdrawn. For Anson this was a grievous blow, and increased his feeling of isolation. Any hopes of joining Vernon's forces in a combined attack on Panama vanished, nor would there now be any British presence on the isthmus to help Anson with reinforcements and supplies.

To offset the disappointing news from the Caribbean came the information that Pizarro's squadron had been even more badly mauled than Anson's in attempting to get round the Horn. Two of the Spanish ships were missing, and Pizarro with his remaining three ships had been forced to return to the River Plate 'almost entirely disabled, their Masts, Sails, Yards, Rigging and Hulls in a manner shattered and torn to Pieces'. In time, more grim detail emerged about the fate of the Spanish squadron, which had sailed from the River Plate in late January 1741, for Pizarro was determined to get round the Horn before Anson. Having provisioned and refitted his ships in Chile, he would then be able to intercept Anson's ships as they straggled into the South Sea. By the time the British squadron reached the Strait Le Maire in early March Pizarro had already passed Cape Horn, only to run into the same furious storms that Anson was soon to encounter. The *Herminona* (54 guns) disappeared and was never seen again, while the other ships were blown back along their track and south of Staten Land once more. At some point British and Spanish ships must have passed each other in far southerly latitudes, without ever glimpsing each other. Starvation rather than scurvy was the nightmare on board the Spanish ships, for in his haste to get to sea, and confident of a fast passage to friendly ports in the South Sea, Pizarro had sailed with only four months' provisions on board. Once these were finished, men died in their dozens, often dropping dead at the pumps. Rats were caught, and sold at four dollars each. By the time Pizarro's flagship the *Asia* (66 guns) and the *San Estevan* (40 guns) reached the River Plate they had lost half their men. Even worse was the plight of the *Esperanza* (50 guns), where out of a crew of 450 only 58 survived. Just as horrifying was the fate of the biggest ship, the *Guipuscoa* (74 guns), described in a letter from her captain that was found on board a later prize captured by Anson's men. As Captain Mindinuetta tried to get his ship back to the River Plate he threw overboard all his upper-deck guns to ease the strain on the ship's sides, which had opened in the heavy seas. As the vessel continued rolling and jolting, the masts went, one by one, first the main-mast, then the foremast, and finally the mizen-mast. By now 250 out of the crew of 700 were dead. The hundred or so men able to do duty were on a daily allowance of 1½ oz. of biscuit a day, the rest 1 oz. of wheat.

As the crew struggled to get up jury masts the hulk was driven along the coast of Patagonia, past the River Plate and into an anchorage just south of St Catherine's. There the crew abandoned the pumps and, with 30 dead bodies lying on deck, forced the captain to run the ship on shore, where she sank.

At Buenos Aires Pizarro made efforts to refit two of his ships, but after further disappointments only the *Esperanza* reached Chile, by which time Anson was far distant on the coasts of China. Anticipating delays and problems, Pizarro had on his arrival in the River Plate immediately sent advice overland to the viceroy of Peru that in case any of Anson's ships managed to get round the Cape and into the South Sea he should fit out a force to intercept them. In response to this, four armed vessels, the largest carrying 50 guns, had set sail from Callao, three to wait off Concepción, and one off Juan Fernández. They remained on station until early June 1741, by which time it was assumed that if any of the British ships had survived the passage round the Horn they would have long since arrived in the South Sea, and have been spotted. As the *Centurion*'s officers heard more about the movements of the Callao ships, they realised that the man-of-war stationed off Juan Fernández had given up her watch only days before the *Centurion* arrived there. With only a few officers and eight seamen left on deck to work the ship, any resistance would have been useless; and the same would have been true of the *Gloucester* and *Tryal* when they came in sight. Pascoe Thomas picked up a rumour from the *Carmelo*'s crew that the Spanish force had orders 'to put us all to the Sword without any Distinction', and however improbable this story it brought home to Anson's men the narrowness of their escape. In retrospect, the navigational error that led Anson to miss Juan Fernández on his first sweep, and then to lose 70 or 80 men on the terrible second attempt to beat westward to the island, saved the squadron. Were it not for that miscalculation the *Centurion* would have reached Juan Fernández before the end of May, and there found the Spaniards waiting.

When the *Centurion* returned to Juan Fernández with her prize, the documents from the *Carmelo* were scrutinised more closely, and gave renewed cause for optimism. The cruising squadron from Callao had been so damaged by storms that it would be unable to put to sea again for at least two months. Meanwhile, with the seas apparently clear of foreign intruders, normal coastal trade had been resumed. The *Carmelo* was one of three ships that had sailed in company from Callao for Valparaiso – another was the sail sighted from Juan Fernández on 8 September – and several others were ready for sea. With the capture of the merchantman and her news the balance of advantage had for the moment tilted Anson's way. There were no men-of-war scouring the seas for him, and the presence of his squadron so near coasts of Chile and Peru was unknown. How long this cloak of invisibility would last was uncertain, for the failure of the *Carmelo* to make port would set alarm bells ringing again. But Spanish apprehension of renewed danger, and action to follow that apprehension, would take time; and meanwhile there was no reason why this first prize should not be followed by more. It was the limited ambition of the buccaneers of a past age, rather than that of the commodore of a King's squadron; but for the men that was more than enough. In three months they had passed from being the wretched, half-dead survivors of a ruined enterprise to a situation where there was every prospect of rich pickings in prize money. And the dreadful casualties carried a grim consolation, for the fewer the crew the more prize money each individual would get. A new energy was evident in the operations at Juan Fernández as Anson rearranged his forces for the weeks ahead. The modest armament of the *Anna* was put on board the prize before the pink was sunk, and some of the Spanish prisoners were sent on board the *Gloucester* to help work the ship. It is true that all the ships were under-manned. On the prize Saumarez had only three petty officers, twelve seamen and six prisoners to sail the ship and work the guns. Even so, as he pointed out, although a man-of-war would make short work of him, he would be more than a match for any merchantman they met.

Anson's final dispositions sent Captain Michell in the *Gloucester* to cruise off the small Peruvian port of Paita, where he was to take care to keep out of sight of land. All was not well between Anson and Michell. Entries in the latter's journal show that he resented Anson's refusal to send any men to the *Gloucester* except Spanish prisoners. There were 29 of these, but seven of them were unhandy merchants. They all had to be guarded, and the ship's officers and warrant officers went fully armed.

Anson with the *Centurion* and his prize intended to join the *Tryal* off Valparaiso. With the net thus spread, further prizes should follow as the unsuspecting Spaniards resumed normal trade. For eight weeks Anson's ships struggled to keep station. They had to remain far enough out to sea to avoid being sighted from the land, yet not so distant that a merchantman could slip between them and the coast. Matters were not helped by the hazy weather, which prevented the usual astronomical observations to establish their position. On at least one occasion the ships were blown so near an unseen and unsuspected shore in the darkness that only the sound of the surf alerted the crew to the danger. The logs reflect a constant apprehension that any sail sighted might be one of the men-of-war from Callao, refitted and at sea once more, rather than an unarmed merchantman. In the event, most of the sightings in these weeks proved to be another ship from the squadron; but since the first reaction of Anson's ships to the sight of a sail was to hoist Spanish colours mutual identification was often not made until after tense hours of preparing for action.

Even the successes of this cruise brought problems. The first prize was the *Arranzazu*, taken by the *Tryal* after a chase lasting 36 hours at a time when the rest of the squadron had not yet left Juan Fernández. At 600 tons the *Arranzazu* was one of the largest Spanish merchantmen in the South Sea, but since she was virtually unarmed her crew surrendered after the *Tryal*'s first shots. She carried a mixed cargo, but only £5,000 in coin and plate. Among this were ornaments for a church, including two-foot images of saints 'finely wrought' in silver, which 'we beat up close to make them lye snug in the Chests'. During the long chase in stormy weather the *Tryal* had sprung both her mainmast and foremast, and when the *Centurion* came up with her six days later the sloop was wallowing helplessly in heavy seas with the pumps unable to cope. Once the weather improved, the crew and the twelve guns of the *Tryal* were moved to the prize, and the sloop was scuttled. It was a sad but inevitable end for the smallest vessel in the squadron, one that had weathered Cape Horn and had played a full part in the action since. The *Arranzazu* was an imposing-looking ship, with ports cut for 32 cannon, and she had been used by the Spaniards as a frigate in times of emergency; but neither of the prizes that were armed and commissioned by Anson at this time could be considered as anything but hastily improvised men-of-war.

A few days after the *Centurion* reached her station off Valparaiso the first rumblings of discontent about prize money were heard. The incident is reported only by Pascoe Thomas, but there is no reason to doubt the details given in his account. Some among the crew demanded that the treasure from the *Carmelo* should be divided up there and then. Almost every buccaneering and privateering expedition to the South Sea had experienced disputes over this issue, and the men had usually won. Anson summoned the crew on deck to explain why things were done differently in the navy. The rights of the crew were secured by Act of Parliament, he pointed out, and all the money and plate taken on the prize had been weighed and marked. He would allow a representative from the crew to inspect the inventory of the *Carmelo*'s cargo, but was not prepared to go any further. With references to the Articles of War and the dangers of mutiny, Anson then dismissed the crew.

With this issue out of the way, the watch was resumed for Spanish ships, but during the weeks that followed the sea remained empty. Inevitably, concern grew on Anson's ships that one or other of them had been spotted. Not until 5 November was another Spanish sail sighted, the 300-ton *Santa Teresa de Jesus*. Sensibly, her crew surrendered once the *Centurion* opened fire. Again, the captors were frustrated by the sight of an assorted cargo that was of no value to them, since the Spaniards had strict instructions not to ransom either goods or individuals. And this time the silver on board amounted to only £170. Also on board were passengers, including three women. Even more than the others, they were terrified 'at the falling into the hands of an enemy, whom, from the former outrages of the Buccaneers . . . they had been taught to consider the most terrible and brutal of all mankind'. These words in the authorised account were followed by several pages in praise of Anson's humane treatment of his prisoners in general, and of these three women in particular. They were allowed to keep their own cabins on the *Santa Teresa*, and Anson allocated the ship's pilot as their guardian. In this, as in other ways, Anson was intent on demonstrating that a King's officer was of a different stamp from his disreputable buccaneering predecessors, whose cruelty had been vividly described by Esquemeling, Defoe and others.

The taking and plundering of *PAYTA*.   *Page 51.*

The plundering of Paita. Engraving in Anon., *An Authentic and Genuine Journal of Commodore Anson's Expedition* (1744). This lively scene, almost certainly not based on a first-hand drawing, strikes a contrast between the riotous behaviour of the sailors and the sedate stance of the officers in the foreground.

His behaviour had benefits that he could not have anticipated; two years later Byron thought that the good treatment he and other survivors from the *Wager* had received in Chile owed much to reports of Anson's conduct towards his prisoners.

The third and final prize taken in this stage of operations was the *Nuestra Señora de Carmin*, seized the day after she left Paita on her way south to Callao. Prisoners taken off the ship included an Irishman in the

Spanish service, John Williams, whose rough treatment at his employers' hands made him eager to pass on all the information he had. The *Gloucester* had been sighted by a merchantman coming into Paita, and officials in the port had already taken precautionary measures. Dispatches had been sent to Lima alerting the viceroy; some of the treasure in Paita was being removed to Piura, about 40 miles inland; the rest had been loaded onto a fast ship that was to leave for Mexico the next day. With secrecy gone, Anson decided on an immediate attack on Paita. It was a small town of less than two hundred low houses built of sun dried brick, together with a few larger buildings such as the custom house, the governor's dwelling and two churches. It was defended by a small fort and eight cannon. Situated on a desert coast with no vegetation or water, Paita's main feature was its large harbour, where passengers bound for Lima could disembark to complete the remaining 600 miles of their journey by road, rather than spend weeks in a vessel trying to beat south against the headwinds. Paita was unlikely to put up much resistance, and its capture promised booty and a place where surplus prisoners could be left. It was hardly one of the great citadels of Spanish America but, as the authorised account put it, the proposed assault was 'the only enterprize in our power to undertake'. With his land forces wiped out by disease and his field guns lost with the *Wager*, Anson's options were as limited as those of his predecessors, who from Cavendish onwards sacked Paita when they could think of nothing better to do.

Small and unimpressive though it was, Paita was the only Spanish town stormed by Anson's men; and the authorised account, without indulging in false heroics, made the most of it. The attack was a night landing by four of the ships' boats, carrying about sixty men between them under the command of Lieutenant Peircy Brett. As guides they had two of the Spanish pilots who had been taken prisoner, and who were threatened with death if they gave the alarm. For one of them there was nothing new in this; twenty years earlier he had been taken prisoner by Shelvocke's consort ship, the *Success*, and been forced to direct an assault force towards Trujillo, just south of Paita. In 1741 the action was over almost as soon as it started. There were a couple of cannon shot from the fort, both fired (it transpired later) by a visiting official from

REFERENCES.
Prizes *taken by the* Centurion.
a. *Nostra Seigniora del monte Carmela.*
b. *The Santa Terressa de Jesus.*
c. *Nostra Seigniora del Carmene.*
d. *The Aransace taken by the Tryal Sloop.*
1.2.3.4.*Vessels belonging to Merchants.*

The burning of Paita. Engraving in *Anson's Voyage* (1748) after drawing by Peircy Brett. This detailed sketch by Brett was drawn on the spot, and was careful to show that amid the damage and wreckage the church and convent were unscathed.

REFERENCES.

e e. Two of the Vice Roys Gallies of 36 Oars each.
f. { The Fort with eight Guns mounted, and capable of mounting thirteen.
g. The place where the Boats landed 49 Men.
h. The Convent of Mercenarians.
i. The Parish Church.

Piura, and some desultory small arms firing; then the inhabitants fled, some of them still in their night clothes. To Anson's anger, the governor escaped at this time, quickly followed by his young bride, and in doing so wrecked Anson's hopes of negotiating a ransom for him and the valuable goods in the town. In the authorised account, this was the only blemish in an operation that left one crew member dead (Anson's steward, Peter O'Brien), and another, the Hon. Augustus Keppel, slightly wounded. There was some pillaging, but this was put in a light-hearted context with long descriptions of Anson's sailors dressed in plundered finery, often women's clothes. Otherwise, the emphasis was on the discipline of the men; only one unnamed individual became drunk – to such an extent that he almost missed the evacuation of the town, and when he staggered to the beach had to wade in the water up to his chin before the last boat took him off.

This is probably not the whole story about the taking of Paita. As in many such operations there was much going on at the margins that was either not officially known, or at least not officially reported. Pascoe Thomas was told that the men on landing fired so wildly that the two casualties might have been caused by them rather than by the Spaniards. Thomas was not one of the attacking force, but the pseudonymous narrative by 'John Philips' has what seems to be a first-hand account of the landing. It gave a rather different description of the behaviour of the men after the attack as they drank and smashed their way through the streets and houses of Paita, raping a dozen Indian women they found still in the town. The two churches that were the first targets for the looters stood in splendid contrast to the surrounding shanty town. They were 'large and fair, with great Beams, Posts, and Doors, all adorned with carved Work, besides good Pictures, brought hither from Spain, and rich hangings of Tapestry, or printed Calicoes'. A Spanish account, not first-hand, described how Anson's men became so drunk that slaves of the fleeing Spaniards returned to Paita to retrieve or hide many of their masters' valuables. The authorised account admits that the slaves returned, but insisted that several of them deserted to the English side. Some credibility is added to this by the note that one of the slaves was known from his Panama days by 'a Gentleman' on board the *Centurion* – clearly Henry Hutchinson.

The Spaniards meanwhile were behaving as though following a well-rehearsed script. As on innumerable occasions in the days of the bucca-neers, they assembled on a hill overlooking Paita, and were joined there by two hundred mounted militia from Piura. During the three days that the English were in possession of the town, the growing Spanish force paraded backwards and forwards, every now and again making threatening sallies down the slope before returning to safety. Meanwhile the treasure from the custom house was ferried out to the ships, which were now at anchor in the harbour and covering the town with their guns. All attempts to negotiate a ransom for the other goods in the custom house, mostly fine fabrics, failed. Some were taken on board the ships, with rather more useful cargoes of live hogs, sheep and fowls. On the third day, as the Spaniards showed signs of mounting a serious attack, Anson gave orders to burn the town except for the churches, to sink the vessels in the bay except the largest (which he took with him), and to land the prisoners. Once the shore party was back on board the ships put to sea, leaving behind the blazing port and sinking ships shown in Brett's drawing. It was a sign of how high Anson's reputation was among the Spaniards that at least some of them believed that the firing of Paita was done contrary to his orders, and that he was angered by 'such unjustifiable behaviour'. Eighty years later a British naval officer, Captain Basil Hall, discovered during a visit to Paita that Anson's attack was still talked about by the inhabitants, but that they dwelt not upon the destruction of their town but on the kindness with which Anson had treated their forebears who had been taken prisoner.

Once at sea, Anson's priority was to find the *Gloucester*, which should be cruising in the area. First he had to settle a dispute that threatened both discipline and harmony. Predictably, it concerned prize money, and was between those who had been in the shore party that attacked Paita, and those who had remained on the ships. By the rules governing the distribution of prize money, all were entitled to a share, and rightly so, for the men aboard the ships and guarding the prisoners were as essential to the success of the operation as the men who went off in the boats. The official prize money amounted to about £30,000, together with an assortment of rings and jewellery not yet valued. The problem concerned the personal plunder brought back by the men of the shore party, which they insisted was theirs and theirs alone. Even though the amount taken in this way was not known (it was probably not very much) feelings ran so high that the morning after sailing from Paita Anson called all hands on deck. He pointed out the role that the whole crew had played in the taking of Paita. He then ordered the officers and men of the shore party to produce their plunder on the quarterdeck, and warned them that their chests and hammocks would be searched. Once displayed, the booty was divided among the crew according to rank – not a very straightforward job since little of it would have been in cash – while to soothe any resentment among the shore party Anson gave them his share.

The next day the *Gloucester* was sighted. She had taken only two small prizes, but between them they produced specie amounting to £19,000. The smaller vessel had the larger amount of specie, most of it hidden in jars holding cotton. This boat was heading for Paita, and there is another echo of the prize-money dispute when the authorised account pointed out that if the boat and money had reached Paita it would then have been taken in the attack and added to the *Centurion*'s prize money. Perhaps in retaliation, some of the *Gloucester*'s crew reported that they saw 'a great Smoak' in the direction of Paita on 15 November, the day the town was set on fire. This was confirmed by Michell's journal, and was sufficient to bring them within the rules of the allocation of prize money since they would have been present at the action – just. At this, Anson was alleged to have sent for the officers' journals and to have sealed them, ordering them to begin new books. No evidence exists for this assertion, and journals such as those kept by Michell on the *Gloucester* and Saumarez on the *Centurion* have no obvious break at this point. But the allegations and counter-allegations were a sign of things to come.

From the coast of Peru Anson intended to sail north to Mexico in quest of the only worthwhile objective left to him – the Manila galleon. It would probably be two months before the galleon arrived at Acapulco, ample time to cover the distance, or so it was thought. The only delay would be to get water, for it was running dangerously short, and Paita had provided little. Shelvocke's narrative, and the reports of some of the prisoners with knowledge of the coast, pointed to Quibo in the Bay of

Panama. This double recommendation was thought necessary because the reports by Dampier, Shelvocke and the others had by now lost all credibility. They were 'legendary writers, of whose misrepresentations and falsities, we had almost daily experience'. By contrast, the authorised account of Anson's voyage would be full of carefully observed navigational and hydrographic detail, supplemented by charts, views, coastal profiles and plans. In this sense it looked forward to the more scientific surveys of the Cook era rather than back to the rumbustious narratives of the buccaneers and privateers.

On the first leg of the passage north Anson's squadron of eight vessels would have made an imposing sight for any watcher on shore. The reality was that only the *Centurion* and *Gloucester* were ships of force, and with many of their crews dispersed among the six prizes they were pitifully under-manned. As Michell wrote in a worried journal entry, the prisoners on board the *Gloucester* outnumbered the crew. By the time the squadron reached Quibo in early December with the help of the Spanish pilot of one of the *Gloucester*'s prizes, three of the slower merchantmen had already been scuttled. The island proved to be a good choice. A few degrees north of the Equator, it bore all the hallmarks of what later generations would regard as a tropical island paradise: sandy beaches, fresh water, tall trees where parrots, parakeets and macaws swooped and screeched, deer in the woods, and turtles on the seashore. In a boat trip around the island Anson and his officers came across a cascade rushing through a rocky, tree-shrouded chasm before it tumbled into the sea over a series of water-falls. So vivid an impression did it make on the boat party that when they returned to the ships they were in 'a kind of transport' as they tried to describe the sight. At a more practical level, the giant turtles, some weighing 200 lb., provided plentiful fresh meat. Many were taken on board, where they were kept alive until a new supply was found in the warm shallows off the Mexican coast. The accounts agree that they played an important part in the health of the crews – 'dress'd several different Ways, as roasted, baked, stew'd, boil'd, and the like. The Broth of them is good and nourishing.' In a remarkable contrast to what had gone before, during the seven months after the ships left Juan Fernández only two deaths were reported.

After nine days at Quibo the ships left for Acapulco. Calms and headwinds made the progress north infuriatingly slow, not helped by the fact that the *Centurion* and *Gloucester* were each towing a prize. The logs are full of detail about tow-ropes snapping, ships running aboard each other, and all the other problems associated with towing. Given the necessity to reach Acapulco as early in January as possible, it might have been better to abandon the sluggish prizes. In the event, it was 26 January before the ships reckoned themselves in the latitude of Acapulco, and turned east towards the coast, as yet out of sight. At 10 p.m. that evening a light was seen on the larboard bow. Confident that it was the galleon, showing a light in her tops to guide her consort, Anson ordered the *Centurion* and *Gloucester* to cast off their tows, make full sail, and prepare for action. On the *Centurion* the heavy 24-pounders on the gun deck were to be loaded with two round shot for the first broadside, then with one round shot and one grape. The round shot would damage the hull of the galleon, then the grape would sweep the decks. Soon the sharper-eyed thought that they could make out the sails and rigging of the ship ahead, but throughout the hours of darkness she stayed just out of range, and with their bottoms foul with weed the men-of-war could not close with their prey. Daylight brought disbelief and disappointment as it revealed an empty sea. The light was still visible, but it came from a fire on a mountain 30 miles distant. The three prisoners on board, a pilot and two Indians, who claimed to know the region, had a consoling message for their captors. The fire was a sign that the galleon had not yet arrived, for it was intended as a direction beacon; and the two high hummocks or paps visible to the north marked the port of Acapulco. This last seemed to be confirmed by Dampier, whose first-hand report of this coast referred to 'two Hillocks like two Paps on its Top' behind the town.

Whether all this was correct or not, Anson had no way of knowing. He was uneasy about the fact that the two hummocks in sight were in about latitude 18°N., whereas Dampier and other accounts placed Acapulco in about latitude 17°N. Captured Spanish charts and pilots' guides did nothing to clarify the matter. After cruising off the coast for several days Anson suspected that the galleon had already made port, but he was reluctant to leave his station until he was certain. On 6 February he ordered the *Centurion*'s barge to sail inshore and look into the harbour at Acapulco. The boat returned after five days with depressing news. It had run along 100 miles of the coast without being able to locate Acapulco or even a landing place; but at their farthest point its crew could see two hummocks just visible to the east. At this the ships sailed along the coast and the boat was sent off again. A week later it returned to report that it had located Acapulco, and had reached the entrance of the harbour during the night. As the crew lay on their oars, weighing up whether to risk discovery by venturing further in, they came across a canoe with three fishermen. These they seized and brought back to the ships, where they reported that the galleon had made harbour on 9 January, about three weeks before Anson arrived on the coast. This was disappointing, but hardly unexpected, and was more than balanced by the news that the galleon was preparing for sea. The date had been announced, 3 March, only two weeks away. With five ships at his disposal, Anson intended to draw a cordon outside the port which the galleon would not be able to escape. Moreover, her cargo would be much more valuable to her captors than that brought from Manila – luxury goods from China and the East Indies – for on the return voyage the cargo consisted mainly of silver.

By the time of Anson's voyage readers in England would have had at their disposal a fair degree of reliable information about the galleons that sailed between Manila and Acapulco, leavened with some more fanciful detail. The trade had been established on a regular basis following the founding of Manila in 1571, and linked the East Indies, Philippines and China with the silver-rich markets of Spanish America. Each year a ship from Lima laden with silver reached Acapulco at the end of December, and after the arrival of the galleon from Manila took on board a cargo of spices, silks and other eastern commodities for her return voyage to Peru. The arrival of the galleon was eagerly awaited, with sentinels keeping watch on the hills, and beacon fires burning. An account of her lading in one of the journals kept by Anson's men left nothing to the imagination.

The cargo of this Ship consists of Diamonds, Rubies, Saphires, and other precious Stones found in the East

Indies; of Cinnamon, Cloves, Mace, Nutmegs, and Pepper; of the rich Carpets of Persia; the Camphire of Borneo; the Benjamin and Ivory of Pegu and Cambadia; the Silks, Muslins, and Calicoes of East India; the Gold Dust, Tea, China Ware, Silk, Cabinets &c. of China and Japan; all which amounts to a prodigious Value, this one Ship having more Riches in it than some whole Fleets.

At Acapulco, apart from the transhipment of goods across to the waiting Lima ship, the galleon's cargo was split up into individual loads to be carried by mules and pack-horses across Mexico to Vera Cruz, and from there to Europe. Once emptied, the galleon was loaded with silver coin and plate for the return voyage to Manila, together with reinforcements for the garrison there. It was this cargo of treasure that made the westbound galleon 'the most desirable prize that was to be met with in any part of the globe'. At Manila the silver helped to sustain the spider's web of trade that radiated from the Philippines to the East Indies in one direction and the Asian mainland in another. Despite the intrinsic value of the cargoes carried, the Manila–Acapulco link was usually maintained by single galleons, sometimes with a smaller ship sailing in company. Whether one ship or two, the annual voyage was dictated by the pattern of the prevailing winds. The eastbound galleons followed a northern semicircular track from Manila to Acapulco, and returned along a route 3,000 miles farther south. East or west, it was the longest unbroken trading voyage in the world. The eastbound galleons usually took five or six months, from July to December or January. Those following the more direct westbound route could make the voyage in two, sometimes three months, from March to June, and unlike the eastbound galleon they had a port of call at the island of Guam in the Marianas. While one or two ships were making the twelve-month return voyage, others were being prepared at Cavite, the port of Manila. The name given to the galleon was that of her port of departure, so she was known as the Manila galleon on her eastbound voyage, the Acapulco galleon on the return voyage.

The galleon had twice been taken by English ships, the first time by Thomas Cavendish in 1587 when he encountered the *Santa Ana* off Cape

San Lucas, the usual American landfall of the galleons. The ship was between 600 and 700 tons, but she carried no cannon and her decks were encumbered with cargo. Apart from a couple of arquebuses the only weapons available to the crews were stones picked out of the ballast. Cavendish's two ships simply stood off, firing into the helpless vessel until after six hours the Spaniard surrendered. When Cavendish arrived back home in September 1588 he staged a spectacular entry up the Thames to where the Queen and court were waiting at Greenwich. Each sailor had a gold chain round his neck, the sails were made of blue damask, and the ship flew a standard of gold and blue silk. A Spanish official explained the lack of armaments on the galleon by pointing out that 'they have always sailed with as little fear from corsairs as if they were on the river of Seville'. After Cavendish this complacency vanished, and the lightly armed buccaneers and privateers of a later period rarely provided a serious threat to the galleons. In 1704 Dampier was beaten off in an encounter in which his privateer was armed only with five-pounders, while the galleon could bring hull-smashing eighteen- and 24-pounders to bear. The sole further English success came in 1709, when the privateer Woodes Rogers intercepted two ships from Manila, and captured the smaller one. The larger vessel proved quite beyond his reach, but the ship that was taken, with her cargo of gold plate and coin, textiles, silks and other oriental luxury goods, was brought back to England. There newspapers reported how 'the Aquapulca Ship' reached the Thames in October 1711, the very incarnation of the wealth of the South Sea.

Tales of both the wealth and the size of the galleons grew over the years. In the authorised account of Anson's voyage the largest of the galleons were described as giant vessels carrying crews of more than 1,000 men. Even the smaller ships on the voyage were said to be 1,200 tons or more, and it was commonly believed that their sides were so thick that no cannon ball could penetrate them. It is true that Woodes Rogers claimed to have fired 500 shots without much effect at the galleon he had tried unsuccessfully to take in 1709, but his cannon were only six-pounders. The frigate-built ship he captured was not unusual in either size or firepower, but undoubtedly the larger of the ships built at Manila were outstanding in strength and durability, and had to be to survive the long voyage ahead. The greatest of them, the *Santíssima Trinidad*, taken by the British off Manila in 1762, was 2,000 tons, but carried a crew of 384, less than the full complement of the *Centurion*. The inflated numbers quoted in the English accounts invariably included passengers, soldiers and convicts, often more of an encumbrance than a help in sea actions.

According to the captured fishermen, the galleon in harbour mounted 58 guns and carried 400 men. Whatever feelings of apprehension there might have been among Anson's men off Acapulco as they waited for this formidable adversary to come out of harbour, their actions were dominated by the determination to seize 'the immense treasure'. Lieutenant Peter Denis thought that the cargo would be worth £1,000,000 sterling, while his fellow lieutenant Philip Saumarez worked out that his individual share would come to no less than £10,000. Anson's preparations were meticulous. Of the five ships under his command only the *Centurion* and *Gloucester* would fight in the action that lay ahead. His own men were concentrated in the two ships, and they included slaves taken at Paita and from Spanish merchantmen, trained to man the cannon, and promised their freedom later. The three prizes had only skeleton crews, but they now justified Anson's retention of them by acting as lookout vessels, part of the cordon strung 40 miles off Acapulco, just out of sight of land. With the five ships stationed nine or ten miles apart they covered a 50-mile arc of sea, and double that in terms of visibility in clear weather. In case the galleon slipped out under cover of darkness, two cutters were stationed nearer inshore, with orders to get close to the harbour entrance each night. The trap had been set; it remained to be seen if the Spaniards would spring it.

The ships were on station by the beginning of March, and the waiting began. At first there were moments of excitement when men scrambled into the tops or raced below deck to the cannon as lights were sighted during the night and fires during the day, or ships in the cordon veered

OPPOSITE: The Harbour of Acapulco. Engraving in *Anson's Voyage* (1748). The chart shows the difficulties that Anson would have faced if he had gone ahead with his plan of a night assault by boats supported by the ships' cannon. Even if the attackers had stormed the fort at the mouth of the harbour, it would have been difficult to cut out the galleon, moored close to the shore three miles away, with large numbers of Spanish troops and auxiliaries to hand.

A PLAN of the
HARBOUR of ACAPULCO
on the Coast of Mexico in y South Sea,
in the Latitude of 16.° 45' N. and West
Longitude from London 108.° 22'.

A. The Harbour.
B. The Town.
C. The Castle of St. Diego, having .... 100. Guns
D. 4 New Bastions with .... 5 each.
E. A Battery with .... 7.
F. The Watering Place.
G. Punto del Grifo, where they are
   building a New Fort which is to mount 30.
H. The Road to the City of Mexico.
I. The Governors Plantations.
K. Look-out Houses.
L. The Island without the Harbour.
M. Port Marquis.
N. A Plantation.
O. Two Trees, which y Manila Ship
   always has a Cable to.

A Scale of Miles

off station as though in pursuit of a sail. Slowly the initial optimism faded as the days passed, and all the lookouts could see as the ships rose and fell in the long Pacific swell were the tips of the twin hills ('Cerro Tetas de Coyuca') above Acapulco, shimmering in the heat. Philip Saumarez's journal marks the change of mood. On 2 March he was 'in hopes of seeing her soon'. By the 14th a note of pessimism had crept in as the lieutenant wrote, 'expecting the galleon out shortly or we shall begin to despair of seeing her'. By the 19th he 'had several conjectures concerning the galleon's not appearing, but in general are all on the desponding side'. And by the 23rd Saumarez had 'began to give up all hope of seeing the galleon'. As Anson had feared, despite all precautions the Spaniards had sighted the *Centurion*'s barge, a large eighteen-oared boat, in its search along the coast for Acapulco; and they had decided to hold the *Pilar* in port. There would be no Acapulco galleon leaving for Manila that year. For a moment Anson considered the possibility of a night attack on the port. This would be a very different and more hazardous operation than at Paita, for during the galleon's stay Acapulco was full of armed men – 1,000 militia, 200 regular troops and a large number of Indian auxiliaries, according to the three fishermen. All thoughts of such a desperate venture were abandoned when the crews of the cutters stationed off the harbour reported that at night it fell calm, and when the wind got up again towards morning it always blew offshore.

From thoughts of action and treasure, Anson was reminded of his own perilous position when his officers reported that all the ships were running short of water. The daily ration was reduced to four pints, only just adequate in the sweltering heat. On an unknown and hostile coast, Anson had no recourse but to turn for guidance to Dampier, one of the despised buccaneer writers. Less than 100 miles from Acapulco, Dampier wrote, was the small settlement of Chequetan (the modern Zihuatanejo), with a good harbour and a river of fresh water. Leaving a cutter under Lieutenant John Hughes on watch outside Acapulco in case the galleon appeared, Anson abandoned his vigil. On 7 April he found the harbour of Chequetan where Dampier had described it. There were only six days' water left on board.

The ships remained at Chequetan for a month, for watering proved a difficult and laborious business. It had become a characteristic of the voyage that all its operations took longer than anticipated. At Chequetan the local topography had changed since Dampier's visit in 1685. The river no longer ran into the sea, but formed a large land-locked lake behind the beach over which waves from the sea often broke at high tide. Only at the far end of the lake, a half-mile from the beach, was the water reasonably fresh; and it took much ferrying of water in small canoes across the lake and the mangrove swamps behind the beach before the ships' casks were full. Even so, both Millechamp and Thomas had doubts about the water taken on board. It was not only brackish but, according to Thomas, 'full of nauseous live Worms'.

The day after reaching Chequetan, Anson sent a party of forty armed men inland to make contact with the inhabitants. They were to be invited to trade any fresh provisions they had for the valuable cargoes still in the holds of the prizes. For men who had not set foot on land since Paita, the march in the heat became a fearsome ordeal, and some became so exhausted that they had to be carried back to the ships. Nor, apart from one startled horseman, did they come across any people. They had to content themselves with fixing messages written in Spanish to posts encouraging the inhabitants to visit the ships. Not surprisingly, there was no response to this offer. To prevent any such visit from being turned into an ambush, trees were felled across the path leading inland from the lake, and guards posted there. Despite this, Anson's cook, a Frenchman named Louis Leger, wandered off on 14 April, and never returned. A Frenchman, and probably a Catholic, he was assumed to have deserted. Anson entered in the *Centurion*'s log, 'Lews. Legear my Cook deserted', and against his name in the ship's muster book is the damning initial 'R' (Run).

Three days later there was the only direct contact with Spaniards on land since the attack on Paita. It was not an affair of great moment, but the way in which it was treated in the authorised account is another example of how that was written to show the expedition's actions in the most flattering light. It described how Lieutenant Brett was sent with two boats and sixteen men to investigate the coast east of Chequetan. As he prepared to land at Petatlán Bay, he saw on the other side of the bay three squadrons of armed horsemen, in all 200 men, coming down towards the beach. Brett immediately put off in his boat and stood across the bay towards the horsemen. As he drew nearer the horsemen opened fire, but when the boat crew returned the fire they fled. This sequence of events was presumably intended to show how the pacific intentions of Anson's men were thwarted by the Spaniards, but the version in the authorised account finds little support elsewhere. Brett's own log put the number of Spaniards at eighty, and made it clear that they 'had no sooner come within shot, but the boats fired at them, which made them all fly into the bushes'. The official log of the *Centurion*, under Anson's signature, is even more explicit: 'They discovered a party of horsemen upon which my lieutenant ordered his men to give fire and fired several volleys, they did not return one shot but fled to the woods.' It was Millechamp who pointed out the contradiction between pinning up messages inviting the inhabitants to trade, and then opening fire on the first Spaniards sighted.

More serious problems were about to surface as Anson prepared to leave Chequetan on the first stage of his homeward voyage. Determining a route was not a difficult decision. To have retraced his track back along the coasts of Spanish America, now fully on alert, and to attempt once more the fearsome passage round the Horn, would have been suicidal. Instead, Anson intended to follow the suggestion made in his instructions and to return home by way of China, following the route of the Acapulco galleon for most of the time, except that as he neared the Philippines he would swing northwest into the China Sea. At the mouth of the Canton River was the Portuguese settlement of Macao; at Canton itself the factory of the English East India Company. With the regular trade winds in their favour, the ships should make the crossing of the North Pacific in two months or less.

Before sailing, Anson had to reach a decision about the prizes. He had already decided to destroy the *Carmelo* and the *Carmin*; but the *Tryal Prize*, the former *Arranzazu*, was a different proposition in more ways than one. A large 600-ton ship, not only was she 'in good repair and fit for the sea', as the authorised account admitted, but her officers and warrant officers came from the *Tryal*, scuttled in February. She was, in a sense, their replacement ship, and a more imposing vessel altogether than the sloop which had brought them into the South Sea. But with the *Centurion* and more especially the *Gloucester* short of men, Anson decided to burn the prize and distribute her men among his two remaining vessels. On the *Gloucester* Michell had warned Anson that he did not have enough men to work the ship if the weather worsened. When Anson announced his decision Michell's only reaction was one of impatience: 'It was what I should have done a great while ago.' There is no mention in the authorised account of the strenuous opposition of the warrant officers of the *Tryal Prize* to this decision, for their position now that both their original ship and her replacement had gone would be as super-numeraries on the *Centurion* and *Gloucester*. Anson, as letters copied by Millechamp into his journal show, did his utmost to reassure those involved. First he made it clear that the decision was forced upon him by the lack of men to crew the three ships. In total their number was less than the complement of a fourth-rate man-of-war, he pointed out, and none of the ships would have enough crew to work them in bad weather. In a letter to Charles Saunders on the *Tryal Prize* Anson was explicit: 'I therefore think it as well for the safety of His Majesty's subjects as for the security of both His Majesty's ships to destroy His Majesty's ship *Tryal Prize*, notwithstanding her being in repair and fit for the sea, to reinforce the said ships with her men.' This was to be the basis of future claims by the officers of the *Tryal Prize*, not that Anson was wrong to destroy their ship and allocate them to the two remaining ships; but that the decision was taken in order to save the squadron, and that accordingly they deserved equal treatment with the regular officers on the *Centurion* and *Gloucester*. Of the officers, seamen and marines, Indians and Negroes on board the *Tryal Prize*, forty-five were sent to the *Gloucester*, seventeen to the *Centurion*. The officers, Anson added, were to be entered as supernumeraries, but would be entitled to their pay as officers 'until their arrival in England'. Time, and court action, would show whether this included prize money.

As the *Centurion* and *Gloucester* sailed from Chequetan on 30 April one further worry prevented Anson, already in danger of missing the navigable season, from heading out to sea. There had been no sign of his cutter, left on watch outside Acapulco, and now long overdue. Anson felt that he had no alternative but to sail slowly back along the coast in the hope of finding it. When the ships drew near Acapulco without any sign of the missing boat, the best that could be assumed was that it and its crew had been captured by the Spaniards. On this assumption, Anson sent a boat into Acapulco with a half-dozen Spanish prisoners, and a message to the governor offering to release all his prisoners in return for Lieutenant Hughes and his six men. Three days later a small boat was sighted, not coming out from Acapulco with the Spanish reply, as was first thought, but the cutter itself. Its crew were in a dreadful condition, having being blown along the coast, unable to land because of the surf, and without water. Only a squall of rain had kept them alive, and after six weeks in a small boat they were badly sunburnt and had lost the use of their legs. Once he got his men on board, Anson decided to go ahead with the release of most of his prisoners. All the Spaniards on the ships were sent ashore, together with some Indians and sick Negroes, fifty-seven in all. He kept forty-three of the strongest Indians and Negroes, together with a few mulattos. Among them was a Filipino from Manila who spoke Chinese, and who would be useful as an interpreter on the coast of China.

With this remaining business completed, the ships at last left the coast and headed out to sea. It was 6 May, two months later than the normal departure date of the galleons.

V

'Words Cannot Express the Misery'

'Sent on board the *Centurion* the sick Men, most of which were hoisted out of the Ship on Gratings and were in so miserable a Condition with the Scurvy, that words cannot Express the Misery they were in.'

Captain Michell, 15 August 1742

'I have but five-and-forty men before the Mast and some of them have not recovered their senses, for numbers turned Mad and Idiots with the Scurvy.'

Anson, 7 December 1742

THE DELAY IN LEAVING the Mexican coast had unexpected and disastrous results for the hapless crews of the *Centurion* and *Gloucester*. Relying on the accounts of former navigators, Anson anticipated an easy run across the North Pacific to the coast of China. He later admitted that 'he had no apprehension that the season was too far advanced'. Whereas the eastbound six-month voyage of the annual galleon sailing from Manila to Acapulco was a byword among mariners for hardship and danger, the shorter westbound passage was regarded as comparatively straightforward. From Acapulco (in latitude 15°51'N.) the Manila-bound galleon dropped a few degrees in latitude until she picked up the northeast trades between the fourteenth and tenth parallels. The Italian traveller Gemelli Careri had made the eastbound crossing in 1697 and, in an account translated into English, had contrasted that voyage, 'the longest and most dreadful of any in the world', with the return route to Manila taken by the galleons. 'They always run in a streight line in a smooth Sea, before the wind, as

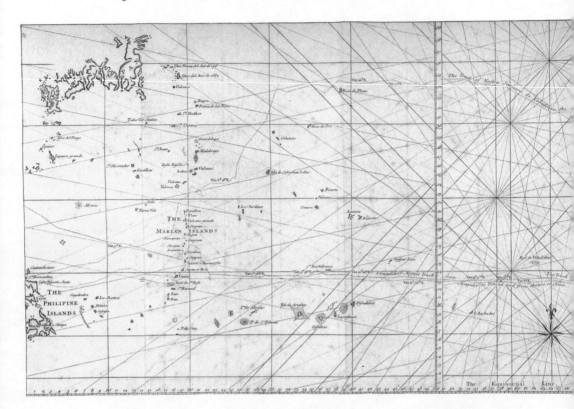

A chart of the North Pacific ocean. Engraving in *Anson's Voyage* (1748). This is a revised version of one of the charts taken from the *Nuestra Señora de Covadonga*, and shows for the first time in published form the great circle route of the galleon on its eastbound voyage, and its much flatter southerly track on the return voyage to Manila. On the right-hand edge of the chart Anson's track from Acapulco reveals the southward detour of his two ships that caused them to miss the trade wonds.

if they were in a Canal,' he wrote, and normally reached the Ladrone Islands (the Marianas) in 60 or 65 days. By contrast, his voyage to Acapulco had taken 204 days (and five hours, he added).

Among the books on the *Centurion* were the accounts of Dampier and Shelvocke, and probably that of Woodes Rogers as well. All made much of the length of the crossing, and the dangers from scurvy and from the shortage of food and water, but their experiences were generally reassuring. As usual, it was Dampier who gave the fullest navigational detail. His ship, the *Cygnet* (Captain Swan), left the coast of Lower

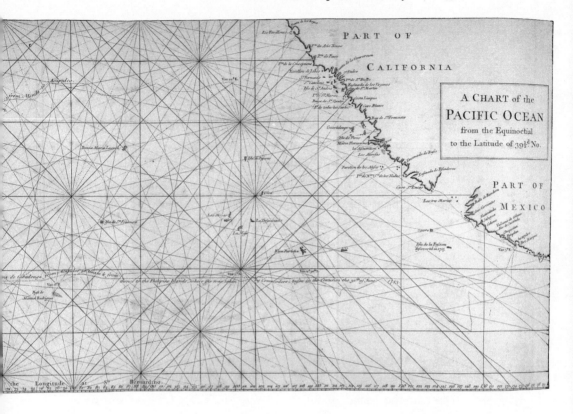

California on 31 March 1686. At first the winds came off the sea, but as the vessel got into latitude 13°N. they swung to a more easterly direction, and then became a steady east-north-east trade that took the *Cygnet* to within 40 leagues of Guam in only 50 days. At no point did the ship go farther south than latitude 12°50'S. Much the same course was followed earlier in the season by Woodes Rogers in 1710. Leaving Lower California in mid-January he reached Guam in 51 days. His farthest south was latitude 12°54'N. The fastest voyage of the three was Shelvocke's in 1721: at a different time of year, August and September, he made the run from Cape San Lucas in Lower California to Guam in 42 days. Although daily observations have not survived for Shelvocke's track, his journal shows that he picked up the northeast trade wind in latitude 13°N., and apart from a brief foray into latitude 14°N. kept to this track.

Anson and his officers drew the wrong lesson from these narratives. They read of ships sailing south and southwest from the coasts of Mexico or Lower California until they found the trade wind, and they decided to do the same. But there was no example of a ship leaving the American coast in May, by which time the trades were moving north with the coming of summer. 'As if an evil genius possessed us', one crew member wrote later, the ships kept on a southerly course, right across the path of the trades. As the ships reached down to equatorial latitudes they found themselves in a region of calms, light winds and blistering heat. Day after day the journals record bafflement at the failure of the winds to follow the rules as Anson's officers understood them. On the *Gloucester* one lieutenant suspected after only a week that they were sailing too far south, but not until the middle of June did the senior officers come to the same conclusion. After falling as far south as latitude 6°40'N., Saumarez wrote on 13 June, 'we steered NWbW, concluding it was most likely to meet the trade wind to the northward.' It was 23 June before the wind settled down to blow steadily from the northeast, and by then seven weeks had passed since the departure from Acapulco. In about that time Anson's privateering predecessors had completed the voyage from the American coast to the island of Guam in the Marianas; his two ships were less than a quarter of the way across.

What to ships and crews in good condition would have been an inconvenience turned into catastrophe. Only three days after the departure from Acapulco the *Centurion*'s foremast split, while a few days later Michell recorded an ominous entry in his journal: 'all our Sails extreamly bad much wore and Rotten, all the Indians and Negroes taken with the Scurvey'. Worse was to follow. In the middle of June, in only moderate seas the mainmast of the *Gloucester* split with a loud crack. It had to be cut down to 26 feet, and although a topmast was fixed to the stump to make a jury mast, this task took eight days. By the end of the month the first cases of scurvy had appeared among the regular crew members on both the *Centurion* and *Gloucester*, and on 5 July the first death was recorded. In his annotations written on the pages of the authorised account, James Naish later suggested that the expedition's misfortunes of these months could have been avoided. With the advantage of hindsight, he wrote that Anson's mistake was to sail north along the coast from Quibo to Acapulco in the hope of intercepting the galleon as she entered the Mexican port. If the *Centurion* and *Gloucester* had instead made their North Pacific crossing at that stage, they would have arrived at Guam in good condition, and could have waited off the island for the galleon to appear on her return voyage to Manila. Moreover, the galleon would then be laden with silver, not the bulky luxury goods of the eastward crossing.

The new outbreak of scurvy on the *Centurion* and *Gloucester* was both terrifying and inexplicable. Most men on the two ships had already suffered from scurvy on the voyage around Cape Horn, and all had seen its ravages as their messmates sickened and died. The causes of the first outbreak seemed obvious in retrospect: ships crammed with invalids and landmen in unventilated quarters; cold, wet weather; lack of fresh provisions. None of these problems applied to the voyage across the North Pacific. In the half-empty ships the men had the luxury of space and ventilation unknown on most men-of-war. The weather was warm, and the squalls of rain brought plenty of good drinking water. There were still live hogs and fowls to provide fresh meat, while each day fish were caught and distributed among the crews. Whether much in the way of fruit and vegetables had been taken on board is less certain. The surgeon of the *Centurion*, Henry Ettrick, according to Pascoe Thomas 'a very good practical surgeon, but in the theory part vain and pragnatical', had developed his own explanation of the causes of scurvy, that it was a disease of cold climates which thinned the blood. Confronted with the new outbreak in warm weather, Ettrick declared himself helpless. A layman's view came from Saumarez, who wrote – not very helpfully under the circumstances – that land was man's proper element, and that no physician's remedy was 'equal to the smell of a turf of grass or a dish of greens'.

As a last resort, Anson turned to Ward's drop and pill. It had not been used during the first outbreak of scurvy, and it was a sign of desperation that Anson went against his surgeon's advice in distributing it now. A violent purgative, this quack medicine brought momentary relief to some, but then left them weaker than before. Pascoe Thomas, who seems to have escaped the worst of the earlier outbreak of scurvy, was struck down this time, and his description shows its impact on one sufferer out of the many affected on the voyage.

> I was first taken about the beginning of the month [July 1742] with a small pain on the joint of my left great toe; but having hurt that a little time before, I imagined it to be the effect of that hurt, and minded it the less . . . but in a little time a large black spot appearing on the part affected, with very intense pains at the bone, gave me to understand my case. I now took physick often by way of prevention, but to little purpose; several hard nodes now began to rise in my legs, thighs, and arms, and not only many more black spots appeared in the skin, but those spread until almost my legs and thighs were as black as a Negro; and this accompanied with such excessive pains in the joints of the knees, ankles and toes, as I thought, before I experienced them, that human nature could never have supported. It next advanced to my mouth; all my teeth were presently loose, and my gums, overcharged with extravagated blood, fell down almost quite over my teeth. This occasioned my breath to stink much, yet without affecting my lungs; but I believe, one week more at sea would have ended me.

The only cure for the sick was to get them ashore, but with the crippled *Gloucester* making little way this seemed a distant prospect. Even though the ships had at last reached the northeast trades, the *Centurion* rarely had more than her topsails set as she waited for her consort, and as much as a month was wasted through the subsequent delays. By now the fresh food taken on board along the Mexican coast was finished, and the men were back to a more familiar diet. As Pascoe Thomas described it, their biscuit was 'so much worm-eaten, it was scarce anything but Dust . . . no Beef, and Pork was likewise very rusty and rotten'. The officers, he added sourly, 'had always soft Bread new baked'. By 24 July the situation was so dire that Anson sent a new and startling order to Michell. To save the sick he intended to land at Guam, although there was known to be a Spanish garrison there. According to the published narratives of the privateers, Guam had only a small fort and a company of soldiers but, given Anson's weakness, there was no prospect of an armed assault on the island. The most that could be hoped for was that the appearance of two large men-of-war off the island would terrify the Spaniards into submission or flight before they realised the state of the crews. A final problem was that the accounts disagreed on the distance across the North Pacific. With uncertainty about the longitudes of ports at both the American and Asian ends of the sailing route, and difficulties in calculating the distance to be allowed for a degree of longitude in different latitudes, there was a gap of almost a thousand miles between the various estimates. To avoid running onto unseen land during the night, Anson decided to sail three or four leagues ahead of the *Gloucester* during the day, and then to lie to during the hours of darkness while his slow-moving consort came up with him.

At the end of July even this stuttering progress came to a halt. As the *Gloucester* pitched and yawed in the great oceanic swells, her fore-topmast came crashing down, followed by a tangle of yards, sails and rigging. The *Centurion* at first sent men across to try to repair the damage, and then took her consort in tow; but Anson had to let the tow go when during a storm the *Centurion*'s hold began to fill with water and all hands who had any strength were sent to the pumps. On the *Gloucester* each day brought further damage: the foretopmast broke away, then the mizen-yard, while sails were ripped and blown to pieces. In the chaos the chest containing the azimuth compass was knocked out of its deck lashings and fell overboard. When water gushed in through a huge leak near the stern the end was clearly near. The ship, repaired and patched up so often, was literally falling to pieces. On 10 August Michell wrote in the ship's log, 'the Men extreamly ill and I fear we will all dye if we dont get soon to some land.' By 13 August there was seven foot of water in the hold and it was gaining on the pumps. The men working them were so exhausted that they were unable to get the cutter out to send across to the *Centurion*, but a distress signal to Anson was answered with the message that the flagship's own leak was so serious that she also was in danger of foundering. On board the *Gloucester* Michell and his officers agreed that it was impossible to save the ship, and set out their reasons in writing. They are written out in full in Michell's journal, opposite the log entry that shows that the ship had sailed 2,203 leagues (or about 6,600 miles) from Acapulco with no sight of land, the equivalent of a return voyage across the Atlantic. Michell had a melancholy story to tell. The leak at the stern was gaining on the pumps, where officers, men and boys had worked 24 hours without a break and were exhausted. The seawater swirling around in the hold was over the tops of the water-casks, so there was no drinking water on board. The only masts standing were the foremast and mizen; two main beams were broken amidships; and the upper works of the ship were so loose that the quarterdeck might collapse at any moment. Of the 97 crew still alive, only sixteen men and eleven boys could keep the deck, and even they were weak from scurvy. Anson took the only possible decision: the crew and any useful stores were to be taken off the *Gloucester*, and the ship set on fire lest she remain afloat long enough to drift ashore at Guam.

This operation was carried out, in the words of the authorised account, 'with as much care as the circumstances of that time would permit'. Something of the reality behind this cautious statement was revealed in the other journals. Michell's described how, as the sick were hoisted out on gratings, 'words cannot express the misery they were in'. As the heavily laden boats rowed back from the *Gloucester*, Saumarez on the *Centurion* realised that most of their crews were drunk from the liquor they had found on the sinking hulk. They arrived on the deck of the *Centurion* just as a squall struck, and as they were ordered aloft to shorten sail the sick and dying were left on deck among the stores from the *Gloucester* and running ropes. It was a nightmare scene as darkness fell, with the *Gloucester* blazing only two miles away. Little had been salvaged from the sinking ship, though care had been taken to bring across the chests of bullion taken from Spanish prizes. For the ship's purser, Millechamp, the end of the *Gloucester* was a dramatic and moving sight. She burnt all night, with her guns firing so regularly as the flames reached them that they sounded like mourning guns at a funeral. It was six in the morning when the fire reached the powder magazine and the ship blew up, leaving behind a great column of smoke that hung over the scene for an hour. 'Thus ended the *Gloucester*, a ship justly esteemed the beauty of the English navy,' Millechamp wrote.

The *Centurion* was now alone in an empty ocean, crippled, and with men dying, eight and ten a day, 'like rotten sheep'. All the officers, including Anson, worked at the pumps. Pascoe Thomas described their 'miserable Condition, the Ship considerably lumber'd with Prize Goods, and the small Room we had left throng'd with the Sick, whose Numbers were now very much increas'd with those from the *Gloucester*; the Dirt, Nauseousness, and Stench almost every where intolerable'. The sick on board, more than a hundred, had only a surgeon's mate (Keating, a former apothecary who had been surgeon of the *Anna*) to look after them; but even he was forced to take his turn at the pumps, leaving his charges completely unattended. Still the water gained and it became a race against time to find port, even a hostile one. Storms had forced the *Centurion* north of her intended track towards Guam, and into the northern fringes of the Ladrone (Mariana) Islands. On 23 August, just as fears were growing that the ship had missed the archipelago altogether, islands were sighted; but it was another four days before the *Centurion* found an anchorage. She had been at sea sixteen weeks, and so serious were the leaks that it would be only a matter of days before the crew took to the boats. The island ahead was Tinian, about which little was known. From the deck men thought that a white speck on the land might be a church, an ominous sign that the island was inhabited. Weak though they were the crew stood to arms, with Spanish colours flying, in the hope that their ship would be mistaken for the Acapulco galleon. A strange-looking outrigger proa put off from shore, and was seized as it came alongside. It contained one Spanish sergeant and four Indians. To the immense relief of the *Centurion*'s crew, he was the only Spaniard on the island, where he had been sent with a small bark from Guam to kill cattle for the garrison. Otherwise, Tinian was depopulated, the result of disease among the native inhabitants and the forced migration to Guam of the survivors. Reassured by this news, the *Centurion* slowly made her way inshore. Only seventy-one men could manage even the lightest duties, and so few could go aloft that it took five hours to furl the sails, and the Spaniard and four Indians were called on to help. When the anchor was raised to move the ship farther inshore, the only crew members with strength to move the capstan bars were Captains Michell and Saunders, 'the Colonel' (Cracherode) and a few of the junior officers.

After the ship anchored, the sick were carried on shore, 128 in all. Again the officers, including Anson, and the proa's crew helped with this, dropping the sick into the boats still in their hammocks, and then carrying them onto the beach across their shoulders. All the time heavy rain fell, and their bedding was soaked. Once ashore the sufferers had to fend for themselves, for their helpers were exhausted. Pascoe Thomas, one of the sick, wrote how they were dropped on the hard ground, many unable to reach the fruit or get to the fresh water that might be only yards away. A further twenty-one men died during the landing or soon after, but then greens and fruit worked their customary cure. Near the beach were coconuts, guavas, limes, oranges and breadfruit, as well as dandelion, mint, sorrel and other greenstuffs. One of the accounts described how Anson cut up oranges, and squeezed the juice into the mouths of those with the worst symptoms. Within two or three days most of the sick were at least able to crawl and, as at Juan Fernández, were allowed to build their own huts. Tinian attracted extravagant praise from journal-keepers on board, in some cases even before they landed. Millechamp wrote that as they sailed along the shore he could see through his glass orange and coconut trees, cattle grazing, and delightful plains – all in all 'a perfect paradise'. To the writer of the authorised account Tinian was not like 'an uninhabited and uncultivated place, but had much more the air of a magnificent plantation, where large lawns and stately woods had been laid out'.

The experiences of Anson's men, added to those of the solitary castaways such as Selkirk and Crusoe, brought a new dimension to images of the South Sea. Islands were to rival and, in the end, supplant unknown continents as objects of attention. For mariners, islands had always held a double significance. Looming out of open water they posed a threat to any ship, but on the long ocean voyages of the Pacific they were a haven for crews short of food and water. The predicament of those marooned on an island changed as the months passed. For Selkirk an initial moment of regret was followed by one of peace of mind. Crusoe's 'Island of Despair' became a secure refuge in time, even 'Deliverance' when he managed to struggle back to it after drifting away in his canoe. On Anson's voyage Juan Fernández, Quibo and Tinian were life-saving island ports of call whose natural beauties called forth superlatives from the pens of the journal-writers. But it was beauty as beheld by observers with eighteenth-century ideas of order and harmony, whose most lavish praise of a view was to compare it to an English park, a gentle landscape laid out with lawns, woods and paths. Even the awesome wonder of the rocky cascade at Quibo could be related to the artificial grottoes and waterfalls which were beginning to grace noble estates at home. In the narratives from Anson's voyage we have a premonition of a new vision of the South Sea, 'A Dream of Islands'. Before long there would be Tahiti, Hawaii and much else. Perhaps too much should not be made of this anticipation, for the island refuges of the buccaneers and other predators were unin-habited. There were no welcoming, garlanded islanders thronging their beaches. They were deserted, silent places, except for the beating of the surf and the calling of the seabirds, a reminder that for Europe the Pacific remained a vast, empty ocean.

Soon after landing, Brett sketched the double-ended, outrigger proa, often described but rarely drawn by earlier visitors. In 1686 Dampier had taken a log-line on board one of them, and estimated that it was sailing at about twelve miles an hour, but that in favourable conditions it might do double this. In 1710 Woodes Rogers was presented with one by the governor of Guam, and brought it back to England, though nothing seems to have come of his suggestion that it should be dis-played on the water in St James's Park. He left a vivid description of how it skimmed past his ship 'like a bird flying'. At Tinian Brett took the captured proa to pieces before making a detailed scale plan which appeared in the authorised account, with an accompanying text that noted that with a following wind this remarkable craft could sail at twenty miles an hour. In such boats, the writer speculated, the inhabitants of the Ladrones might have island-hopped as far as New Guinea – a

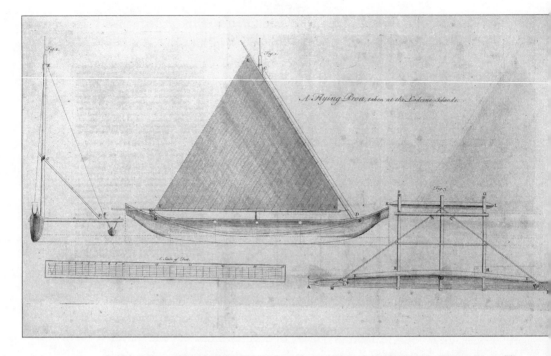

A flying proa. Engraving in *Anson's Voyage* (1748) based on drawing by Peircy Brett. These plans of the outrigger proa that was captured off Tinian were the first detailed drawings of this craft, so strange to European eyes, to be published. The accompanying text noted that 'The construction of this proa is a direct contradiction to the practice of all the rest of mankind. For as the rest of the world make the head of their vessels different from the stern, but the two sides alike; the proa, on the contrary, has her head and stern exactly alike, but her two sides very different.' It then went on to describe at length the principle and practice of the outrigger construction that gave the proa such remarkable speed and handling capacity.

perceptive guess about the remarkable long-distance voyages that had helped to explore and people the Pacific long before the arrival of the Europeans.

Amid the delights of island life on Tinian, marred only by swarms of mosquitoes, the priority for Anson was to locate and repair the *Centurion*'s leak. All the fit members of the crew were employed man-handling cannon astern to lift the bow out of the water, so that the carpenters could get at the leak. They ripped out the rotten sheathing, replaced it, and caulked and leaded the seams. But as the guns were moved back, the water rushed in as rapidly as before. A second attempt was made; this time powder-barrels from the forequarter storeroom were moved as well as the guns – back-breaking work even for fit men. The ship's stem was now three foot out of the water, and the carpenters were able to replace the sheathing lower down than on the first repair. The result was the same: once the guns and powder were moved back the water burst in again. The main leak was clearly well below the waterline, and could only be reached with proper dockyard facilities. During this time Anson had remained on board, but with scurvy taking hold of him just as most of the crew were recovering he at last went ashore. It was further evidence, if any were required, of his tenacity and devotion to duty.

As at Juan Fernández, Brett drew the scene, with its picturesque ruins, a well, the commodore's tent, and in the foreground a large breadfruit tree. His drawings represent the image of a paradisial tropical island that was to blossom in full splendour in the paintings of William Hodges on Cook's second voyage. Brett's sketch also reveals one of the drawbacks to Tinian – the open roadstead at the southwest end of the island, which was the only place where ships of any size could anchor. During the night of 18 September a furious storm blew the *Centurion* and her skeleton crew of 109 men and boys, commanded by Lieutenant Saumarez, right out to sea. The waves crashing over the vessel were so mountainous that they exceeded anything Saumarez had seen in the turbulent waters off Cape Horn. At one moment they hurled the longboat, moored at the stern, clean out of the water and sent it smashing into the gallery of Anson's cabin high on the quarterdeck. As the giant seas threatened to poop the ship, the bower cable snapped, and with the sheet anchor running free out of the hawse, the *Centurion* drove out to sea. Saumarez ordered flares to be lit and signal guns to be fired as signs of distress. Many of the cannon were rolling loose in the after part of the ship, where they had been moved during the search for the leak, while the water poured in through the open gun ports. In the bow the leak opened again. For those on the ship and on the island it was a time of 'the utmost despair'.

On shore the violence of the storm was such that the *Centurion*'s signals of distress went unheard and unseen. With daylight came the

The watering place at Tinian. Engraving in *Anson's Voyage* (1748) after drawing by Peircy Brett. There is much of interest here – the open roadstead where the *Centurion* lay at anchor, Anson's tent, the well in mid-picture, and the ruins of an edifice built by the former inhabitants of the island. Palms and citrus fruit trees are also shown, but dominating all is the breadfruit tree in the foreground. Its fruit, the text noted, was eliptical in shape, and seven or eight inches long. 'It was constantly eaten by us during our stay upon the Island instead of bread, and so universally preferred to it, that no ship's bread was expended.'

chilling sight of an empty anchorage. First fears that the ship had sunk during the night were dispelled when no wreckage was found strewn on the beach, but those stranded on the island had little hope that they would ever see the *Centurion* again. Given her condition, the odds were that she had foundered. Even if she kept afloat, in the strong easterly winds she would surely be unable to beat her way back to Tinian. The best that could be hoped for was that she might get to Macao and there refit. For the 107 men on the island, the options were limited and depressing. It was unlikely that any ship would call at the island, and if one did she would be Spanish. The little bark used for carrying beef could hold 20 or 30 men, and Guam was within reach. But again, that meant a Spanish prison, and perhaps worse, for all would remember the orders allegedly given to the cruising squadron from Callao to put Anson's crews to the sword. The only alternative was to lengthen and refit the bark, and attempt to reach Macao, almost 2,000 miles away. Even this desperate expedient was easier said than done. The carpenters of the *Centurion* and *Gloucester* were on the island, with some of their tools, but bellows had to be manufactured from a gun-barrel and ox-hides. Nor were there any navigational instruments from the ship on shore, although this problem was at least partly overcome when a small compass, no more than a child's toy, was found on the Spanish bark, and a quadrant was put together from separate bits and pieces. In this respect they were worse off than Robinson Crusoe on his lonely island, for Defoe's castaway had 'three or four compasses, some mathematical instruments, dials, perspectives, charts, and books of navigation'. Apart from a jar of salt, no food had been brought ashore from the ship, although that was the least of the crew's worries in a location with abundance of meat, vegetables and fruit. For the first time, bread-fruit came into its own, at first boiled, and then baked in an oven built for the purpose. Its taste was something between that of a potato and loaf bread, but better than either. So highly did Anson regard it that it formed the central part of the design of a specially commissioned porcelain dinner service he brought home from Canton. Later in the century the praise by Dampier and by Anson's men of the breadfruit was to result in Joseph Banks's scheme to transfer breadfruit plants from Tahiti to the slave plantations of the Caribbean, in Bligh's *Bounty*.

Meanwhile the work on the bark progressed. In an echo of the operation carried out by the *Wager*'s crew a year earlier, the carpenters and their assistants began to lengthen and refit the tiny craft. First the hull was moved on rollers made out of coconut trees into a dock on the beach, and then cut in half. Trees were felled and the laborious business began of sawing them into planks. Anson and the other officers once more joined in the tasks, handling axes and saws, and carrying timber. As the enlarged craft began to take shape, so worries about it grew. At 40 tons, it would have more than 100 men crammed into it. There would be room for only half below deck. The rest would be exposed to wind and weather, and if men came rushing up from below in any kind of emergency the boat would probably capsize. Provisions for 100 or more men for a 2,000-mile voyage would also be a problem, for few of the foodstuffs found in such abundance on shore would keep at sea. Finally, there was only enough gunpowder for 90 musket charges, a worrying prospect if any enemy craft were encountered. As the officers fretted about these problems, so uneasiness seems to have grown among the men. Although there was to be no repetition of the lurid events on Wager Island, there was clearly some challenge to Anson's plan, if not to his overall authority. Millechamp referred to objections and arguments, and Pascoe Thomas later picked up a rumour that most of the crew intended to desert and live in the woods, not being prepared to risk their lives in the tiny barque. Even the authorised account hinted at problems, though these were made more controllable by the fact that no wine or brandy had been landed from the ship. The only drink on the island apart from water was coconut juice, 'and this, though extremely pleasant, was not at all intoxicating, but kept them [the men] very cool and orderly'.

Then, nineteen days after disappearing, the *Centurion* was sighted. So far had hope faded that the ship would return that Anson appears to have posted no lookouts. The distant sail was seen by chance by a marine officer who had abandoned his work on the beach and climbed a hill inland. For the first time Anson's famed reserve broke as he threw down his axe and rushed down to the water's edge with his men 'in a kind of frenzy'. Saumarez's story on his return was laconic in its telling, but it indicated heroism and endurance by the *Centurion*'s skeleton crew exceptional even by the standards of this troubled voyage. The ship was almost unmanageable as she was driven off Tinian during the night of the 22nd. The sea poured in through the open ports, unlashed cannon careered across the decks, the sheet anchor was trailing far below, and only the mizen mast was rigged. Later, Saumarez penned a sardonic note on his desperate situation, wondering 'whether I should not be a captain in spite of my teeth at last'. Slowly the crew gained the upper hand. After five days they had got up the foreyard and mainyard, and had managed to bring up and secure the sheet anchor. After straying perilously near Guam and its garrison, the ship beat her way against the wind to within sight of Tinian.

The saga of Tinian was not quite over. Three days after her return the *Centurion*, held only by her single anchor, was again blown off the island, this time leaving just forty men ashore. Within five days the ship was back, to find a scene of purposeful activity. The Spanish bark, cut and lengthened with so much labour, had been taken to pieces again and almost restored to its former and, it was hoped, stronger state. The men were preparing to put to sea, with all the more urgency since two proas had just been sighted off the island, and it would not be long before the Spaniards at Guam would be aware of the Englishmen on Tinian. Taking on board water and fresh fruit the *Centurion* put to sea on 20 October. Just before sailing Anson sent one man from each mess back on shore to collect as many oranges for the voyages as he could carry. Under more normal conditions the ship would not have been regarded as seaworthy. Much of the rigging was rotten, and the leak was as bad as ever. Even more worrying, given the intricate navigation that lay ahead on the unknown coast of China, the ship had only one anchor, the heavy sheet anchor, used for anchoring in deep water. Again, improvisation was the answer. Two light anchors taken from earlier Spanish prizes were joined together and two four-pounder cannon fixed between their shanks to make an ungainly but effective best bower anchor. A similar operation produced a small bower anchor. Almost ninety years later a whaler at Tinian hooked up one of the *Centurion*'s lost anchors. Although covered in rust, and with the wooden stock rotted away, the huge anchor was in surprisingly good condition, and was beaten into bars and bolts by ship-wrights on Guam.

For Anson, the navigation of Chinese coastal waters proved as fraught as he had feared. The *Centurion* had some Dutch charts on board, and Anson had been given some general navigational hints by James Naish before he left England; but once Formosa was sighted the ship's progress was slow and uncertain. After months at sea without a sail in sight, it was strange to be moving through waters crammed with craft of all shapes and sizes. Most were small fishing sampans, numbered in their thousands. To Anson's men there was something uncanny about the scene, for the boats carefully avoided all contact with the *Centurion*, and efforts to find a pilot from the larger junks failed even when purses full of silver coin were dangled from the ship's side. It was as though the towering warship was invisible. Finally, as the *Centurion* came to within twenty miles of Macao, the Portuguese settlement at the mouth of the Pearl (Canton) River, a local pilot agreed to guide the ship in. By 11 November she was at anchor off Macao, and the next day a Portuguese pilot took her into the harbour at Typa.

For Anson's weary crew the worst of the voyage must have seemed over. After two years in which they were rarely free of danger from the elements, disease and the enemy, 'we once more arrived in an amicable port, in a civilized country'. A Portuguese settlement since 1557, Macao had at first enjoyed a privileged position of extra-territoriality on the margins of the Chinese empire. By the time of Anson's visit it had lost much of its commercial significance to the European factories seventy miles upstream on the Pearl River at Canton. The city retained its Portuguese governor, and for most of the year offered shelter to the supercargoes of the European trading companies, who were allowed to remain in Canton only during the time of the East Indiamen's stay there. But if Macao was a more relaxed place for European traders and seamen than the tightly controlled river strip of the Company factories at Canton, it was just as firmly under Chinese control. In time, Anson would discover this, but for him and his men the first priority was news – both of events in Europe

Chinese junks. Engraving in *Anson's Voyage* (1748) after a drawing by Peircy Brett. The left-hand vessel was of about 120 tons, used in the river and coasting trades. Two craft of this size were used to help hove down the *Centurion* at Typa in the early months of 1743. The other two sketches are side and bow views of a sea-going merchant vessel of about 280 tons. War junks, the text noted, were not much larger, and were armed only with 4-pounder cannon.

and of the more personal matters that would fill the letters from home that were on the East Indiamen newly arrived at Canton. To Anson's surprise and anger, the only letter for him was from James Naish, the former East India Company supercargo who had had much to do with the planning of the expedition. 'Not a line from my brother nor any other friend; no orders from the Admiralty, from whom I expected a supply of men and stores,' Anson wrote to Naish. Clearly feeling a forgotten man, he went on to describe his despair. 'What an opportunity I lose,' he told Naish; for how could he hope to seize the galleons heading for Manila from Acapulco the following spring since he had 'but five-and-forty men before the Mast and some of them have not recovered their senses, for numbers turned Mad and Idiots with the Scurvey'. This letter is the only private communication written by Anson on the voyage that has survived; its uninhibited language is very different from the dispassionate prose of Anson's long official report of the same time to the Duke of Newcastle. In revealing for a moment the frustration Anson was feeling after the disasters of the previous two years, the letter to Naish lifted the edge of the close mask of reserve and composure with which he normally faced the world.

One nagging worry for Anson and his men was their assumption that no reports about their fate had reached England, and that they had been given up for dead. It is a sign of the difference between this expedition and its privateering predecessors to the South Sea that Anson and his ships had in fact not disappeared from view. A surprising amount of news had filtered back to England long before the first letters from Anson's men arrived in London on East India Company ships from Canton in the summer of 1743. In the Caribbean Vernon had intercepted and sent home dispatches from Panama and elsewhere about Anson, while Jamaica proved a sensitive seismograph for picking up Spanish tremors about Anson's exploits on the other side of the Panama isthmus. By the spring of 1742 ministers and newspapers in London knew about the wreck of Pizarro's squadron, Anson's stay at Juan Fernández, the attack on Paita, and the turning back of the *Severn* and *Pearl*. By the autumn news had reached London of the wreck of the *Wager*. In contrast, Anson at Macao knew nothing of the *Wager*'s fate, and among the letters he wrote at this time was one addressed to Captain Cheap at Batavia (Jakarta). This was not as bizarre as it might seem, for Anson had picked up a Spanish report of a strange vessel seen off the Philippines, and he hoped against hope that she might be the *Wager*. In England, first-hand information about the expedition came from an unexpected source – Louis Leger, the *Centurion*'s French cook who was thought to have deserted at Chequetan. Instead, he had paid the penalty for wandering off in the woods – looking for limes for Anson's table, or so he indignantly maintained – and had been captured and taken to Acapulco. From there he was sent to Vera Cruz and then Havana, before being put on ship for Europe. Escaping at Lagos, he arrived in England on board a British warship in April 1743 with his news, at about the same time that Anson was preparing to leave Macao; and his account of the voyage up to the time of his capture was printed in the *London Gazette* and other papers. It was a sad postscript to a remarkable story that, within weeks of his arrival, Leger was killed in a gaming brawl in London. In May 1746, far too late for him to benefit personally, the 'R' was removed from Leger's name in the *Centurion*'s pay book, and the sum of £20–6–10d. paid to his executors. During his final weeks Leger must have been sought after by families of those on the voyage, anxious for first-hand news about their relatives. Among the papers of the de Saumarez family there is a jubilant letter from this period passing on Leger's reassurance that both Philip and Thomas Saumarez had been in good health when he last saw them. The letters, official and private, written at Macao and Canton, were of course welcome. Their contents were summarised in newspapers and periodicals; but even before these arrived an outline of the expedition's fortunes up to the time it headed across the North Pacific was known in England.

Whatever feelings of relief were apparent among Anson's men on their arrival at Macao, they evaporated in the months of frustration that followed. In the later published accounts anger was expressed at what was seen as the pusillanimous attitude of the Portuguese authorities at Macao and the obstructive Chinese officials upriver at Canton. There was more to the situation than this, for lying in the river at Canton were four ships of the East India Company. Ever since its establishment a half-century earlier the Company's China trade had laboured under difficulties. At this time it depended on an awkward triangular relationship between the Company factors at Canton, the local Hong merchants who supplied its cargoes of tea, silk and porcelain, and the watchful Chinese authorities. Subject to stringent restrictions and sometimes under the threat of suspension, the Company's trade was a delicate enough plant to be uprooted by any display of force by an impatient naval commander unfamiliar with local conditions. The dislocation of the Company's trade in 1744 with the arrival off the coast of China of Spanish warships from Manila was to provide a sharp reminder of the damage that commerce could suffer from the spread of war to a region previously unaffected by European conflicts.

From first arrival off Macao Anson behaved with circumspection, but equally he showed an unbending determination that he should be regarded as commander of a King's warship, exempt from the various dues and restrictions imposed on trading vessels. As soon as the *Centurion* reached Macao, Anson sent an officer ashore to pay his compliments to the governor, and to seek his advice. His preference was to take the *Centurion* upriver to Canton for her refit, but he made it clear that he was not prepared to pay port charges there. When he heard this the governor nervously advised Anson to leave the warship at Macao, where she could be careened and repaired. Despite all his private assurances of goodwill, the Portuguese official warned Anson that he could not supply his ship with any stores or provisions without the explicit consent of the viceroy at Canton. Some indication that this might not be an altogether straight-forward business came when a Chinese official at Macao refused per-mission for Anson to board the boat he had hired to take him to Canton. In the end consent was obtained – by the threat of force, according to the authorised account; by the solicitations of the Portuguese and a bribe, according to a private note by Anson – but it was a sign of things to come. The small junk with Anson and several officers on board took three days to reach Canton. The river was busy with boats, and the banks were dotted with villages. Set against the delights of what Michell called 'a beautiful landskip' was the irritant of continual inspections of Anson's pass by guard boats and posts on the banks. His destination was the East India Company's factory at Whampoa, a few miles short of Canton itself. There he was persuaded by the English factors that he should allow the Hong merchants to act as intermediaries and submit his request for permission to refit the *Centurion*, but after a month nothing had been achieved. According to the authorised account, the 'perfidious' Chinese merchants never even attempted to pass on Anson's request, but the diary kept by the Company supercargoes puts a different slant on the story. The Hong merchants insisted that the mandarins were totally unable to understand the status of a ship that had sailed round the world destroying other ships. Millechamp complained that he and other crew members were abused as 'ladrones' or pirates, and stones thrown at them in the streets. James Naish, far distant in England, had another explanation for the delays, which he put down to the machinations of the French and Dutch supercargoes at Canton. In his letter to Naish, Anson admitted that all the European traders at Canton except the English were against him, because the holding of the galleon for Manila at Acapulco that spring had disrupted the normal pattern of trade between Canton and Manila. In the end the East India Company supercargoes probably came nearest to the heart of the problem when they acknowledged that 'a King's ship coming being without precedent, everybody avoided being concerned in the affair'. Their own priority, the factory diary makes clear, was to get their ships away before Anson's patience ran out.

Letters from Anson to Saumarez, left in charge of the *Centurion* at Macao, reveal his fury at the situation as the weeks passed. 'Of all the places I was ever in this is the most disagreeable,' he wrote on 24 November. With one of the Swedish East Indiamen about to leave for Europe, Anson was anxious to get a report of the voyage on board, but the Chinese refused to allow any of his party to go down to the *Centurion* to bring back his log book and other documents. In the end he had to ask Saumarez to copy out the relevant dates and other information for him. On 5 December things were no better: 'I am cursedly plagued with these people and am afraid all will not come out right at last.' The reference this time was to an attempt by the Hong merchants to persuade Anson to return to Macao, where they assured him supplies would reach him. Not only Anson was disinclined to believe this; the English supercargoes thought the suggestion was 'no more than a piece of farce and chicanery'. It was just as well for the supercargoes' peace of mind that they were not aware of Anson's instructions to Saumarez to look out for two Spanish trading vessels expected from Manila. If they came in sight he was to send out the *Centurion*'s barge to seize them; and all considerations of diplomacy and the East India Company's trade would have gone by the board. Perhaps fortunately for all concerned, no Spanish ships appeared, while at Canton the stalemate was eventually broken, though in a not very satisfactory way. Anson persuaded the Hong merchants to smuggle some extra provisions on board the East India Company ships which were waiting to leave

Canton. When they reached Macao they would transfer them to the *Centurion*.

Also on board the East Indiamen were Captain Michell, Lt.-Col. Cracherode, Hubert Tassell, marine officer Charles Herriot and the Revd Richard Walter, all bound for England. Captain Saunders had sailed earlier in a Swedish ship, carrying Anson's dispatches. Other officers from the *Gloucester* and *Tryal* had also requested permission to return home, but given his shortage of crew Anson was adamant that they could only leave if they found seamen to take their places on the *Centurion*. The obvious source for trained seamen were the East Indiamen at Canton, but their captains refused either to assign men to Anson as he requested, or to exchange any of them for officers. This behaviour Anson condemned as 'Cruel Usage to the Kings Servants in Distress', and it reflected the differing priorities of the naval commander and the Company traders. Even Richard Walter was told by Anson that he must find a replacement, presumably on the grounds that he had done the work of an ordinary seaman on the desperate voyage across the North Pacific, though eventually Anson let him go. It would be difficult to apply a strict replacement rule to the most senior officers such as Michell and Saunders, and in any case, save in the most exceptional circumstances supernumerary officers were likely to be more of an embarrassment than help on shipboard. Unlike ordinary seamen, it was not every day that a naval captain could be expected to man the capstan or cut wood. There seems little justification for Millechamp's later allegation that Anson had sent Michell and Saunders home so that he would not have to share any future prize money with them. On the issue of prize money Millechamp was not a disinterested party, and for Saunders at least there is evidence that he fully expected to return to England as soon as possible. His final entry as captain in the log of the *Tryal Prize* on the day she was scuttled (1 May 1742) read: 'went my self on board Commodore Anson for Passage home'.

In mid-December, after a wasted four weeks at Canton, Anson returned to Macao where, as he came on board the *Centurion*, he was told that not only was the leak worsening but that the mainmast was defective. Regardless of whether provisions were obtained from the passing East Indiamen it was out of the question to put to sea, and the matter of the ship's refit took on a new urgency. Anson now regretted his circumspect approach at Canton, and his deference to the advice of the East India Company factors. The day after his return he wrote to the viceroy at Canton explaining his attempts to obtain an audience with him, and requested permission to repair and provision his ship. The English original of Anson's letter survives, and shows that it was couched in uncompromising, not to say peremptory, tones. It began with a 'Demand' for goods and help, including two large junks, 'Provisions of all kind', timber, 3,000 yards of canvas, pumps and other stores, and, finally, 'Carpenters, Caulkers, Bricklayers and Smiths'. To the surprise of those who had advocated a conciliatory, submissive approach, the new directness paid off. Two days later a high-ranking mandarin arrived from Canton to inspect the condition of the British warship. The occasion was one of considerable pomp and ceremonial. The mandarin was accompanied by a retinue of lesser officials and their attendants in a fleet of eighteen junks, which drew abreast the *Centurion* with streamers flying and music playing. Confronted with this splendid sight Anson found himself in a quandary. Neither Royal Navy officers nor seamen at this time had a regular uniform. A brief burst of generosity by Elizabeth I, who had supplied blue coats to the seamen fighting Spain and the Armada, was soon put to an end by the more austere James I, who refused 'to clothe the men to make them handsome to run away'. At sea, once their shore clothes were worn out, the men either made canvas trousers, shirts and jackets out of old sailcloth, or bought 'slops' from the purser. These varied from ship to ship, but usually consisted of baggy trousers or drawers, checked shirts, with waistcoats, woollen stockings and shoes for those who could afford them. After two and a half years at sea the *Centurion*'s crew must have presented a particularly shabby appearance, so Anson ordered 100 of 'the most sightly' of them to put on the regimental uniforms of the dead marines, and with drums beating they made an improvised guard of honour to welcome the mandarin on board. The inspection of the *Centurion*'s hull was a thorough one, made by two Chinese carpenters who came on board with the mandarin. While they were deep in the bowels of the ship the mandarin was shown around the more accessible parts of the *Centurion* from Anson's great cabin to the gun deck. There he seemed particularly impressed by the size of the 24-pounders and the weight of their shot. This was the hidden threat behind the courtesies of the occasion, though how many of Anson's expostulations about his treatment and what would happen if it continued were actually conveyed by the 'linguist' or translator to the mandarin is a matter of doubt. The Chinese-speaking Filipino captured in the South Sea had not survived the Pacific crossing, and Anson was dependent on local translators who were only too aware of the fate of messengers bearing unpleasant news. After a formal dinner on the ship and a fifteen-gun salute the mandarin departed for Canton – and the waiting began.

It was without surprise that Anson learned that in the discussions at the viceroy's council in Canton the French used their influence to prevent the British warship being given any special treatment or dispensation. He himself was convinced that his hints that the *Centurion* could destroy every vessel in the river was responsible for the eventual decision to grant the necessary permission. In his letter to Naish, Anson managed to extract some humour from an unpromising situation as he recounted how in answer to the viceroy's query about what action the British might take if denied help, the mandarin 'said I had told him that in case I received a refusal I should then consult with my people whether to eat one another or the Chinese, and that I had desired him to put himself in my circumstances and consider whose lot it would fall to! Upon which the viceroy declared I must be supplied.' More probably the change of heart came from the realisation in Canton after the mandarin's inspection that without a refit the *Centurion* might remain indefinitely at Macao, an awkward and threatening presence, a challenge to Chinese sovereignty. At the anchorage at Typa 100 local caulkers arrived, while Saumarez was allowed to hire two junks at Canton to help with the unloading and careening of the ship. There was still much haggling over costs and wages, and despite the numbers of workmen swarming over the *Centurion* the refit proceeded too slowly for Anson's peace of mind. With the ship helpless on her side, it would be an easy prey for an enemy, and rumours of Spanish warships in the offing did nothing to calm the situation. By the beginning of April all was ready for sea. The elusive leak had at last been found, deep below the water level, and plugged; fresh sheathing had been fixed to the hull; decks and sides had been caulked; masts repaired and new rigging put up. Now it was the turn of the Chinese to show impatience for the ship to be gone. Anson, however, had his own agenda and his own timetable, and it was another two weeks before he left the roadstead for the open sea.

VI

The Prize of All the Oceans

'A man who would not fight for a galleon would fight for nothing.'

Admiral Sir Charles Wager

THE *CENTURION* HEADED OUT TO SEA from Macao roadstead on 19 April 1743, refitted and careened, ready for the long haul back to England. If the ship was once more in good shape, the same could not be said of her crew. There were only 227 on board (among them 27 boys), and these included 23 Lascar and Dutch sailors taken on at Macao as well as the survivors from vessels of the original squadron. Of more than 500 crew, marines and invalids who had sailed on the *Centurion* from Spithead three years earlier, almost 400 had died. Down in numbers, the crew was also low in spirit. All had lost shipmates during the terrible Pacific crossing; and a sense of failure hung heavy over officers and men alike. So depressed was Anson as he contemplated the fate of his squadron that while at Macao he had not been able to bring himself to write a single line to his patron, Lord Hardwicke. When he did write, after his return to England, he explained that his 'misfortunes gave me an uneasiness I could not express to your Lordship'. The *Severn*, *Pearl* and *Wager* had disappeared in tempestuous seas off Cape Horn, and with their hulls and rigging damaged and many of their crews dead or sick it was doubtful if any had survived. In the Pacific the *Gloucester*, the *Tryal* and the *Tryal Prize* had all been scuttled. To set against these losses, Anson could show only the capture of a few Spanish trading vessels off the South American coast and the sacking of Paita, an unimportant Peruvian settlement. His ambitious instructions to attack the great cities of Spanish America, encourage rebellion against the rule of Spain, and open the region to British traders, had become a mockery.

Only one exploit could redeem this dismal story – the taking of the Acapulco treasure galleon on her way into Manila. In 1742 Anson had arrived off Acapulco three weeks too late to intercept the Pilar as she made port at the end of her eastbound voyage from Manila. Now, despite his shortage of men, Anson was determined to make one last effort. During the stay at Macao he had asked Joseph Allen, surgeon of the *Tryal*, to get intelligence about the galleon from a Manila Jesuit he knew. In the end, Anson was able to do better than this, for he took on board a newcomer, one Collet, who despite his 'sottish Attachment to strong Liquors' was to be of inestimable value in the weeks to come. Collet was an Englishman who had been in the Spanish service at Manila, but had deserted his ship at Macao and joined the *Centurion*. He was a mine of information about the galleon, and advised Anson on her usual route into the Philippines, and where she could be best intercepted. For his part, to keep up the pretence that he was sailing direct to Java on his homeward passage, Anson had taken letters and gifts on board at Macao to be delivered at Batavia (Jakarta), and had written to the Dutch governor there in anticipation of 'the pleasure of waiting upon your Excellency'. Essential though it was to keep secrecy if Spanish forces in Manila were not to be alerted, Anson told his officers about his intentions. In his journal the first lieutenant, Philip Saumarez, wrote on the day the ship sailed from Macao that they intended to make for Cape Espiritu Santo at the northeast tip of the island of Samar (farthest east of the Philippines group). The cape was the normal landfall of the westbound galleon, and there the *Centurion* hoped to intercept both galleons from Mexico. Like Anson, Saumarez assumed that there would be more than one galleon because the *Pilar*, which should have made her return run to Manila in the spring of 1742, had been held at Acapulco once it was realised that Anson was lying in wait off the port. Unknown to the English, the *Pilar* had made the ocean crossing early in 1743, and was already safe at Cavite, the port for Manila. But the likelihood that the undermanned *Centurion* would be faced with two galleons made Anson's decision all the more

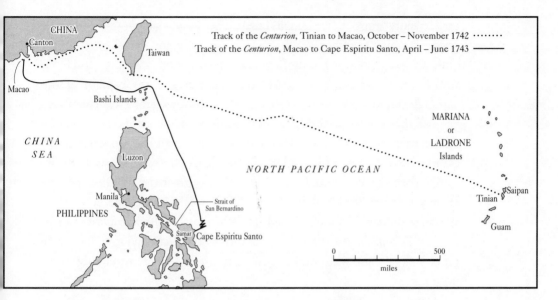

courageous, or foolhardy. It could be seen as an act of desperation by a commander who faced professional ruin, a last throw by a gambler who had lost all. If so, it was a popular move as far as the crew were concerned, summoned towards the quarterdeck once the ship was clear of land to hear the news.

Characteristically, Anson made only a short speech. He began by describing the wealth of the galleons before refuting the 'many ridiculous tales' about giant ships with sides so thick that no cannon ball could penetrate them. He promised his listeners that he would bring the *Centurion* so close to the galleons that her shot would smash through one side of their hulls and out the other. Such reassurance was the more necessary since there had been a unnerving moment as the *Centurion* saluted a Swedish East Indiaman on the day of sailing from Macao, only to find that the cannon fired with so little force that the wads were thrown only a few yards. When checked, the powder in the guns fired was damp; the rest proved to be full strength. Even so, there may have been those on the *Centurion* who had read, and remembered, the account from Woodes Rogers's voyage of the engagement with the Manila ships in 1709. The prize that was taken was a vessel of 400 or 500 tons, with only twenty guns and a small crew. The larger galleon beat off the privateer's attack with ease. She was a new 900-ton vessel of 40 guns, with a crew of 600. One of Rogers's officers wrote that they might as well have tried to take a castle. And according to the captain of the captured ship, the towering galleon, and not his own craft, was characteristic of those making the long voyage; he went on to describe one so strong that she had beaten off a Dutch attack even though she had 90 cannon balls sticking in her sides. On the surface at least, all was enthusiasm and confidence, and Anson's speech was greeted with three cheers. If only half the stories about the galleon's wealth were true, a share in the prize money would be enough to set up for life the humblest seaman on the *Centurion*. As the veteran admiral Sir Charles Wager had once remarked, a man who would not fight for a galleon would fight for nothing.

From the Chinese coast the *Centurion* sailed eastwards, south of Formosa and through the Bashi Islands before bearing south to run down the east coast of the Philippines towards Cape Espiritu Santo. This was the signpost pointing the galleons into the Strait of San Bernardino and on to Cavite. The round hummocks of the Cape came into sight on 20 May, and Anson immediately ordered the topgallant sails to be taken in to avoid discovery from possible watchers on land. Each June lookouts were posted on the Cape to give notice of the approach of the galleon. It was now a time for waiting, and for patience. Day after day the *Centurion* tacked backwards and forwards as her lookouts scanned the eastern horizon for sight of a sail. Below them the crew practised at the great guns, and with small arms. Their deficiency in numbers could only be made good by rapid, accurate fire. So targets were hung from the yardarm, and successful marksmen were rewarded for their efforts.

Powder and shot were in too short supply to allow practice firing of the ship's cannon, but the incessant daily exercising of them continued. In the heat of action, speed and coordination by the gun crews were essential as they obeyed the thirty-eight separate commands that directed a single firing of a cannon. After each round the bore and touch-hole of the gun had to be cleaned; it was then loaded and primed, and the gun port lifted before the gun was run out with the help of tackles and levers.

The same levers were used on the rear of the gun to nudge it into aiming position before a slow-match was applied to the touch-hole. As the recoil from the explosion brought the gun crashing back inboard, it was halted by ropes fastened to iron bolts on the ship's side. Finally, the gun port was swung down again to give the men some protection from flying shot and splinters, and the whole cumbersome operation was repeated. It was muscle-straining, hot work, with the gun crews blackened by powder and deafened by the blast of the explosions and the rumble of the gun carriages. There was the more need for Anson's crew to practise, even without powder and shot, because the shortage of men prevented him from manning the cannon in the normal way. Instead of the standard size crew posted to each cannon (eight to ten men to a 24-pounder, seven or eight to a nine-pounder), only two men could be spared to each piece to sponge it out after firing, and then to reload. Gangs of a dozen men ran along the gun decks opening the ports, laying and firing the guns, and bringing up the ammunition for the next loading.

For a month the drills, the exercises, the watching went on in hot, sultry weather. The ship was ready for action, and more than ready. It was a tense, difficult time, for there had been too many disappointments on the long voyage for doubts not to creep in. 'All hands began to look very melancholy,' Saumarez entered in his log for 19 June. The galleon, they had been told, always arrived during the month of June; and 19 June on board the *Centurion*, reckoning by the Old Style Julian calendar, was the last day of June for the Spaniards and their New Style Gregorian calendar. The next day, at sunrise, came the long-awaited moment. A midshipman high in the tops saw a sail, far away to the southeast. Although it would be hours before those on deck could see what Charles Proby had spotted, all the pent-up feelings of the previous month were released. Cheering and whooping, 'mad with joy', the crew raced to the guns and into the tops, throwing overboard everything that lay in their way, regardless of its value.

As the morning wore on, the distant flicker of sail began to take shape, even for watchers at deck level, as a large three-masted ship, sailing straight at the *Centurion*. In those waters, at that season, it could only be the Acapulco galleon. The firing of a gun by the galleon at 7.30 a.m.

was assumed to be a signal to a consort following astern, but no other vessel came into view. Difficult though Anson and his officers found it to believe, the galleon intended to fight, and the two ships closed steadily. The hours of waiting took their toll on the crew, some of whom suddenly doubled up with 'Dry Gripes', and had to be steadied by Anson's words of reassurance. At noon the *Centurion* swung across the wake of the galleon to come up from astern on her port side, so cutting off any escape to the nearby land. Soon after, the galleon hoisted Spanish colours and hove to, waiting, it seemed, for the action to begin. Through squalls of wind and rain the *Centurion* closed with the galleon, firing her bow guns at a half-mile range, to which the Spaniard replied with her stern-chaser, loaded with chain-shot that 'cut about' the warship's sails and rigging. It was at this moment that the *Centurion*'s crew carried out two routine procedures for action that, they discovered later, caused consternation on board the galleon. First, they got the spritsail-yard fore and aft so that if ordered they could run the ship alongside for boarding without entangling the rigging. Given Anson's lack of men, and the protective netting stretched across the galleon's main deck, it was unlikely that he would ever give that order, but the Spaniards were not to know that. They had been told a few days earlier at Guam about the helpless condition of the *Centurion* when she had arrived in those waters the previous year. Now, too late, they wondered whether the ship had got reinforcements in China or the East Indies. Even more alarming to those on the galleon was the sight of the *Centurion*'s lower gun ports slowly opening, and the muzzles of the heavy 24-pounders coming into view.

At 1 p.m. the *Centurion*, with colours and Anson's broad pennant flying, came alongside the galleon, and crossed her bow to open fire with the starboard guns at only a pistol-shot's range. Whereas the *Centurion*, lying across the galleon's bow, could pour the fire of almost all her starboard guns into the Spaniard's forequarters, the galleon could bring only a few of her broadside guns to bear. In the tops Anson had stationed 30 of his best marksmen, and their first volley killed or quickly drove down their opponents in the galleon's tops. As they switched their fire to the exposed decks, they picked out the galleon's officers and the gun crews as their special targets. After a half-hour the *Centurion* lost her original position across the galleon's bow and instead lay alongside at about three boat-lengths' distance, but her grape-shot continued to sweep the galleon's decks while the heavy cannon balls crashed into her hull. On the gun decks of the *Centurion*, as the cannon waited their turn to be serviced by the running gangs of men, there was no possibility of conventional broadsides. Each gun fired as soon as it was ready; unlike regular broadsides, which would have allowed the Spaniards to take cover as they saw the *Centurion*'s gun ports opening, the sporadic but deadly fire of the English ship gave them no intervals of safety.

All the accounts agree that for almost an hour the Spaniards fought bravely, but then panic set in as men were mown down, seven or eight at a time. Among those left alive, some jumped down the hatches, while others lay flat in the scuttles, covering their heads. The galleon's officers tried to stop the flight, but when their commander was hit and taken below resistance collapsed. Five or six cannon were fired for the last time, and then the galleon struck her colours after 90 minutes of fighting. It was at this moment that clouds of thick smoke pouring up from below decks seemed to show that the *Centurion* was on fire. Some cartridges had blown up and set alight oakum between the planks, but the small blaze was soon put out. As the helpless galleon crashed against the *Centurion*'s hull, and then fell away again, it was clear that the action was over. Philip Saumarez and ten men were sent across in the cutter, the *Centurion*'s only undamaged boat, to take possession of the prize.

As he climbed on board the galleon Saumarez found a scene of horror, for the decks were 'covered with carcasses, entrails and dismembered limbs'. Some bodies had been thrown overboard; others were lying in heaps down the main hatchway. Milling around on deck or sheltering below were several hundred confused and frightened men – and the task of Saumarez and his tiny prize crew was hindered by the strengthening wind. The galleon was the *Nuestra Señora de Covadonga*, 72 days out from Acapulco, and twelve days from Guam, where she had called for water and other supplies. The vessel was a sorry sight, with her hull, masts and rigging shattered by gunfire. Her 'general' (the title always given to the galleon's commander) was an experienced Portuguese officer, Don Gerónimo Montero, who had served on the galleons for fourteen years.

He had been wounded by musket-fire towards the end of the action, and could not be moved. On board, Saumarez was told, was treasure amounting to one and a half million dollars, together with money and valuables in private hands.

Anson quickly sent across to the galleon another 40 men, including two surgeons, and with them blocks and rigging. By nightfall Saumarez had completed the most urgent running repairs, and had sent 300 prisoners on board the *Centurion*, together with the first of the treasure. Among the prisoners was the governor of Guam, who had been slightly wounded in the action. By a quirk of fate he was greeted on board the *Centurion* by Captain (Acting) Alexander Crowden, the last survivor amongst the invalid officers, who thirty-six years earlier had been captured by the Spaniard at the Battle of Almanza. The two dozen or so boys on the *Centurion* must have been much in evidence as the prisoners came on board, for when the Spaniards saw the number of 'striplings' among Anson's crew they were alleged to have complained that they had been beaten 'by a handful of boys'. The remaining Spaniards, less than 200, and the wounded, were kept on board the *Covadonga*. Since at any moment Spanish guard ships might appear at the mouth of the nearby Strait of San Bernardino to confront the *Centurion* and her prize, both of which were damaged and encumbered with prisoners, Anson had no alternative but to head back to the Chinese coast. He took the *Covadonga* into the King's service, and appointed Saumarez as her captain. A week was spent rowing the treasure across to the *Centurion* – the coins alone filled 256 chests – and to compensate for the weight of silver taken out of the prize Saumarez had to shift cannon into the hold.

For the prisoners on board the *Centurion* the crossing of the South China Sea was a nightmare ordeal. All except the officers and the wounded were crammed into the hold. Two hatchways were left open to provide air, but at the edges of each one four swivel guns manned by gunners with lighted matches pointed down at the masses below. On deck the ship's crew went about armed, while the officers slept fully dressed, weapons at their sides. The English accounts made no attempt to conceal the sufferings of the prisoners. In the stifling confines of the hold they could be spared only a pint of water a day, and although none of them died, when they were brought up on deck after a month's captivity even the strongest had been 'reduced to mere skeletons'.

The galleon proved a slow sailor, and when the weather allowed she was towed by the *Centurion*. It was 11 July before the two ships reached Macao, and it took another three days to work them round into the Canton River. It was time to take stock, not least of the treasure. Most of it was now on the *Centurion*, but not all, for at the same time as the English sailors had been ferrying their booty across from the *Covadonga* to their own ship, so the prisoners on the galleon had also been busy. Once the ships were safely at anchor in the Canton River, the English made a close search of the prize. They found valuables hidden everywhere: in nooks and crannies, behind beams, even concealed in scooped-out cheeses. When the final sums had been done, it was clear that on board the *Centurion* was one of the richest treasures ever seized by an English ship: 1,313,843 pieces of eight, and 35,682 oz. of virgin silver and plate. These were the figures, to be repeated over and again in accounts of the voyage, that stirred imagination in England. The capture of the Acapulco galleon, coming as it did after extraordinary hardships and disasters, laid the foundations of both Anson's private fortune and his public reputation.

Accounts of the action, at the time and since, have depended heavily on a single source, the authorised narrative of the voyage published in 1748 under the name of Richard Walter, chaplain on the *Centurion* (but since shown to have been 'ghosted' in part at least by a writer who was not on the voyage). The book indulged in no melodramatic exaggerations. Its description of the taking of the galleon was, to outward appearance, analytical and dispassionate. It rightly laid stress on the measures taken by Anson to overcome his deficiency in numbers. With only 227 men – instead of a normal crew of 400, plus marines – he clearly could not man the guns in the conventional way, and leave enough hands to work the ship, act as marksmen in the tops, carry ammunition, and take away the wounded. Anson, as we have seen, adopted unconventional emergency measures. He gave priority to the tops, where he sent 30 of his best men to harass the Spaniards with musket-fire, while down below the 24-pounder cannon on the lower gun deck and the nine-pounders on the

Engagement between the *Centurion* and the *Nuestra Señora de Covadonga*. Engraving in *Anson's Voyage* (1748) based on a drawing by Peircy Brett. Brett's sketch of the action formed the basis for later representations of the action by artists such as John Cleveley (see jacket): the ships are shown stern on, and even allowing for possible quirks of perspective the galleon appears a larger vessel than the *Centurion*.

upper gun deck were manned on the starboard side only, and then by skeleton crews. In the action itself no outstanding feats of seamanship were displayed, or indeed called for, as the *Centurion* battered the galleon into submission at point-blank range.

The writer of the authorised account went on to assess the Spaniard's strength. The galleon was much larger than the *Centurion*; she had 550 men on board, and 36 cannon mounted for action, together with 28 swivel guns. Many of the Spaniards, he admitted, were inexperienced, but he then described how the prisoners, when they were brought on board the *Centurion* and for the first time saw her crew, cried out with anger that they had been beaten by a handful of boys. The image is clear. It was one accepted in England almost as a natural right since the days of Drake and Grenville, of an English vessel facing overwhelming odds. Peircy Brett's drawing of the action shows the tall masts and high hull of the galleon looming large over the low-lying shape of the *Centurion*. If the image is clear, it is also distorted. This was not a case of an English David bringing a Spanish Goliath to his knees, and unpublished sources from both sides modify the accepted version of the famous engagement. Whatever Walter's role in writing the authorised narrative, one thing is certain – the chaplain was not present at the taking of the galleon, for he had sailed for home from Macao in December 1742. That section at least of the book was written under Anson's close supervision; it represents the evidence of a commander justifying his own conduct, understandably making the most of one of the few successes of an expedition scarred by failure.

Spanish documents reveal that Anson's confidence about the secrecy of his intentions once he had left Macao was misplaced. Letters from a Chinese merchant in Canton gave Gaspar de la Torre, governor of the Philippines, details of Anson's arrival at Macao. The first, written in December 1742, listed Anson's misadventures: the fruitless wait for the galleon off Acapulco; the loss of the *Gloucester*; and the dreadful casualties – almost all the marines, and some 1,200 seamen. 'They are in a wretched state,' the informant concluded, having little in the way of men, equipment or stores, and with the ship falling to pieces. A second, undated letter from the same merchant (probably written in March 1743) told a different and more worrying story. Despite all difficulties, the *Centurion* had been refitted and provisioned. In public Anson had made much of his problems and his intention to make for Batavia and home, but the letter-writer suspected that his real intention was to cruise for the galleon as she neared the Philippines. In a final shrewd guess he wrote that the *Centurion* was likely to leave Macao in mid-April, as indeed she did.

In Manila a council of war held at the beginning of May (about 20 April by the English calendar) considered this alarming news, and decided to fit out one of the galleons then in port, the *Pilar*, and send her to escort the incoming galleon through the danger zone. The preparation of the *Pilar* was a protracted business, unnecessarily so if the critical tone of later Spanish accounts is any indication. The port commander at Cavite made much of the leaks discovered in her hull, problems with the rigging, and the lack of heavy cannon. Once all this had been put right, the galleon's commander insisted that her keel should be surveyed – a fort-night's job since the cannon would have to be landed, the ballast removed, and the ship unrigged before she could be propped up to expose her keel. In the end it was decided simply to 'boot-top' the sides – a process that involved cleaning and tallowing as much of the lower hull as could be reached by tilting the ship while she was still afloat. By 28 May (NS) the galleon was deemed ready for sea, but there were further delays, and it took another six days before she finally sailed. The *Pilar*'s progress through the tortuous channels of the archipelago towards the San Bernardino Strait was slow despite news that a three-masted ship had been seen cruising off the coast, which could only have been the *Centurion*. When the galleon ran aground, entering the harbour of San Jacinto on the island of Ticao, she had not even reached the western entrance of the strait. It was in any event too late: a week earlier the *Covadonga* had surrendered to the *Centurion* a hundred miles to the eastward. It was a sorry story, and after long drawn-out judicial investigations in 1749 Gaspar de la Torre was found guilty of negligence.

If the escort force betrayed a lack of urgency, the Spaniards on the *Covadonga* showed a complacency bordering on the reckless. When the galleon reached Guam near the end of her long run, the news that Anson had been in the area the previous autumn was treated by most of the officers with a contemptuous lack of concern. The galleon's Portuguese commander, Don Gerónimo Montero, counselled caution; but he was outvoted in the junta or council of officers that he was obliged to call in cases of dispute or uncertainty. Even though the galleon's lower gun ports were too near the waterline to allow them to be used, the council rejected Montero's prudent suggestion to make for Manila by a more circuitous route than usual. Two years later the *Santo Domingo* did just that when she reached Manila northabout around Luzon; but the *Covadonga* sailed along the regular galleon track to her doom.

The sequence of events on board the galleon on the morning of the 20 June is not at all clear. Different sources support different interpretations of the galleon's failure to veer away when she sighted that distant sail at sunrise off Cape Espiritu Santo. The most likely explanation is that the *Covadonga*'s officers assumed that it was an escort vessel sent out from Manila to bring them in. Some support for this comes from the early morning cannon shot mentioned by the English, which might well have been a signal gun fired by the *Covadonga* to the escort which she supposed she could see ahead. There is a different explanation advanced in some of the Spanish and English accounts: that the *Centurion* was recognised as a foreign ship, probably Anson's, but that she was thought to be so weak that she posed no serious threat to the galleon. Lawrence Millechamp wrote that the news picked up by the galleon at Guam was that Anson had only 120 or 130 men left, while Pascoe Thomas has much about the supposed bravado of Montero, who on the morning of the action boasted to his officers that he would entertain Anson to dinner before the day was out. Even if true, this story takes nothing away from the sense of apprehension that Montero clearly felt from the time he arrived at Guam. Together with his courage during the engagement this helped to clear him (but not until eleven years after the event) of charges of cowardice and negligence.

Other puzzles remain. The log of the *Covadonga*'s first pilot, which was seized by the English, shows that on 10 and 11 June (NS) – that is, about three weeks before the action – the galleon's crew were clearing the ship and knocking down the cabins on the quarterdeck and waist, so as to keep the guns clear. Yet the English accounts state that not until noon on the day of the action, when the ships were almost within long-distance cannon range, did the galleon's crew suddenly begin clearing for action, throwing lumber and cattle overboard. By then it was too late to do anything about the piles of stores and rubbish between decks which, one of the galleon's mates who was taken prisoner complained, made it impossible to fight the lower-deck guns.

Once the engagement began, the odds were stacked against the Spaniard. Saumarez entered in his log that he was 'amazed to think what he could propose against our weight of metal and a ship of our appearance'. Millechamp's 'Narrative', written long after the event, treated the whole affair even more coolly: 'The particulars of the engagement that ensued are hardly worth mentioning ...' The fact was that the *Centurion* was a vessel built and fitted for war. She carried 60 guns, 24 of them 24-pounders. Set against the 42- and 32-pounders of the great three-decker battleships of the day, these would not be decisive in a full-scale naval battle. But in any other circumstances the 24-pounder was a fearsome weapon, firing a solid iron ball that smashed through a ship's sides and sent a hail of splinters across the decks to kill or maim all in the way. Although the *Covadonga* was pierced for 64 guns, only 44 were on board, and twelve of these were lying useless in the hold or between decks. The 32 guns that were in position were all on the open decks, and they were a miscellaneous collection, ranging from six- to twelve-pounders. Rather than picking out the galleon's cannon, which were unlikely to inflict serious damage on the *Centurion*'s hull, the English focused on the 28 light pedreros or swivel guns as the weapons most to be feared, especially in close-range fighting. Mounted on the gunwales and in the tops, each of them was loaded with up to 70 musket balls, rusty nails and other bits of metal. Since the *Centurion*'s crew made no attempt to board, and many were under cover on the lower gun deck, these man-killers wrought less execution than might have been expected, and those firing them were soon struck down or driven away by grape-shot and by musket-fire from the *Centurion*'s tops.

In terms of size the *Covadonga* was not one of the bigger galleons used on the Acapulco–Manila run. The *Santíssima Trinidad*, captured by the British just inside the San Bernardino Strait in 1762, was at 2,000 tons one of the largest vessels afloat. She was hit, it was estimated, by more than 1,000 shot, none of which penetrated her timbers. By contrast, and despite the assertion made in the authorised account, the *Covadonga* was smaller than Anson's ship. Philippines-built at Cavite in 1731, she was about 700 tons burthen compared with the 1,000 tons of the *Centurion*. Measurements taken by one of Anson's carpenters showed that the galleon's gun deck was 124 feet long, twenty feet shorter than that of the *Centurion*. More serious than the discrepancy in size was the fact that the *Covadonga* was essentially a trading vessel. Her low bulwarks gave little protection to the men on deck, and the narrow gun ports made it difficult to slew the cannon round at any kind of angle.

Even the numerical superiority of the Spaniards was more apparent than real. Montero's deposition after the action shows that of the 530 men on board the galleon only 266 were reckoned as crew, about half of them Filipinos. Apart from a company of soldiers (three officers, 40 men), there were servants (a huge number at 177), convicts (24) and passengers (20). The galleon's handwritten 'Plan de Guerra' for the voyage has survived, and although Montero allocated battle stations on it to more than 400 men, the capabilities and steadiness of many of these were doubtful. Pascoe Thomas was among the second party of the prize crew to board the *Covadonga* after the action, and the first thing he noticed was how few of the dozens of muskets that had been thrown down on the decks had actually been fired. Later he found that most of the long pikes for resisting boarders were still stacked below decks. For his part, Montero made no attempt to board the *Centurion*, although the two ships lay within pistol-shot of each other for most of the action, and this suggests that he had no great confidence in the fighting spirit of his crew. That they endured 90 minutes of continual cannon and small-arms fire that killed or wounded more than a quarter of them was as much as could be expected. Certainly they did not have the incentive to fight of Anson's men. Of the original crews of the *Centurion*, *Gloucester* and *Tryal*, only the toughest had survived. No fewer than forty-eight of them were officers (including warrant officers and midshipmen). Of these, twenty-six were supernumeraries – that is, officers who were not part of the ship's regular complement, 'extras' who could be called on to do any duty required. More, much more, would be heard of them in the courts of law after the voyage. But whatever their rank or status, confronted with the alternatives of a fortune in prize money or the inside of a Spanish prison, Anson's men fought with grim determination.

The Spanish accounts give a frightening impression of the effect of the *Centurion*'s fire as it swept across the exposed decks of the galleon. They show that Spanish resistance was already weakening when Montero was struck down by a musket ball in the chest. His second-in-command took over, and remained on deck though hit in the thigh; but as another officer was killed, and a cannon ball blew off the leg of the captain of soldiers, the demoralised crew began to desert their posts. The galleon's steering failed, and as the *Centurion* once again moved ominously across her bows Montero's last despairing order from the cockpit to blow up the ship was ignored, and the Spaniards struck their flag. In his account of the action, Juan de la Concepción later criticised the crew for failing to throw the silver overboard or scuttle the ship. Given that it took a week to shift the silver from ship to ship, the first was hardly a practical proposition in the few minutes left to the crew before Saumarez and his men arrived. There was not even time to destroy all the ship's papers, for some of the most important have survived, including cargo lists, Montero's 'Plan de Guerra', the pilot's log, and the chart of the North Pacific that was later to grace the authorised account of the voyage. And that Montero's order to blow up the ship was disregarded is not surprising. The senior officers were dead or wounded, and those of the crew still on their feet had done their best against the odds. The casualty figures tell their own story. The *Centurion* lost one man killed in the action, two more died of their wounds, and seventeen were wounded. She took 20 or 30 shot in the hull, had two boats smashed and her rigging cut about. The *Covadonga* had 67 killed, 84 wounded and, in Anson's words, 'her masts and rigging were shot to pieces, and 150 shot passed through her hull, many of which were between wind and water, which occasioned her to be very leaky.'

Barring some extraordinary accident of war, there could be only one result to a duel between the *Centurion* and the *Covadonga*. This is not to denigrate Anson's achievement, simply to suggest that it lay not so much in the events of 20 June 1743 as in his determination in preparing his ship and surviving crew members for action after one of the most gruelling voyages in British naval annals. That he was to encounter a poorly armed ship was his good fortune, but clearly he was prepared for something more formidable – two galleons of unknown strength sailing in company. If the pseudonymous account by 'John Philips' is to be trusted, when Anson first turned his glass on the distant sail early that morning he thought that he could see two ships, and 'with great Sedateness and Composure said, My Lads we'll fight them both'. Although Anson was to be described as a second Drake by newspapers after his return, he had none of the Elizabethan sailor's sense of the dramatic or flair for publicity. Instead, the characteristic that stands out in the accounts is his imperturbability. A report of the capture of the galleon that appeared in a London newspaper soon after the *Centurion*'s return included a description by one of her officers of a heart-stopping moment during the action. As Anson was giving orders on the quarterdeck a young officer came running up shouting in panic. The commodore finished his instructions before turning to rebuke the unnamed officer for not making his report in proper form. Having heard the news that there was a fire, he then gave the culprit his orders, direct and simple, to go away and put it out. Other accounts described Anson standing on deck, exposed to the Spanish fire, and 'black as a Mulattoe with the Smoak of the Powder', while Pascoe Thomas, by no means an uncritical admirer, confirmed Anson's calmness throughout the action. On some ships, Thomas wrote, he had observed six times more noise and confusion in hoisting out a cutter than was noticeable on the *Centurion* during the whole thunderous action.

What began as a gamble turned into a near-certainty on the morning of 20 June. After the months of frustration Anson's luck had turned. The galleon was both rich and vulnerable, and her seizure brought him fame, fortune and promotion. Unremarkable as a feat of arms, Anson's capture of the Acapulco galleon in the distant Pacific had long-term effects on British naval fortunes more important than many a great fleet action.

VII

Confrontation at Canton

'Every body was apprehensive this would be a year of great
Troubles ... What follows is a little Secret History (which I
intend not to make Publick).'

Edward Page

ANSON REACHED the Canton or Pearl River in mid-July 1743 with
relief but also with some apprehension. He had no alternative but to
return to a coast where he had experienced so many difficulties on his
first visit. The year before he had met nothing but frustration in his
efforts to get supplies and refit his damaged ship during his five-month
stay at Macao and Canton. Notions of total war were still largely
unfamiliar in the mid-eighteenth century, and nowhere more so than
in a trading centre as remote from Europe and its conflicts as Canton.
There ships from nations officially at war ignored each other's presence,
and concentrated on the lucrative business of trade. When in April 1743
the *Centurion*, repaired and restocked, left the coast for Batavia and home
it was a mighty relief to British traders and Chinese officials alike at
Canton.

Her reappearance three months later towing the shattered hull of a
Spanish galleon was at once unbelievable and shocking, and Anson's clear
determination to sail with his prize upriver to Canton sent tremors of
alarm through the riverside factories. In all ways the situation was even
more fraught than it had been when he arrived at Macao the previous
year. Not only had Anson clearly outstayed his welcome on his first visit,
when he could legitimately claim that he was in distress, but he had now
engaged in open warfare not far from Chinese coasts. Worse, he had

attacked and captured a ship whose cargo was an essential link in the trade between Canton and Manila.

There was a new determination about Anson as he again entered Chinese waters. A hint of his uncompromising approach came when a French vessel, which from a distance looked like a man-of-war, was sighted off Macao. Anson knew from the reports he had picked up from the officers of the *Covadonga* that relations between Britain and France were strained, but he had no idea whether the two nations were yet at war. Instead of hurrying into port with his precious cargo, Anson prepared the *Centurion* for action, brought back most of the prize crew from the galleon, and gave chase. The *Centurion* fired two shots at long range before the strange sail veered away to the east. Anson turned back towards Macao, where he anchored on 11 July with the aid of two local pilots who had come on board. He stayed there only long enough to land as many of his prisoners as he could, sending 60 or 70 ashore before Chinese officials put a stop to the operation. To negotiate the awkward approach into the Pearl River Anson was dependent on his Chinese pilots. Once in the river he blustered his way through the Bocca Tigris, the Mouth of the Tiger, a narrow passage guarded by forts on each side. The forts' cannon, six-pounders at most, were unimpressive compared with the *Centurion*'s 24-pounders, and there was no attempt to challenge the warship. The mandarin in charge of the forts came on board the *Centurion*, but having begun bravely by demanding to know her armaments, 'seemed to be terrified with the bare recital, saying, that no ships ever came into the Canton River armed in that manner'. The best he could do was to put pressure on the pilots not to guide the warship through the Bocca Tigris, a ploy that collapsed when Anson threatened to hang one of the pilots from the yardarm if the *Centurion* grounded on her passage upstream. Nor would Anson have any truck with the mandarin's demand that his ship, like all others, must be measured and pay duties to the Emperor. For what higher authorities regarded as their craven behaviour both mandarin and pilot were punished: the one by dismissal, the other by a bastinadoing that left him half-crippled and begging for Anson's charity.

The ships, still with most of the prisoners on board, spent two weeks at anchor beyond the forts, waiting for a chop or permit to proceed further upstream. Here the crew had ample time to view – at a distance – the neat charms of a Chinese landscape of buildings, woods and fields stretching from the riverbank inland as far as the eye could see. Such contemplation was broken on 16 July by the ominous sight of two European ships coming through the Bocca Tigris. Even though she was in neutral waters, the *Centurion* was once more cleared for action. The vessels were French East Indiamen, heavily armed like all their kind. They had no news of whether Britain and France were at war, but they revealed that the ship chased by Anson off Macao a week earlier was another Indiaman, commanded by the senior captain of that year's French fleet. Anson's ships lay close on shore, where paddy fields came down to the water's edge, and the shallow channels were busy with junks and sampans. A location that Pascoe Thomas found 'pretty and delightful' was full of menace and uncertainty to Anson. He might be trapped, far from open water, by warships sent from Manila, and his efforts to fight would be hindered by the hundreds of prisoners sweltering below deck. The day after encountering the French East Indiamen Anson gave orders for an evening and morning gun to be fired, its ominous boom a reminder to all within earshot that a new and frightening force was in the river.

In an attempt to persuade the chuntuck of the urgency of the situation, Anson sent Lieutenant Peter Denis to Canton in the *Centurion*'s barge with an explanatory letter. The chuntuck, or viceroy (the term used by the English), was the highest civil officer in the two provinces of Kwangtung and Kwangsi, and divided his time between Canton and Shiuhing, where he had his official seat. Denis was received 'very civilly' by the chuntuck, according to the authorised account, but other sources speak of the 'contemptuous manner' with which he and his men were treated. References to shops being closed on their appearance indicate that this reaction probably came from the merchants along the Canton waterfront, anxious about the effect Anson's arrival might have on their trade. Philip Saumarez noted in his journal that both the European supercargoes and the Chinese merchants were reluctant to be seen even talking with officers from the ship.

Anson's response was to stop the East India Company's *Harrington*, just arrived from the Malabar coast, from going upriver past the *Centurion*. This game of bluff and counter-bluff seems to have had some effect on the Chinese authorities, for a few days later Anson received permission to sail beyond the second bar, though only as far as a spot four miles from the Indiamen's normal anchorage in the roadstead at Whampoa. The shallowness of the river prevented the Company ships from sailing the further dozen miles to Canton itself, and all goods had to be shifted by sampan. The bringing of the necessary permit for Anson was attended with a good deal of ceremony, with three mandarins and their escorts coming on board the *Centurion*. Of the chuntuck himself, or of an invitation from him to visit Canton, there was no sign; and Anson assumed

Macao. A rather fanciful engraving in John Campbell, *Navigantium atque Intinerantium Bibliotheca* (1744), showing the *Centurion* and *Covadonga* lying off Macao. In contrast to Brett's sketch of the two vessels (p. 168), the artist here has turned the *Centurion* into a massive two- or possibly even three-deck man of war.

that he was waiting from instructions from Peking on how he should proceed. Once again the mandarins demanded that Anson should pay harbour dues, and once again Anson refused. On the matter of the prisoners, however, the interests of the two sides seemed to coincide. 'A great incumbrance' to Anson, the subjects of a friendly nation held captive on Anson's ships represented to the Chinese authorities an intolerable affront to their sovereignty. After some haggling, most of the prisoners were transferred onto junks on 28 July, and taken down to Macao. Eighty were kept to work the prize, and another fifteen were retained on the *Centurion*. For the prize crew on the galleon the prisoners had been less trouble than their wounded commander during the time he was on board. Montero accused the crew of stealing his commission and a valuable, bejewelled sword-belt. Anson took his fellow-officer at his word and, unable to find the items in question, imposed a collective punishment on his men on the galleon. They were forbidden contact with the shore, and any provisions or other supplies they needed had to be bought on the *Centurion*, at enhanced prices. Bitterness among the prize crew was increased when a later report from Macao noted that Montero had arrived there with the 'stolen' items safely in his possession.

For Anson the departure of the prisoners was a relief and a necessity, but a later Chinese account, which telescoped the handing over of the prisoners in July with Anson's later audience with the chuntuck in November, reveals deeper implications to the affair. It described Anson, 'the commander of the red-haired people', as being totally intimidated by the Chinese authorities, who demanded his Spanish prisoners as tribute. Weeping, grovelling on the floor, and finally crawling into the presence of the chuntuck, Yin Kuang-jen, with his crossbow tucked under his arm, Anson agreed to the Chinese demands; and was then allowed to refit and depart. Written more than twenty years after the event, this account seems to have been a retrospective attempt to put a gloss on what, from the Chinese point of view, had been a vexing and irritating episode. On the *Centurion* Pascoe Thomas made some effort to explain the Chinese attitude when he wrote that since the Emperor was regarded as the greatest prince in the world, his representatives could not negotiate with subjects of other powers unless they gave clear signs of submission to his authority.

Happily unaware of the possible implications of the shedding of the prisoners, Anson sailed beyond the second bar and anchored. By staying off Whampoa rather than coming into the roadstead, Anson kept a distance between his ships and the normal measuring and assessing activities of the Chinese customs officials. At the *Centurion*'s new anchorage Chinese officials imposed a state of quarantine on the warship: guard boats were stationed along both banks of the river to prevent any of the crews from the two ships landing, or any letters being sent ashore. There was nothing unusual in this; among Anson's papers is a copy of an order from the chuntuck restricting the movements and trade of the Indiamen in the river under thirteen different headings. At least Anson was allowed a daily supply of provisions, but with a voyage to Europe ahead he needed far more. The following weeks were taken up by prolonged negotiations with local merchants and Chinese officials over the question of supplies for the voyage. To give the crew ready cash for their personal purchases, about 28,000 silver dollars or pieces of eight from the prize money were distributed. Some indication of the way in which prize money was allocated in the navy came in Pascoe Thomas's note of the distribution – 10,000 dollars for Anson, 101 dollars apiece for petty officers. To offset any resentment at this inequality of treatment, when Anson before the share-out ordered a 'general Search' of persons and possessions for concealed booty he insisted that he be searched first. A cynic might argue that given the disproportionate amount of prize money that came to the officers there was little temptation for them to conceal small items of treasure; but if Anson's action was only a gesture, it was not one that all commanding officers would have thought of making.

Daily assurances throughout September that the supplies were being collected, biscuit baked, and so on, were found to be worthless. Irritated by the haughty manner of Chinese officials, Anson began to cultivate 'as grand and distant a Manner as themselves'. On one occasion he refused to come on deck to meet a visiting mandarin on the grounds that such a step would be demeaning to his position as captain of a King's ship. The writer of the authorised account was highly critical of the behaviour of the Chinese throughout this time, their greed, frauds and dishonesty. The examples were reeled off with increasing indignation: of fowls

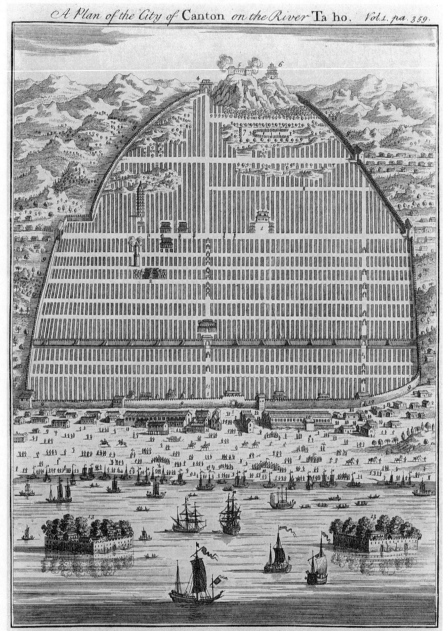

A Plan of the City of Canton on the River Ta ho. Vol.1. pa. 359.

1. The Old Kings Palace. 2. The Young Kings Palace. 3. A Chinese Tower. 4. The Land Gate. 5. The Fort. 6. The Banqueting House. 7. The Place of Exercise for the Tartars. 8. The Quarters for the Tartars. 9. The City Wall. 10. The Armoury. 11. The Vice Roy's Palace. 12. The Watergates. 13. Floating Castles.

crammed with stones to increase their weight; of hogs injected with water for the same purpose, and then prevented from urinating; of every sort of chicanery practised on innocent purchasers. Other observers might have been reminded of the black arts of unscrupulous pursers in the Royal Navy.

For Anson the main frustration lay in his inability to secure 'sea-provisions' from the Chinese merchants. His continued difficulties in this respect made him more determined than ever to see the chuntuck in person, his earlier request for an appointment soon after he arrived having been turned down on the grounds that the mid-summer weather was too hot for ceremonial visits, and that September would be a better time. Taking the bull by the horns, Anson sent a message that he would come up to Canton by boat on 1 October. As at Macao the previous year when the *Centurion* was visited by a high-ranking mandarin, Anson improvised a naval uniform for his men. The barge's crew of eighteen were dressed in a uniform modelled on that of Thames watermen, with scarlet jackets, blue silk waistcoats, and silver buttons and cap badges. As this gaudy entourage was about to set off on the morning of 1 October, an interpreter brought a message that the chuntuck had asked for the visit to be postponed. That evening, when it was too late to retrieve the situation, another interpreter came on board to tell Anson that the chuntuck had waited all day for him, and was 'highly offended' by his non-appearance.

This fiasco prompted Anson to go by barge to Canton itself and stay at the English factory. The English East India Company, along with the other European companies, rented premises on Canton's waterfront outside the south wall of the city. These served as offices for the transaction of business with the Hong merchants, warehouses for the storage of goods, and living quarters for the supercargoes and their staff. There the fan kwae, or foreign devils, lived under tight restrictions. They were

OPPOSITE: The city of Canton. This plan, although published in 1744 to accompany the account of Anson's voyage in John Campbell, *Navigantium atque Itinerantium Bibliotheca*, is of uncertain date and dubious accuracy. Several European ships are shown lying off the city, whereas they anchored at Whampoa, twelve or so miles downriver. The buildings outside the city wall are presumably the European factories, but they are not identified as such, nor is there any sign of the shanty town of flimsy houses between the river and the wall that accounts describe.

not allowed to enter the city itself or to bear firearms; their only legal contact was with the Hong merchants; and at the end of the trading season they were forced to leave, for Macao or home. Much of the actual riverbank was taken up by the European factories and the 'hongs' of the Chinese merchants, but in the remaining few hundred yards between the river and the wall were crammed thousands of flimsy bamboo and matting dwellings. Other families lived in sampans moored together on the river. In the forbidden territory on the other side of the wall were more spacious buildings, including the palace or yamen of the chuntuck, set in a deer park, in terms of structure and spacious grounds a symbol of imperial majesty. The Europeans also had their symbols, for paintings of their factories show tall flagpoles in front of the premises flying the national colours. The trade was profitable to Chinese and Europeans alike, but the relationship between the two was never an easy one, and was complicated by the interplay of local officials and individual Hong merchants (not yet brought together into the collective Cohong of the mid-century years).

Although Anson was allowed to collect stores at the English factory, there was no sign of the necessary permission from the chuntuck to send them on board the *Centurion*. All attempts to use the Hong merchants as intermediaries ran into a morass of excuses, delays and misunderstandings. The turning point, at least in the authorised account, came when Anson's crew helped to put out a great fire that threatened to burn down much of the city. The flames shot so high that they could be seen from the *Centurion*, twenty miles downriver, and according to this account only the heroic efforts of Anson and 40 of the *Centurion*'s seamen got it under control. The feckless Chinese, by contrast, 'contented themselves with viewing it, and now and then holding one of their idols near it, which they seemed to expect should check its progress'. Pascoe Thomas has a slightly less dramatic description of the blaze, which he thought destroyed just two or three streets of old houses, together with the Swedish factory on the waterfront, while Justinian Nutt's log put the number of houses destroyed at 110. There is no reason, though, to doubt the gratitude of Canton's principal merchants, some of whom waited on Anson to thank him formally, while the European supercargoes presented him with a porcelain dinner service. Most important of all, a message came from the chuntuck arranging an audience for 30 November.

This first meeting between representatives of the British and Chinese governments was a splendid one in terms of ceremonial. One of the journal-keepers on the *Centurion* set the scene as Anson in his sedan chair was carried through the gate and into the city, accompanied by his officers, the barge's crew in their scarlet and blue uniforms, East India Company captains and Chinese merchants. Outside the palace 10,000 armed men were drawn up in ranks, while all vantage points were crammed with onlookers. Once again the occasion was threatened by misunderstanding as Anson and his retinue were left kicking their heels in an antechamber, a place 'no Ways proper for the Reception of the Representative of the King of Great Britain', Anson protested. Finally, the doors of the great Hall of Audience swung open and Anson, accompanied by Lieutenants Saumarez and Keppel, and his interpreter, James Flint, found themselves in the presence of the chuntuck, seated in a canopied chair of state surrounded by his mandarins. A contemporary engraving shows the delegation of British naval officers and Company captains with their heads uncovered except for Anson himself, who is still wearing his cocked hat as a high-ranking mandarin introduces him to the chuntuck (p. 189). There was no suggestion of the customary 'kow-tow', and Anson was allowed to take a seat. In the exchange which followed he seems to have made all the running as he listed the complaints of his countrymen in the service of the East India Company. An awkward silence followed, until Anson 'asked his interpreter if he was certain the viceroy understood what he had urged; the interpreter told him, he was certain it was understood, but he believed no reply would be made'. Anson then turned to his own position, and asked for a chop to take his stores on board so that he could depart for England. The concession was made, apparently, without any further mention of the bothersome question of harbour dues. This, Anson's official report and the authorised account noted (in almost identical words), was the point which gave 'the greatest satisfaction', for it was 'the authentic precedent' that established that no British warships would be asked to pay dues in Chinese ports. In fact, it was not a precedent. The next British man-of-war that arrived in Canton to refit, the *Argo* in 1764, was measured by Chinese officials and paid the normal harbour dues.

During the first week of December the provisions for the long voyage home were taken on the *Centurion*. Some of them made their own way on board amid a great cacophony of noise, for 'every man now had lain in a stock of pigs, hens, geese, and Mr. Anson had the decks filled with live cattle and sheep, [so] that we lived nobly for almost all our homeward passage'. On 7 December the two ships sailed from Canton, and passed through the Bocca Tigris three days later. The walls of the two forts were lined with soldiers, but their armament of pikes, muskets and stones did little to impress the ships' crews. In a final jibe the writer of the authorised account described how the threatening figure of a gigantic soldier in full armour paced the battlements, battle-axe in arms, but that the glittering appearance of his 'armour' roused suspicions that it was made of tinsel paper rather than steel. At Macao the galleon was sold to local merchants for 6,000 dollars, much less than she was worth, but Anson was in a hurry to be gone. On 15 December the *Centurion* set sail, her crew anxious to get home before the Indiamen arrived from Canton with their tales of the solitary British warship and her huge treasure.

The part played by the East India Company factors during the months of Anson's stay at Canton appears in the pages of the authorised account to have been muted, even unpatriotic. They were rarely mentioned, and never by name. As a group they were held responsible for many of Anson's problems in securing an audience with the viceroy, and for putting Company before national interests. This view has been accepted in the absence of any documentation from the Company side, for there are no Canton factory records for 1743 in the archives of the India Office Library. This gap can now be filled, and explained, by documents that have been discovered in the last few years. They consist of an exchange of letters (sixteen in all) between Anson and Edward Page, the Company's chief supercargo at Canton in 1743, together with a 73-page manuscript by Page, 'A little Secret History of Affairs at Canton in the year 1743 when the *Centurion* Comodore Anson was lying in the River'. Internal evidence

Chinese porcelain dish: part of a dinner service presented to Anson in November/ December 1743 by the European supercargoes at Canton in gratitude for the efforts of his men in extinguishing the fire along the waterfront. The breadfruit tree in the centre suggests that Anson had some say in the design; the rim has views of the Pearl or Canton River, the Eddystone and Macao lighthouses, and Plymouth Sound.

suggests that Page took away some of the Company's factory records when he left Canton, and that he had them by his side when, in 1765, long after his retirement, he decided to write his 'Secret History'. There is a strong element of self-justification in the document, but it enables a much fuller picture to be drawn of Anson's visit to Canton than is available in the self-righteous record of those months in the authorised narrative.

Edward Page was an experienced factor who had served the East India Company since 1722, and had been a supercargo on the Canton voyages at least since 1735. With no resident factors allowed at Canton, the role of the visiting supercargoes was important and their emoluments were high. Page had been at Macao and Canton in 1741–2, but had returned to England before Anson arrived for the first time on the coast of China in November 1742. In 1743 Page sailed for China again, as chief supercargo on the *Haeslingfield*. It was an eventful voyage, for the ship was dismasted in a typhoon while still more than 100 miles west of Macao. Eventually the ship reached Whampoa, with much difficulty, on 8 November, there to join the *Harrington*, which was also under Page's management. Page himself reached Canton on 30 September, passing at the second bar the disturbing sight of the *Centurion* and her prize. As he wrote later, 'every body was apprehensive this would be a year of great Troubles'.

The day after Page's arrival was to be the occasion of Anson's ceremonial visit to the chuntuck, and the collapse of the arrangements for the visit in a morass of misunderstandings and contradictory messages dominated the first phase of the relationship between Anson and Page. In his 'Secret History' Page explained that the 'viceroy' Anson was demanding to see was not in fact the chuntuck, but a temporary replacement, the chuncoon. This lesser official had been in post only three months but was, Page added, 'a strict man in regard to Forms and the punctilios of his Station'. That being so, the fiasco of 1 October was particularly unfortunate, and three days later the English supercargoes wrote to Anson expressing their uneasiness at what had happened.

Anson was less concerned by the sensitivities of the Company traders than by his own inability to make direct contact with the Chinese high officials who alone could issue the necessary permits. His temper was not improved by his realisation that the *Harrington* brought him no men, no stores and no instructions from the Admiralty. Even more so than on their arrival at Macao the previous year, Anson and his crew seemed to be forgotten men. In an effort to put more pressure on officials and traders alike Anson decided to move to the Company factory at Canton. The actual move, on 13 October, was an elaborately ceremonial affair.

Anson meets the Viceroy, 30 November 1743. Engraving in Anon., *An Authentic and Genuine Journal of Commodore Anson's Expedition* (1744). In fact, Anson was meeting the Chuncoon or acting Viceroy; nevertheless the occasion was a historic one. Ceremonial and protocol were important considerations, so although the naval and Company officers accompanying Anson have doffed their hats in deference to the representative of the Emperor, Anson as captain of a King's ship is still wearing his cocked hat. Although the lack of a naval uniform in this period makes identification difficult, Saumarez and Keppel would seem to be the figures immediately behind Anson, with the East India Company officers bringing up the rear.

Anson had asked that as well as Page and his colleagues, the foreign supercargoes at Canton should accompany his barge in their pinnaces. The French were not included in these formalities, for Anson was still smarting from an earlier insult by the French East Indiamen who had refused to lower their topsails (the normal courtesy paid by a foreign vessel to a Royal Navy ship) as they passed the *Centurion* in the river. By now the commodore of the French East India fleet had arrived, a month late after his efforts to avoid the *Centurion* off Macao. He had retreated as far as Amoy, 100 miles to the east, and from there had written to his fellow-captains describing how he had chased two large ships off the estuary. When he finally reached Canton he 'was heartily laughed at for his Gasconade', or so Pascoe Thomas, no lover of the French, wrote.

In the event, the pinnaces of the Swedish and Danish supercargoes formed part of Anson's escort, and although the Dutch supercargoes felt unable to follow suit, they agreed that their ships at Whampoa would salute him as he passed. For the arrival at the factory Page had arranged a guard of honour of musketeers, while at the factory Anson was given the best apartment, where European supercargoes and Chinese merchants came to pay their respects. This degree of attention helped to change the attitude of at least some of the Chinese. No longer were the *Centurion*'s crew called ladrones or thieves, or Anson referred to as the 'Grand Ladrone-Man'. There was grudging recognition that he was something different, 'the Grand King Captain'. To this, however, Pascoe Thomas added a rider: 'but in their Actions and Behaviour otherwise they were much the same'.

Anson's stay of seven weeks at the factory took up very little room in the pages of the authorised account, which quickly moved to the visit to the chuntuck on 30 November. The period of the stay, on the other hand, fills Page's 'Secret History', which offers a fascinating if rambling dissertation on the events of those weeks. Some of the revelations are trivial, but others offer fresh insights into Anson's character – so opaque that neither at this time nor later was it easy to decipher. Page's general tone was hostile and carping, prompted by his anger at the authorised account's strictures on the East India Company and its servants. The book, he noted, was written under Anson's supervision, a role all the more direct for his second stay in China, since the Revd Walter had by then left for home. Some of Page's entries concern the difference between the public and private man. So, within two or three days of Anson's arrival at the factory his outrage at the attitude of the French had cooled sufficiently for him to accept an invitation to a meal and game of cards with the French captains and supercargoes. In other ways Anson 'was pretty hard of Belief, & strongly fix'd to his own Opinion', Page noted. Nowhere was this more evident than in his insistence that his problems would disappear if only he could bypass the Hong merchants, and arrange a personal interview with the chuntuck. An awkward meeting with the senior of the merchants, Seuqua, served only to confirm Anson in this belief. Anson's expostulations to the merchant about his treatment, and his explanations about 'the Dignity and Importance of his Command', cut no ice with the older man, for many years past the most important among the Hong merchants. His forces, Anson was told, were feeble compared with those of the Emperor, and his attempts to see the chuntuck simply interposed 'a foolish Business' before the 'real Business' of the merchants, busy packing their teas and silks on board the European ships. Seuqua, who according to Page spoke fluent English, finished with a snub and a warning to Anson: 'To you it is all one as to see a play, But to others it gives much Trouble and Vexation; and perhaps after all, when you have your Visit, you will not be pleased.'

For Page, close proximity to the commodore did not necessarily bring much exchange of confidences. The two men met on their own every evening before supper, but it was only from a French informant that Page discovered that Anson was trying to arrange a visit to the chuntuck through his own interpreter. He proved no more successful than the merchants, and Anson's frustration vented itself in veiled threats to Page about what he might do if his demands were not met. 'We had many little Altercations of an Evening,' Page wrote. Irritated beyond measure at the delays, Anson decided to communicate directly with the chuntuck through a letter delivered by one of his lieutenants at the city gates. Tired of the problems associated with the Chinese 'linguists' he had relied upon until now, Anson persuaded a Company employee, James Flint, to accompany his lieutenant as interpreter. Flint had been sent to Canton by the Company in 1736 as a boy in order to learn Chinese, and remained there until his expulsion by the Chinese in 1759. Anson's difficulties with his local interpreters were not unusual. An earlier newcomer to Canton, Colin Campbell, captain of the first Swedish East India Company ship to reach China, complained in his journal of 1732 about the inadequacies of his interpreters, who were more concerned with pleasing the mandarins than giving an accurate translation of Campbell's representations.

If the authorised account is to be trusted, all went well with Anson's new initiative. The letter was received by the mandarin in command at the main gateway into the city, who promised that it would be given immediately to the chuntuck. Page tells a different story, and no incident better illustrates Anson's problems in an unfamiliar environment than the fate of this letter. Unopened, still addressed 'On his Britannick Majesty's Service, To the Vice Roy of Canton', it was handed to Page one evening by the landlord of the Company's quarters, who had retrieved it from the top of a 'dusty Cabinet'. Page's return of the crumpled missive to Anson was greeted with a tirade that probably owed more to frustration than to any real intent, as Anson threatened to blockade the river and stop the movements of all junks. When a horrified Page pointed out that the Chinese might take retaliatory action against the Company ships at Whampoa, Anson's only response was that 'he did not mind That, the Nation might make that up some other way'.

Page's most nervous moments came when the possibility of a scuffle, or worse, between Anson's men and Chinese officials loomed. One such incident saw a confrontation between the lieutenant of the *Centurion*'s barge and customs officials trying to check for concealed goods. Since the barge was flying a special flag it was given the same privilege as was granted the boats of the East India Company captains and supercargoes; it did not have to stop at each and every one of the various customs posts on the river, but was simply followed by a customs boat and searched on reaching the factory stairs. But what to one side was a concession, to the other was an affront, and only the intervention of Company traders and Chinese merchants saved the day. As Page recalled, in the previous twenty years there had been three incidents in which Europeans had killed Chinese by accident, and on each occasion the government had insisted on retribution. 'Let any one Judge', he added, 'what would have been the Consequence if any of their Officers had been murdered in the Scuffle for obeying the orders of the Government.'

The climax of Anson's stay was the long-awaited visit to the chuncoon or acting viceroy on 30 November. Even in the authorised account the occasion struggles to live up to expectations; in Page's narrative there is an added touch of farce. The afternoon before the visit, a rather complacent Anson came into the supercargo's apartment and told him about the preparations being made for a grand feast in his honour. The chuncoon had even taken the trouble to borrow a pair of terrestrial globes from the French, and Anson looked forward to explaining their use to him. That evening Anson returned to ask Page whether he had any grievances which should be raised with the viceroy. Page declined the offer in emphatic fashion if his later recollection is correct: 'I told him No; we had carried on our Business very quietly (and indeed there is no countrey that I ever knew, where you carry on your Business with more Ease, if there are no Ugly Accidents).'

The great day seems to have started even less auspiciously than the authorised account suggests, although since Page does not seem to have been present his 'Secret History' is not first-hand evidence for the meeting with the chuncoon. If it is accurate, and Page clearly talked with some of the *Centurion*'s officers later in the day, the delay before Anson was admitted to the Hall of Audience almost ended in disaster. One of the officers made to draw his sword and force his way in before he was restrained, and it was left to the accompanying Hong merchants to calm tempers by bribing one of the palace servants to unlock the door of an antechamber where Anson could wait. The most serious discrepancy between the official account of the actual meeting and Page's version revolves around the issue of Anson's request for a permit so that he could take on board provisions and stores. The 1748 account is quite clear on this: 'The Viceroy replied ... that the licence should be immediately issued, and that every thing should be ordered on board the following day.' Page's manuscript insists that there was never any prohibition, and that large quantities of bread were taken on board the *Centurion* in the days before the visit. Despite Page's efforts the previous evening Anson raised with the chuncoon a number of grievances on behalf of the Company, as well as those he had himself experienced – without, as we have seen, producing any reaction from the viceroy other than 'a profound Silence'. Anson then turned to the assistance his men had provided in the recent fire, assistance the chuncoon acknowledged before rather pointedly wishing Anson a good voyage home.

At the factory Page and the other Company traders had just finished dinner when Anson and his party, thought to be dining in style with the viceroy, unexpectedly appeared. The authorised account explains that Anson, offered 'an entertainment' after his audience, refused when he found that the viceroy would not be there. Page now takes up what had become a slightly risible story as he described how he saw a gloomy Anson and his officers coming through the courtyard of the factory, asking whether Page had yet eaten. In the end Page's cook produced a light meal for the naval officers, which they ate in silence. Only at the end did Anson break out with the remark that he had not anticipated that the mandarins would have been 'such a Pack of Scrubs'. Later in the evening Page heard further details of the visit from Philip Saumarez, who sat in Page's room 'with a broad open laced Hat cocked, & put on a very Big look, and said "Damn them, I'll never pull off my Hat to a Mandareen again"'. As a final insult, Saumarez told Page, the chuncoon had refused to accept the handsome gift taken by Anson, and his own present, sent round to the factory that night, turned out to be two cheap pieces of cloth. Page could not resist pointing out the moral of all this: 'It was as Sequa told him when I went with him, that when he had his Visit very likely he would not be pleased.'

Three days after the visit Anson left the factory and returned to the *Centurion*, now almost ready for the homeward voyage. Page accompanied him on board, and was flattered by the attentions of Anson and his officers. He slept in Anson's own bed, while the commodore made do with a hammock – an unusual kindness and a signal mark of respect. Saumarez took him on a tour of the galleon, 'a very ugly heavy looking Ship', still bearing scars from the action six months earlier. Saumarez pointed out that there was no truth in the report that the sides of the Manila galleons were so thick that shot would not penetrate them. He showed Page a hole in the starboard quarter, matched by one on the larboard side, where a 24-pound ball fired by the *Centurion* had gone straight through the ship's hull. Just before sailing Anson wrote a final letter to Page, half-apologising for 'the trouble I have given you and all the Gentlemen at the Factory', and looking forward to renewing their acquaintanceship in England.

Once back in London Anson called at Page's house and, hearing that he was at a nearby coffee house, sought him out there. To be treated in this way by the new national hero, who was, as Page noticed, 'extremely caressed by the Great people', must have been very flattering. But disillusionment came when the authorised account of Anson's voyage was published in 1748. Page complained that the book was unfairly critical of the Company's officers, and its narrative of events at Canton he thought 'ungenerous'. Much of his 'Secret History' was devoted to setting the record straight. The essence of Page's argument was that an already difficult situation for the Company supercargoes took an abrupt turn for the worse with the appearance of a British warship off Canton that seemed determined not to acknowledge Chinese sovereignty. The newly arrived chuncoon, who had perhaps never seen a European before, could not be expected to understand western distinctions between a merchant-man, a warship and a pirate. Implicit in all this was Page's worry that Anson was just as unfamiliar with Chinese conventions and sensitivities. His own role was 'to act with all the Circumspection we were able, to stave off any fatal mischeif'. To emphasise what was at risk, Page listed the value of the cargo he had brought home with him in the *Haeslingfield* and *Harrington* in 1744: 800,000 lb. of tea, 400 chests of china, 7,000 pieces of wrought silk, 60 chests of raw silk and £20,000 in gold. The cargoes were disposed of at the Company's sale for £240,000, a profit of 116 percent. If the Company made a profit, so did the state. The excise on tea alone, of four shillings a pound, amounted to £140,000 (and this after the drawback on tea that was to be re-exported had been deducted).

> But all these Advantages might have been Sacrificed about a trifling punctilio in a Foreign port, to which the Comodore had No Credentials, Not to mention the Imprisonment of our own persons, where we might have remained to linger out our days, and the future consequences to our Trade, had he offered any Insult to the Port, and any Men had been Slain in the Contest.

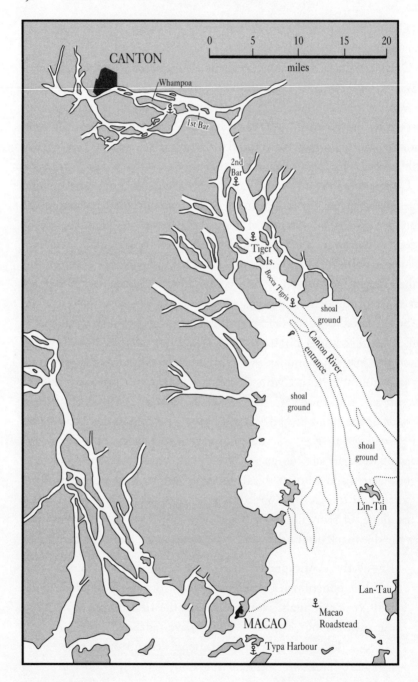

Canton and Macao

The fact, of course, was that in the end no insult was offered, no men were slain. Whatever anger and frustration Anson showed when alone with Page, in public he appeared as cool and dignified as circumstances allowed. In insisting that a King's ship should be treated differently from merchantmen Anson was following conventions accepted throughout Europe and its overseas empires. That the Chinese had different ones was not his concern, and so in the great hall of the viceroy's palace naval officers and mandarins faced each other across a gulf of mutual disdain and incomprehension. As Page wrote, 'the Chinese reckon us . . . the most Ungovernable and Troublesome of any Europeans that come to the Port.' And not only Page had a valuable cargo at risk, for on board the *Centurion* was treasure worth £400,000. For Anson that was as nerve-racking a responsibility as any that Page bore. When he was getting ready for his abortive visit to the viceroy on 1 October, the safety of the treasure loomed large. If he was detained, Lieutenant Brett was to take the prize crew off the galleon, destroy her, and immediately sail the *Centurion* downriver beyond the forts of the Bocca Tigris. That in 1744 the *Centurion* and the Company's ships arrived safely in home waters says something about the utility of the relationship, however strained it was at times, between Anson and Page. King's officer and Company trader were always likely to have different priorities, and nowhere were these more evident than in the charged atmosphere of Canton as Chinese officials and Company supercargoes strove to ignore the distant clamour of European war.

As the *Centurion* left the Chinese coast the journal-keepers on board reflected on what they had learned about China and its people. The general impression was not a favourable one, and was summed up by Millechamp when he wrote, 'The people are of a low stature and of a yellow complexion, in general ingenious, artful and treacherous. Covetiousness seems to be their darling passion, for they will all be guilty of the most infamous crimes to gratify it.' A London newspaper account noted, with heavy-handed irony, that the Chinese merchants generously doubled the prices of all goods sold to Anson's crew because they knew that they had plenty of money. Once the observers probed beyond their limited shipboard contacts with the shore, most of them with traders and shopkeepers, all was mystification. Chinese religion was clearly pagan and idolatrous, but embellished with Roman Catholic pageantry. The accounts were able to agree that the Chinese were numerous – perhaps 100,000 of them living on sampans on the Canton River alone – and were of bizarre appearance. As Millechamp observed, because of foot-binding the women could only hobble, while 'The men indeed make odd figures . . . with long thin beards and whiskers, and a long single plaited lock of hair from the middle of their heads which hangs down almost to their heels.'

The authorised account of 1748 contained the most forthright and widely circulated of the attacks. It acknowledged that the Chinese were industrious, but as far as arts and crafts went they were mere 'servile imitators'. For evidence of the absurdity of Chinese culture one only had to look at their writing, if such it could be called. Whereas other nations had developed logical combinations of letters and words, the Chinese relied on scratched marks and characters, too many for the human memory. The famed morality and equity of Chinese government was another example of 'jesuitical fictions'. Their officials were corrupt and venal, and their people thievish. Even at the most fundamental level of state responsibility – defence of its people – the Chinese government was deficient. The empire was open to the ravages of every invader, and its seapower was contemptible. An engraving of three Chinese junks was appended to show just how crude and awkward their ships were (see p. 150). The largest cannon on the war junks seen at Canton were only four-pounders, proof that the *Centurion* alone was more than a match for the entire Chinese navy.

In these few pages the writer of the authorised account struck at some of the most cherished beliefs about China held among Europeans of the period. In England during the seventeenth century there was an increasing admiration for what seemed to be the wisdom and tolerance of Chinese government. By the period of Anson's voyage the important Jesuit obser-vations on China, based on first-hand experience over a long period of time, had been brought together by Father du Halde. His *Description de l'Empire de la Chine* of 1735 was in English translation in two rival editions within the year. The Jesuit picture of China under the Manchu dynasty was not of a flawless regime. Yet the achievements of the Chinese political and judicial system seemed impressive, with its deference to age and wisdom, to philosophers rather than soldiers. A vast population lived peacefully together, ruled by consent, not repression, and without the bloody civil and international conflicts characteristic of Europe's recent past.

Few attempts to modify this interpretation came from the British traders who reached China in the first half of the eighteenth century. Monopolistic trading companies did not encourage their servants to inform the world at large about their experiences, and in any case the supercargoes' contact with the people of China was limited and fleeting. Whatever frustrations they experienced in their dealings with officials and merchants were set against the backcloth of a lucrative commercial connection. The two East India Company supercargoes, James Naish and Edward Page, both challenged the sweeping indictments of the authorised account of Anson's voyage, but not in any public way. Naish annotated his account of the book (now in the British Library) with notes that supplement or contradict the official version of events. These notes, which were written a year or two after the book's publication, accompany the first chapter on the origins of the voyage, where they elaborate on Naish's own role; and the final two chapters dealing with Anson's stay in Canton. Naish tried to put the accusations about the dishonesty of the whole Chinese nation into some kind of perspective when he insisted that the examples given related to the 'dregs of the people, and such instances as these may be found in every country under the sun'. He was critical of the way in which the account used the term 'mandarin' to refer to every obstructive Chinese official encountered. Many, he pointed out, were low-ranking customs officers with no independent authority. Page for his part supplied some interesting detail on the reality of trade with the Chinese. There was fraud and trickery, he agreed, as in all countries, but in general he found the leading Hong merchants honourable in their dealings. Agreements, he pointed out, were mostly verbal, simply noted down in the supercargo's diary; but in his experience these were not disputed later. He compared the criticisms levelled in the 1748 account with those that might be written by a Chinese visitor to England, who after a few weeks in London picked up gossip in the newspapers and elsewhere on political corruption, cheating shopkeepers and street violence, and used them to condemn the whole nation.

These remarks by Naish and Page were confined to their personal papers, and whatever defence they mounted of life and trade in China there is no doubt that there was a marked difference between the tough reality of China at one level, as experienced by the Company traders in Canton, and the image of China diffused through Europe during the 'chinoiserie' craze of this period. For the tea-drinking English in particular this had the comforting assurance of gentle refinement. Porcelain, wallpaper, furniture and garden landscapes all came under the influence of what were thought to be Chinese forms, until many eighteenth-century Englishmen developed a visual image of China as a land resembling the willow-pattern designs of their dinner services. Ironically, Anson added to this perception when he brought back from Canton a Chinese miniature garden, together with willow-pattern porcelain and lacquered cabinets, chairs and stools, and inspired his brother to erect a Chinese-style pagoda at the family estate at Shugborough based on a design supplied by Peircy Brett. Sinophiles such as Charles Stanhope questioned Anson's overbearing behaviour in China, and his apparent readiness to resort to force. Across the Channel, Voltaire entered the fray, unwittingly echoing the words of Naish and Page as he insisted that an entire nation should not be judged by experiences on the borders of one province.

The debate was just beginning. Sixty years later Lord Macartney's embassy to China, splendid and prestigious though it was in European eyes, experienced the same humbling reception in Peking as Anson had received in Canton. The imperial court was neither impressed nor persuaded by the Macartney embassy, regarded as representatives from a barbarian state who were bringing tribute to a superior ruler. In the long run the clash of cultures and interests was likely to have one end only, and this came with the Opium Wars of the mid-nineteenth century. In this context, Anson's stay at Canton was an early warning of troubles to come.

VIII

Homecoming: Acclamation and Recrimination

GREAT BRITAIN'S TRIUMPH–
(Written extempore as the wagons loaded with treasure passed
through the City of London)

'Less shall proud Rome her ancient trophies boast;
The conquered country, and the captive host.
Her fierce Dominion, Asia, Afric knew;
But round the Globe her eagle never flew,
Thro every clime is Albion's thunder hurled,
And Anson's spoils are from a tribute world.'

Daily Advertiser, 5 July 1744

'We had more terrible engagements in the courts of law than
we ever had in the South Seas.'

Millechamp, 'Narrative'

THE *CENTURION* LEFT the Canton River on 15 December 1743, and
headed out to sea. The rest of the voyage was a welcome anticlimax.
Leaving behind vengeful Spanish forces searching the waters off Juan
Fernández in one hemisphere and the South China Sea in another, the
Centurion slipped home by way of the Sunda Strait and the Cape of
Good Hope. Right at the end, Anson's ship sailed undetected in thick
fog through a French squadron patrolling the English Channel, and
arrived at Spithead on 15 June 1744. Among those on board were only
188 of the original members of the expedition, and these included the
survivors from the *Gloucester*, *Tryal* and *Anna*. The rest of the crew
comprised a mixed bag unusual even by the standards of the omnivorous
appetite for men of the eighteenth-century navy: 'Dutch, French, Spaniards, Italians, Germans, Swedes, Danes, Muscovites, Portuguese, Lascar

Indians, Malays, Persians, Indians of Manila, Timor and Guam, Negroes of Guinea, Creoles of Mexico and Mozambique', as one report listed them. Other survivors, from the *Severn*, *Pearl* and *Wager*, were already back in England; but of the more than 1,900 men who had sailed from Spithead in September 1740 almost 1,400 had died – four from enemy action, a few from accidents, and the rest from disease or starvation.

For the families of the men who had sailed on the *Centurion*, *Gloucester* and *Tryal* almost four years earlier, the return of the flagship in June 1744 brought the first definite news of the fate of their relatives. Given the long list of casualties, for most of those waiting the news would be the worst possible, but their private grief went unnoticed in the jubilation that accompanied the reports of the colossal treasure brought back by the *Centurion*. The calculations of its value given in the first days after the ship's return ranged from £500,000 to £1,250,000. After the Mediterranean fleet's failure off Toulon in February the navy stood in need of a popular triumph, and in the public mind the capture of a treasure galleon was the next best thing to a fleet victory. Anson, an unknown naval captain when he left England in 1740, was a celebrity, and ministers were eager to claim a share of the glory. The Duke of Newcastle, who as Secretary of State had shown no great enthusiasm for the voyage four years earlier, replied to Anson's letter from Spithead with a note conveying the King's approval of his conduct, and added a disingenuous postscript to the effect that he himself took 'a great part' in the honour of the occasion. Of the awful casualties reported by Anson in his letter – 462 dead on the *Centurion* alone – Newcastle made no mention. Heavy losses through disease on overseas operations were the rule rather than the exception, and two years earlier the minister would have received reports that of the 14,000 troops sent to the Caribbean to attack Cartagena, 10,000 had perished (most from yellow fever). The same day that Anson sent his official report to Newcastle, he sent a personal note to his patron, the Earl of Hardwicke, apologising for his failure to write from Canton when he arrived there in December 1742. The disasters of the expedition up to that time, he told him, had given him 'an uneasiness I could not express to your Lordship'. The Lord Chancellor was too astute a politician to let a minor breach of etiquette stand in the way of a relationship that now promised much, and would be strengthened when a few years later Anson married Hardwicke's daughter, Lady Elizabeth Yorke. Meanwhile, Anson was basking in compliments and honours. On 18 June he was received by the King at Kensington Palace, and the following day he was promoted to Rear Admiral of the Blue.

As one of the few national heroes to emerge from a generally dis-appointing war, the highest posts in the navy now seemed open to Anson. First, however, he had to deal with a Board of Admiralty that lived by the rule book. In the months following the capture of the galleon in June 1743 Anson had made two promotions in his capacity as commander-in-chief. After taking the *Covadonga* into the King's service he appointed his first lieutenant, Philip Saumarez, as her captain. The second pro-motion was of Peircy Brett to captain of the *Centurion* during the weeks in late 1743 when Anson together with Saumarez stayed at the Company factory at Canton. Brett's appointment was in no way a formality. If Anson had been killed or imprisoned while ashore, it would have been Brett's responsibility to get the *Centurion* and her treasure clear of the river and out to sea before returning to England. The Lords of the Admiralty confirmed Saumarez's promotion to captain, though they made it clear that this was a considerable concession since such promotions were normally only made when the captured ship was to serve as a man-of-war. But Brett's case was regarded as a promotion too far, and a long letter from Thomas Corbett informed Anson that he had exceeded his powers without good reason. Anson was captain of the *Centurion*, and there was neither practical necessity nor legal grounds for appointing a second captain. Anson's plea of 'extraordinary occasions' was rejected with the dismissive and inaccurate comment that all they involved was 'a journey of a few hours to an audience of the Vice-King at Canton'. If Anson's request was allowed, Corbett went on, it would not only become a precedent but it would mean that 'the Admiralty is no longer master of any rule or order'. By now Anson had declined his own pro-motion, a step that Corbett condemned as being done 'in a sullen fit to fly in His Majesty's face'. That the struggle was over a principle rather than any dispute over Brett's merits was shown by the Admiralty's appointment of him that same week as captain, but it was not antedated

ENGLANDS GLORY. *Being an exact View of the* Waggons *going into the* Tow

AAA *The Tower of London*
BBB *Tower Wharf*
CC *The River Thames*
D *Tower Hill*
E *The Minories*
F *Iron Gate*
G *Traitors Bridge*
N° N° 2. &c. *The Waggons with the Flaggs and guarded by the Sailors some in the Waggons some on Horseback armd with Cutlasses and Musquets.*

England's Glory: the treasure reaches the Tower of London. This very detailed print shows the first sight of the thirty-two waggons laden with treasure winding their way from the Minories to the Tower of London on 4 July 1744.

to his 'promotion' of the previous September as Anson had requested.

This low-key dispute was fought out against a raucous background of public acclamation and celebration. One newspaper picked up a rumour that Anson had refused to accept a commission as rear-admiral, but thought that the explanation might be that he was preparing for another secret expedition. From the moment of the *Centurion*'s arrival at Spithead the London newspapers were full of reports of the voyage and what followed. The treasure was unloaded from the *Centurion* and kept under armed guard at Portsmouth until early July, when it was taken to London in wagons. The escort was provided by the ship's crew, who hired fiddlers to enliven the 90-mile journey. On 4 July a ceremonial procession made its way through the streets of London: 32 waggons of treasure, led by a wind-band and drummers, and guarded by sailors from the *Centurion*. Some of the wagons displayed Spanish colours and other trophies captured during the voyage. Breakfast was taken on Putney Common, and the procession then crossed Fulham Bridge, and passed through Piccadilly and St James's Street to Pall Mall. There Anson, accompanied by the Prince and Princess of Wales, greeted the procession before it moved on to the City, past the Bank of England, and into the Tower, where the treasure was lodged. Prints of the procession show vast crowds lining the streets. The silver, it was announced, would be melted down into coins bearing the inscription 'Acapulco' (when issued by the Mint in 1745 the silver shillings were more appropriately inscribed 'LIMA'). It was, one observer wrote, a triumph worthy of ancient Rome. Newspapers vied with each other in paying tribute to Anson: he was compared to Ulysses by one, to Drake by another; he was 'the glorious Admiral Anson', 'the brave Admiral Anson', even 'our immortal Anson'. Verses commemorating the voyage appeared in the newspapers and periodicals, and broadsheets with ballads in honour of the voyage were soon in circulation. Sailors from the *Centurion* were invited to a performance at the New Wells in Clerkenwell, where they joined in choruses describing the capture of the galleon, while Sadlers Wells responded by putting on an evening's special entertainment for Anson and his officers.

To meet the demand for more detail, narratives giving highlights of the voyage were rushed through the press. A brief anonymous *Authentick*

Account appeared in August, not as triumphalist as perhaps its readers had anticipated. Most of it was devoted to the gloomy saga of the *Wager*, and it finished by pointing out that on the expedition in general 'hundreds of poor Souls' had died, and those few who returned were 'greatly impair'd'. In September a full-length *Authentick Journal* was published, attributed to 'John Philips', said to have been a midshipman on the voyage. The name was a pseudonym, for no John Philips sailed with Anson, but the book was undoubtedly based on a genuine log. It reappeared in two pirated editions in the following months, as *An Authentic and Genuine Journal* (with illustrations), and in another guise as *A Voyage to the South Seas*. In 1745 Pascoe Thomas published his *True and Impartial Journal*, a highly individualistic account by the 'Teacher of the Mathematicks' on the *Centurion* who was not above criticising Anson and his officers. It was also the only one of the published narratives of 1744–5 that did not devote space to the loss of the *Wager*. Another account of the voyage by 'an officer of the *Centurion*' appeared in two long episodes in the *Universal Spectator* and other newspapers. Here for the first time appeared the characterisation of Anson that was to become standard: 'a brave, humane, equal-minded, prudent commander . . . his temper was so steady and unruffled that the men and officers all looked on him with wonder and delight.' The stoicism and imperturbability shown by Anson under conditions of extreme stress were long remembered, and were soon incorporated into the evolving image of the British naval officer that was to reach iconic status in the age of Nelson.

Not all the comment on Anson's triumph was favourable. Horace Walpole, crotchety as ever, watched the resplendent procession of 4 July from his window, and thought it was 'a trumpery sight'. More unexpectedly, the *Daily Post* of 6 July responded to the celebratory verses printed by other newspapers with a poem of rather different tinge. Addressed to 'Deluded Britons', its sentiments, if not literary style, had a surprisingly modern touch.

> Deluded Britons! Wherefore should you boast
> Of treasure, purchased at a treble cost?
> Will this, while centering in a private hand,

Restore to wealth, your much impoverished land?
To purchase this, think how much treasure's gone;
Think on the mighty mischiefs it hath done.
In this attempt, count o'er the numerous host
Of Albion's sons, unprofitably lost.
Then will your boastings into sorrow turn,
And injured Britons, Albion's fate shall mourn.

By the late summer a more general change of tone was noticeable in several newspapers, affronted by the brawls started by the *Centurion's* sailors on their jaunts through the capital. Granted three months' leave by the Admiralty, they had also received an instalment of the prize money (£171, according to one paper). In the newspaper reports of these weeks Anson's men emerge from the anonymity in which they remained on the long voyage, where no chronicler had recorded the lower-deck point of view. For the first time they appear as individuals, celebrating, fighting and dying in the streets of London, prize money in pocket, and all too often knife in hand. John Maddox married Mrs Simms, a widow with a fortune of £1,000, at a ceremony at Dulwich attended by 40 of his shipmates from the *Centurion*; a group of 'the New Gentlemen' from the ship carried out a murderous attack on the Aldgate watch; a Dutch member of the crew stabbed a soldier; Martin from the *Centurion* fell drunk into the Thames and drowned, fifteen guineas and some silver in his pockets; Burton from the *Centurion* was robbed and seriously wounded by a gang between Stratford and Bow. The sad litany of brief news items continued into the autumn when, their leave expired, Anson's crew were once more liable for the King's service.

For the surviving officers their service on Anson's voyage brought mixed blessings. The death rate among commissioned officers on the voyage had been low. On the *Centurion* all the commissioned officers had returned, a fact intriguing enough for someone at the Admiralty in 1745 to make a note at the front of the ship's log that the only officer deaths had been among the warrant or petty officers: Thomas Waller, surgeon (10 December 1740), Robert Wheldon, purser (13 December 1740), Francis Bonny, carpenter (25 May 1741), Henry Kippis, gunner (26 July

1742), Denis Crawly, boatswain (15 August 1742), Henry Ettrick, surgeon (7 September 1743). The lack of deaths among the commissioned officers is striking, but not altogether surprising. Most would have been in better health before sailing than the crew, and one who was not – Captain Richard Norris of the *Gloucester* – had been allowed to return to England early in the voyage. Living conditions on board ship for the officers were much superior to those of the men. However cramped their cabin accommodation would seem to the modern eye, it gave a degree of privacy and space unknown to the men crammed below decks. Officers had their own supplies of food and clothes, and except in emergencies were not subject to the incessant physical labour of many of the crew. They would also have first call on the ship's surgeon – a doubtful privilege perhaps – and more time to recover from bouts of ill health. The low death rate does not mean that the officers were unaffected by the hardships of the voyage. Anson himself returned with his health 'greatly impaired', he told Newcastle, and although he seems to have soon recovered others were not so fortunate. Three years later a whole cluster of letters to the Admiralty told of continuing problems. In January 1747 Captain Saunders requested shore leave since he was still suffering from the 'deep Scurvey' he had contracted on the voyage. In the same month Captain Cheap asked permission to quit the service, for continuing bouts of scurvy had brought him 'so low, that I find my self much weaken'd'. In September 1747 Captain Michell told Anson that 'my South-sea distemper is coming upon me very fast', and the next year he left the navy to become an MP. He died in 1752 'in the prime of life'. Captain Legge died in 1747, and in October the same year Philip Saumarez was killed at the Second Battle of Finisterre while captain of the sixty-gun *Nottingham*. He was thirty-six years old, but the surgeon who embalmed his corpse reported that he would not have survived another year, 'his lungs being grown to his side, and much wasted'.

In one respect at least, Saumarez's influence lived on beyond his death, for the uniform adopted in 1748 by captains in the navy was a modified version of the dark blue uniform designed by him the year before. At least twice on the voyage, at Macao in 1742 and at Canton in 1743, Anson had found himself improvising a uniform for his men in an attempt to impress the Chinese authorities and to distinguish his crew from those of merchant vessels. In the contemporary engraving of the meeting with the viceroy in November 1743 it is not possible to distinguish Anson's officers from the East India Company factors and captains, and in February 1746 a club of naval officers which met at Will's Coffee House in Scotland Yard resolved 'that a uniform dress is useful and necessary for the commissioned officers, agreeable to the practice of other nations'. Until this time, officers wore any form of dress that in terms of style and colour took their fancy. The naval lieutenant in Smollett's *Roderick Random* wore a cut-down soldier's coat, whereas the wealthy captain was resplendent in a silk coat, satin waistcoat, cambric shirt and velvet breeches. A portrait of Saumarez painted soon after his return from the voyage shows him wearing an elegant reddish-brown coat over a loose gold-and-brown waistcoat. To judge from the correspondence of Saumarez, Brett and Keppel, the officers from the *Centurion* were prominent in proposing, and indeed designing, a naval uniform; and in 1748 it was Saumarez's design of a dark blue coat and white waistcoat, trimmed with gold lace, that was accepted as the dress uniform for commissioned officers in the Royal Navy.

However close-knit a group the officers from the *Centurion* remained, a dispute over prize money soon opened up a rift between them and the other officers who had returned on the ship. The legal battle was fought between the ten surviving commissioned and warrant officers of the *Centurion* (the appellants), and the eleven surviving commissioned and warrant officers from the *Gloucester* and *Tryal* (the respondents). Anson himself was not involved in the legal proceedings except as a witness. Since there were no other captains present at the action of the *Covadonga*, his share of the prize money was not in question. Accordingly, the list of the *Centurion*'s officers was headed by the ship's first lieutenant, Philip Saumarez. His view of the matter was expressed in a grim little letter to his elder brother, John, in August 1744: 'The answer as to the survivorship of our countrymen is very concise. They are all dead, few entitled to any prizes, and none to the galleon.' The arguments, which ran on through the courts for almost three years, revolved around two main issues: the reasons for the scuttling of the *Tryal Prize* (to which the officers and crew of the *Tryal* had been transferred) and the *Gloucester*, and the related question of whether the officers from those ships could hold any position on the *Centurion* other than that of supernumeraries. The implications in money terms were considerable because of the way in which prize money was allocated. The total was divided into eight parts. Anson, as captain of the *Centurion* and commander of the expedition, took the lion's share – three-eighths of the whole. The remainder was divided on a scale drawn up according to rank and function. The case of Patrick Baird, first lieutenant of the *Gloucester*, illustrates what was at stake. If he were regarded as carrying out an officer's duties on the *Centurion*, then he would share one-eighth of the prize money with seven others of similar rank at the time of the capture of the galleon – four from the *Centurion* (three lieutenants and the master), and three originally appointed to the *Gloucester* and *Tryal*. If, however, he were regarded as a supernumerary or 'extra', then he would share two-eighths of the prize money with the seamen and other ordinary crew members and supernumeraries, about 200 in all at the time of the taking of the galleon. If we assume £400,000 to be the total sum divided, Baird's allocation would be something over £6,000 according to one ruling, only £500 according to the other. The same proportions applied to the other commissioned officers and to the warrant officers.

All prize-money disputes seem difficult and perplexing at this remove, this one more than most. The evidence, from that presented at the first hearings of the case before the High Court of Admiralty in August 1744, to that considered by the Lords Commissioners for Appeals in Prize Causes in May 1747, runs to several thousand pages. Much of it is repetitive and inconsequential, but amid the mass of detail and formal legal phrases, the main differences between the respondents from the *Gloucester* and *Tryal* and the appellants from the *Centurion* are clear. The case for the appellants rested on the basis that the *Centurion*, as a fourth-rate man-of-war, had a fixed complement of commissioned and warrant officers: 'one captain, three lieutenants, one master, one boatswain, one carpenter, one gunner, two master's mates, and no more'. It was not in Anson's power, even if he so wished, to add to this number. Any other officers taken on board the *Centurion* would be supernumeraries, and since their own ships no longer existed they were not entitled to wages or to an officer's share of any prize money taken after their arrival on board, but only to victuals. This was the hard legal rock against which the respondents' pleas beat in vain.

The case took the High Court of Admiralty back to the dramatic events of the voyage: the scuttling of the *Tryal Prize* and the *Gloucester*, the driving out to sea of the *Centurion* off Tinian, and the capture of the *Covadonga*. Some of the most heroic efforts of Anson's crews, often made in desperate situations, were presented by lawyers for both sides within the narrow confines of naval regulation and precedent. As far as the *Tryal Prize* was concerned, the respondents insisted that the vessel was in good condition, and Anson's decision to destroy her was taken in order the strengthen the depleted crews of the *Centurion* and *Gloucester*. In recognition of this, they claimed, Anson promised the officers of the *Tryal Prize* that they 'would enjoy all the privileges and advantages as fully and effectually as though the ship was actually in being'. All this the *Centurion*'s officers denied. They declared that the *Tryal Prize* was 'out of repair, having neither sails nor rigging fit to trust to', and that Anson had made no pledge to her officers about their future status. This was a shoddy attempt to conceal the true reasons for the scuttling of the *Tryal Prize*, and is contradicted by documents written at the time. Michell's official journal of the *Gloucester* shows that on both 22 and 29 March he made vigorous protests to Anson that he did not have enough men to work his ship, and that on the second occasion Anson responded that 'I should have the *Tryal*'s Men, and he would burn the prize'. The crucial evidence comes from Anson himself in a letter to Captain Saunders of the *Tryal Prize*, dated 14 April 1742. This was one of twenty-two orders whose accuracy Anson confirmed in a hearing before the High Court of Admiralty. In it he explained categorically that he had decided 'for the safety of His Majesty's subjects as for the security of both His Ships [*Centurion* and *Gloucester*] to destroy His Majesty's Ship *Tryal Prize*, notwithstanding her being in repair and fit for the sea, to reinforce the said Ships with her men'. The letter went on to say that her officers would be entered as supernumeraries on the *Centurion* and *Gloucester*, but would be entitled 'to the pay of officers until their arrival in England as the said ship will be destroy'd for the benefit of his Majesties Service'. In the courts it would be argued that such a pledge was beyond Anson's power to make, and it is perhaps significant that in the muster book of the *Centurion* for April 1742 the members of the crew of the *Tryal Prize*, regardless of rank, are entered as supernumeraries, 'for victuals only'. It was a sign of how bitter the legal struggle had become that the respondents challenged this by throwing doubt on the authenticity of the muster book: 'Has not the said Muster Book been wrote and made up since and where and what is become of the Original Muster Book?'

The arguments over the scuttling of the *Gloucester* followed a similar pattern. The respondents alleged that in August 1742 the *Centurion* was in as leaky a state as the *Gloucester*, her masts and rigging rotten, and with few of her crew fit for duty. Without the help of the crew of the *Gloucester*, they argued, the *Centurion* would have foundered. They accused Anson of using the resources of the *Gloucester* to save his own ship, listing the several occasions when Michell was ordered to send spars, hawsers, sails and other materials across to the *Centurion*. At the end of July Anson took the *Gloucester*'s gunner, John Nuttall, regardless of the weakened state of her crew. The *Gloucester*'s lack of seaworthiness, 'rowling and working in the sea', they put down to the weight of iron and other heavy items put on board the ship from the *Carmin* prize before leaving the coast of Mexico. To strengthen their case the respondents made much of the events of 14 August when John Rule, purser of the *Centurion*, came on board the *Gloucester*, and dictated a petition on the state of the ship which Captain Michell and his officers signed. As soon as he received this, and without attempting to return to the *Centurion* to give it to Anson for consideration, Rule took from his pocket an order from Anson to destroy the *Gloucester*. Michell's log is silent on the part John Rule played at this time, but has enough information on the parlous state of the *Gloucester* on 12 and 13 August to remove any suspicion of manipulation by Anson. In a situation as desperate as that of 14 August, when even to get boats from one ship to the other in the open sea was a major operation, speed of decision and action was of the essence. Whatever part the survivors from the *Gloucester* played in saving the *Centurion* in the weeks to come – and there is little doubt of its importance – Anson's decision of 14 August was the only possible one in the circumstances.

The question of the status of the officers of the *Tryal Prize* and the *Gloucester* once they were on board the *Centurion* took up many pages of the documents presented in the legal hearings. The reality was that in the several emergencies of this stage of the voyage they pitched in at every conceivable level to help work, fight and at times save the *Centurion*. The legal implications of their actions were another matter. For the respondents every instance of help – for example, that given by Patrick Baird, first lieutenant of the *Gloucester*, to Philip Saumarez when the *Centurion* was driven from Tinian out to sea – was evidence of their recognition as officers. The appellants countered that such acts were individual and voluntary, carried out without formal appointment. The taking of the *Covadonga* provided another clash both of evidence and interpretation. Early in the action, the respondents claimed, Lieutenant Brett, the officer in command of the upper gun deck of the *Centurion*, was wounded, and replaced by Lieutenant Hughes of the *Tryal Prize*. Some of the evidence given by members of the *Centurion*'s regular crew supported the claimants. For example, Graves Harris, a foremast man who as a periwig maker from Putney had originally sailed as barber to Anson and his officers, asserted that as far as he was concerned the officers from the *Gloucester* and *Tryal Prize* had fought as officers in the action against the galleon. The appellants, by contrast, argued that Brett was wounded late in the action, and in any case was immediately replaced by Peter Denis, third lieutenant of the *Centurion*. Any help that Hughes gave was not as an officer, 'having no appointment under the hand of the Commodore'. Anson's answer to repeated questions was that the officers of the *Gloucester* and *Tryal Prize* on board the *Centurion* 'were usefull and assistant to the said Ship, but not as Officers'.

As the hearings wore on, Anson's evidence came under close scrutiny. He was interrogated in February, April, October and November 1745, and the questioning became increasingly personal. In one heated exchange the officers of the *Gloucester* and *Tryal Prize* challenged Anson's insistence that on 20 June 1743 they had been quartered to the *Centurion*'s guns as foremast men only.

Note well there is not any one Man on board the said ship
but Mr Anson alone (who is the very Person that of all
Men should not have done it) ever once calls us, or imagines
us to be Foremast Men ... in every one of his Orders
constantly requires the duty of officers from us, and directs
every one of his orders to us as officers and that in our ranks
and degrees also, constantly naming an officer of a higher
rank of the *Gloucester* or *Tryal* Prize in his order and degree,
before an officer of lower rank of the *Centurion* itself. And
yet this Geo: Anson is the Man, who says that, in the
Engagement, we did duty as Foremast Men!

In 1745 the High Court of Admiralty ruled in favour of the officers of
the *Gloucester* and *Tryal*, but that decision was reversed on 19 May 1747
by the Lords Commissioners for Appeals in Prize Causes after a hearing
that lasted four days. The decision was a split one. Of the fourteen Lords
Commissioners, eight spoke. Five were in favour of reversal, including
the Lord Chief Justice and also the First Lord of the Admiralty. Two
supported the original decision, including a previous First Lord of the
Admiralty, and one was undecided. But the remaining six commissioners,
none of whom spoke, agreed with reversal. It is possible that a non-legal
factor played a part in the decision, for on the second day of the hearing
news reached London of Admiral Anson's victory over the French fleet
on 3 May at the Battle of Cape Finisterre – the first major naval victory
of the war. The guns at the Tower of London were fired to salute the
occasion, and were joined by dozens of ships in the Thames; that night
the great houses of the capital were illuminated, and there were bonfires
in the open spaces, while jubilant crowds thronged the streets. On the
final day of the hearing Anson himself arrived in London, and was
congratulated by the King at Kensington Palace. A verdict for the officers
of the *Gloucester* and *Tryal* would have been an implicit rejection of
Anson's evidence and his stance; and such a decision would not have
been an easy one for the Lords Commissioners to take on this particular
day.

How the legal decision was translated into cash allocations is still far from clear since – as in other prize-money cases – at that stage the government lost official interest in the business. It was left to claimants, their lawyers and agents to sort things out; and so far at least no records have been found of the general allocation, or even of the total amount distributed. Nor are matters helped by the fact that some estimates of the value of the prize money are given in sterling, others in Spanish dollars or pieces of eight. The reconstruction that follows rests on a variety of sources, but it is advanced in tentative fashion, and with an awareness that much is missing in the way of supporting detail.

Before the capture of the *Covadonga* a considerable amount of prize money had already been taken by the expedition, and recorded in the journals in sterling: £18,000 from the *Centurion*'s capture of the *Carmelo*; £5,000 from the *Tryal*'s capture of the *Arranzazu*; £30,000 from the plundering of Paita by the combined crews of the *Centurion* and *Tryal*; £19,000 from two prizes seized by the *Gloucester*. The distribution of this prize money, totalling about £72,000, would have been relatively straightforward. Some of it had in fact already been given out on the voyage, for the *Centurion*'s log shows that on 5 June 1743 part of the plunder from Paita (amount unstated) was distributed among the officers and crews of the *Centurion* and *Tryal*. What was at stake in the legal proceedings of 1744–7 was the enormous treasure from the *Covadonga*, and we have precise figures for this. Anson's letter of 14 June 1744 to the Duke of Newcastle gave the total as 1,313,843 pieces of eight, and 35,682 oz. of virgin silver and plate. These figures were later repeated in the authorised account of 1748. More detail is given by Justinian Nutt, appointed lieutenant on the *Covadonga* after her capture, and responsible for the counting and weighing of the treasure as it was shipped across to the *Centurion*. His log book for 23 October 1743 shows that the coin was in 256 chests, and that in addition there were six chests of virgin silver of 12,288 oz., three chests of run silver at 10,452 oz., and 13,236 oz. of wrought plate. The whole treasure amounted to 'near a million and half dollars', according to the authorised account, put in terms of sterling at 'not much short of £400,000'. This was a lower but more realistic figure than some of those being bandied around in London in the public prints of the summer of 1744, which ranged as high as £1,600,000. Pascoe

Thomas gave a lower figure still for the total amount of prize money taken by the *Centurion*. Using a conversion rate of 4s. 9d. per Spanish dollar or piece of eight (a ratio in line with modern research on eighteenth-century currency equivalents), he arrived at a figure of £355,324, of which £313,121 came from the *Covadonga*.

We know from a notice printed in the *London Gazette* that the prize money was paid about a month after the legal decision of 19 May 1747. From Monday to Friday of the week 15 to 19 June claimants were invited to attend the offices of a private firm on Tower Hill. First in line were the officers of the *Centurion*, who were to receive their remaining shares of the *Covadonga*'s prize money on the Monday. Any seamen from the *Centurion* who had not been paid earlier were also to attend that day. Later in the week the *Centurion*'s officers were to return to collect prize money from other ships taken on the voyage, and days were also set aside for paying the officers from the *Gloucester* and *Tryal*. The list suggests that most survivors among the seamen had already received much or all of their prize money, and that the *Centurion*'s officers had received a proportion of what was owing to them. The best indication of the actual amounts distributed is contained in the will and accompanying accounts of Philip Saumarez, who died in action in October 1747. This indicates that in June 1747 he received the final instalments of the prize money taken on the voyage. The total amounted to £7,605 12s. 0d. In one respect this would overestimate the amount Saumarez received from the *Covadonga*'s seizure, for it would include the sums due to him from the other captures on the voyage. On the other hand, the amount actually credited to him would not include the fees deducted by his agent. In the lack of any firm information about the size of either of these amounts, I have assumed that they cancelled each other out. If this guess is wrong, then the following calculations are wrong to the extent of the error.

If Saumarez's share was £7,605, then since he shared one-eighth of the total with three other officers, that would put the one-eighth share itself at £30,420, and the total amount of prize money from the *Covadonga* available for distribution £243,360. Even taking into account the three-year legal dispute, with its lawyers' and court fees, this would seem an excessive erosion of the authorised account's original valuation of 'not much short of £400,000', but a more realistic one if Pascoe Thomas's figure of £313,121 is correct. The value of the prize money resulting from the capture of the Manila ship by Woodes Rogers in 1709 was £148,000, but the final amount distributed was only half that. It is true that, in addition to legal fees, there were also deductions in the form of customs duties on the goods sold and compensatory payments to the East Indian Company, neither of which applied in the case of the *Covadonga*. If we take the sum of about £243,000 as a best estimate, then the allocation to individuals is straightforward. At one extreme Anson would have received three-eighths of the whole, about £91,000. This compares with the £719 11s. 4d. the *Centurion*'s pay book shows him receiving as captain during the voyage, and gives some idea of why the hope of prizes was such a lure for naval officers. At the other end of the scale a seaman present at the capture of the *Covadonga* would have received about £300, derisory compared with the fortune going to his captain, but still representing about twenty years' normal pay. In the same way as Anson profited from collecting shares both as captain of the *Centurion* and commander-in-chief of the expedition, so seamen gained from the relatively low numbers of survivors at the time of the engagement of 20 June 1743.

The decision that the officers and warrant officers of the *Gloucester* and *Tryal* were entitled only to a seaman's share of the prize money was probably correct in law, since at no time does Anson seem to have formally appointed any of the claimants to carry out officers' duties on his ship. In other ways it was rough justice, for it is unlikely that the *Centurion* would have survived the rigours of the Pacific crossing, and gone on to take the *Covadonga*, without the help of the experienced officers from the other two ships. Long before the end officers on both sides were heartily tired of courts, lawyers and disputes. Philip Saumarez, first named of the appellants, referred to 'this fatal law suit' that had separated him from his friends, railed against 'the scheming Jesuitical person' that had persuaded him to go to law, and longed to be at sea again. For the unsuccessful claimants, Lawrence Millechamp of the *Gloucester* had the last, bitter word: 'We had more terrible engagements in the courts of law than ever we had in the South Seas.'

IX

Past and Future

'We are talking in England of making new discoveries in consequence of Mr. Anson's voyage.'

Benjamin Keene, May 1749

IN BRITAIN Anson's epic voyage was one of the few memorable episodes
of the European hostilities of 1739–48. However insignificant in strategic
terms, it stood out as a dramatic highlight in a drab, protracted war that
seemed to have no obvious winners. The final triumph of the capture of
the Acapulco galleon after repeated disasters caught the public imagination in a way few of the continental campaigns had done. On his return
Anson was compared with the immortal Drake, and his exploits with the
old, misty feats of arms against the Spain of Phillip II. In the sailors'
ballads of the period he became 'lucky Anson', especially when the booty
from his May 1747 victory at Cape Finisterre brought a second triumphant
procession of treasure through the streets of London. His brother,
Thomas Anson, begged the loan of the royal standard seized from the
Covadonga to embellish the family home at Shugborough, while the
Centurion's battered lion figurehead, removed when the ship was rebuilt,
found a well-earned resting place outside an inn on the Duke of Richmond's estate at Goodwood. Its stone pedestal carried a faintly ironic
inscription:

> Stay traveller a while, and view
> One, who has travell'd more than you,
> Quite round the globe; thro' each degree

> Anson and I have plow'd the sea:
> Torrid and frigid zones have past,
> And safe ashore, arriv'd at last,
> In ease and dignity appear:
> He – in the house of lords, I here.

Despite the comparisons with times gone by, not all the reaction to the voyage was nostalgic and celebratory. The year of Anson's return saw the publication of the first volume of John Campbell's revised and enlarged edition of John Harris's *Navigantium atque Itinerantium Bibliotheca* (the second volume was to follow in 1748). These monumental volumes, running to more than 2,000 pages of small print, had a purpose as weighty as their appearance: the promotion of British overseas enterprise in all parts of the globe. The first volume squeezed in an account of Anson's voyage based on the *Authentick Journal* just published under the pseudonym of 'John Philips'. This last-minute insertion was designed by Campbell to show his readers the opportunities offered by the unknown vastnesses of the South Sea. He advocated projects extending British influence throughout the ocean, using bases on Juan Fernández and New Guinea to probe towards the undiscovered southern continent, *Terra Australis Incognita*, in one direction and the (equally undiscovered) Pacific entrance of the Northwest Passage in another. His arguments for the replacement of Spain by Britain in the Pacific resembled the sentiments of Hutchinson and Naish in 1739, and were summed up in lines that were at once exhortation and warning: 'History affords us no example of a maritime power that remained long at a stay. If we do not go forward, we must necessarily go backwards.'

For Campbell the most important single step towards British domination of the Pacific would be to find the Northwest Passage, 'a kind of maritime Philosopher's Stone'. With memories of Anson's clear run along the South Sea coasts of Spanish America still fresh, Campbell pointed out how British naval vessels could sail undetected through a northern passage to Spain's Pacific possessions. No longer would they have to brave the rigours of Cape Horn. New and lucrative trading areas would be opened up: the coasts north of California where legend placed the fabulous

The *Centurion*'s figurehead: shown here on the contemporary model of the *Centurion* made for Anson, and certainly in better condition than the original, which was presented to the Earl of Richmond after the ship was rebuilt in 1745. In 1832, William IV had the figurehead set up at the head of the Grand Staircase at Windsor, but in 1836 it was sent to Greenwich and over the years gradually disintegrated. The only significant relic of the figurehead is one of the lion's legs, now at Shugborough Hall.

cities of Quivira and Cibola, the rich islands rumoured to lie between the American coast and Japan, and parts of the East Indies. In 1745 Parliament passed an act offering a reward of £20,000 for the discovery of a navigable Northwest Passage; by chance, perhaps, it was the same amount that Parliament had offered in 1714 for a reliable way of determining longitude at sea (still unclaimed at this time). Similar arguments were expressed in another compilation, the *Complete System of Geography*, published in 1747, whose editor assumed that lack of news about the latest expedition sent the year before to Hudson Bay to look for the Northwest Passage was evidence that it had been successful, and would be returning home by way of the Pacific and the East Indies.

It was in the context of this renewed interest in the Pacific – among merchants, geographers and parliamentarians – that in May 1748 the long-awaited official or authorised account of Anson's voyage was published. The first edition of *A Voyage Round the World by George Anson*, in a handsome quarto volume, attracted more than 1,800 advance subscribers, including some of the leading figures in the land, and was followed before the end of the year by four further editions. In September 1748 Henry Legge, the diplomat brother of Captain Edward Legge of the *Severn*, wrote to Anson from Berlin with news of the reception of the first copies. 'All people here who have the least smattering of English (and many have) are at work with Grammars and Dictionarys to read over your S Sea Voyage.' Extracts from the book were given in serial form in the newspapers and periodicals of the day, the fullest in the popular *Gentleman's Magazine*. In its original form, the book was a sumptuous and well-illustrated production. It included 42 plates, available separately as a set, and these were also widely copied and pirated.

In many ways the book resembled the narratives of voyages and discoveries published by Hakluyt in the late Elizabethan period. It was at one level a stirring story of adventure on the high seas, at another a reasoned plea for the expansion of British enterprise in the South Sea. To a modern reader the literary style may seem to veer uneasily between the pedestrian and the turgid, but the narrative has unmistakable power as it unfolds its terrible story of catastrophe and death, redeemed near the end by the capture of the galleon. The circumstances of its composition are reflected in the fact that it is eulogistic in tone when it refers to Anson. Compared with the slipshod literary efforts of most of Anson's buccaneering or privateering predecessors in the South Sea, the book was a detailed, unsensational work; and although the expedition was bent on war, not exploration, the number of charts and views showed Anson's concern to provide a guide to future voyagers in a region that was still largely unknown to British seamen. There were no professional artists on board Anson's ships, but the drawings of Lieutenant Peircy Brett formed the basis for most of the forty-two engravings. To judge from the lack of ethnographic subjects, Brett had no confidence in his ability to draw the human figure, but his careful depictions of coasts, harbours and ships were a considerable step forward. Earlier voyage accounts had suffered from hack artists and engravers, working in a studio with only a textual description before them. The difficulties this could cause had been shown in the English edition of a best-selling work of travel and imagination, *New Voyages to North-America* by the Baron de Lahontan. The illustrations were taken from the Dutch edition, based in turn on the original French edition. In the English edition of 1703 almost all had to be redone, 'for the Dutch gravers had murdered 'em, by not understanding their explications, which were all in French. They have grav'd women for men, and men for women; naked persons for those that are cloath'd, and e contra'. Dampier's *Voyage to New-Holland*, also published in 1703, had some good drawings of antipodean plants, and rather crude ones of birds, fishes and views. He had with him 'a Person skill'd in Drawing' whose identity is unknown, and whose official position on board, like Brett's on the *Centurion*, was probably something other than that of artist. Among the unofficial accounts of Anson's voyage published in 1744 and 1745 were several illustrations, with detail of considerable interest, but they were almost certainly drawn in England by an artist working from textual descriptions of the events depicted: the squadron rounding Cape Horn; the landing place at Juan Fernández; the plundering of Paita; Captain Cheap's pistolling of midshipman Cozens; and Anson's audience with the chuntuck.

Although the engravings published in the authorised account of Anson's voyage were limited in subject-matter, they anticipated the visual dimension of the later narratives of the discovery voyages of Cook and his contemporaries. Above all, they were drawn from direct observation, not, as the Introduction noted, 'composed at home from imperfect accounts, given by incurious and unskilful observers . . . the greatest part of them were drawn on the spot'. They added both to the appeal of the book for the reader and to its usefulness for future navigators. In this context pride of place among the illustrations went to the Spanish chart of the North Pacific seized on the *Covadonga*. It marked the great northern swing of the eastbound route of the galleons, and the twin tracks of the *Centurion* (1742) and the *Covadonga* (1743) sailing from Acapulco towards Guam and the Philippines. The *Centurion*'s disastrous southern dip, which took her out of the path of the trade winds as she left the Mexican coast, is clearly shown, while at the chart's western edge stands Cape Espiritu Santo, the meeting place of galleon and warship in June 1743 (see pp. 132–3). The book was above all a work of information, whose intention was explained in the Introduction as the encouragement of 'the more important purposes of navigation, commerce, and national interest'. In this task the author (of this part certainly Benjamin Robins) stressed the value of accurate charts, global recordings of magnetic variation, and proper surveys taken from naval vessels. It is one of the puzzles of the period that despite Anson's growing influence the navy failed at this time to establish any surveying service, or even a hydrographic office on the French model to keep, correct and publish charts.

Given that part of the purpose of the Introduction was to contribute to 'the safety and success of future navigators', one quite mystifying omission in the book was any discussion of the threat posed to oceanic voyages by scurvy. It was as though the pessimistic, almost fatalistic, comments in the body of the narrative about the impossibility of either prevention or cure represented the final word on the subject. Dr Richard Mead, who in 1740 had been consulted by the Admiralty about the medicines to be taken on the squadron, discussed the incidence of scurvy on the voyage with Anson after his return. He also saw the notes – long since disappeared – kept by Henry Ettrick, the surgeon of the *Centurion* who had died at Canton, and Joseph Allen, who had sailed as surgeon on the *Tryal* (and later became master of Dulwich College). Some time before,

Mead had heard from Sir Charles Wager about the beneficial effects of lemons and oranges on the crews of the fleet Wager had taken many years earlier from the Mediterranean into the colder waters of the Baltic; but in his *Discourse of the Scurvy* (1749) Mead gave citrus fruit no especial attention. He placed most emphasis on 'the hurtful qualities of the sea-air', and the only example of a cure he quoted from his conversation with Anson related to the landing at Tinian. Two accounts of the voyage had mentioned the importance for the sick of oranges picked on the island, but Anson's own anecdote sent Mead, like many of his predecessors, stumbling into a medical cul-de-sac. One of the crew was near death when he reached shore at Tinian, Anson remembered, but 'desired his mates, that they would cut a piece of turf out of the soft ground, and put his mouth to the hole: upon doing this he came to himself, and grew afterwards quite well'.

Even to those familiar with terrible losses at sea from disease, the ravages of scurvy on Anson's ships seemed particularly difficult to explain or accept. Far worse than on any previous English voyage to the South Sea, they threw doubt on the practicality of the schemes put forward by Campbell and other projectors of the period. One of the unforeseen consequences of Anson's losses from scurvy was that they helped prompt James Lind in 1747 to begin his investigations into the disease. Lind was a surgeon on the fourth-rate man-of-war *Salisbury* when in 1746 and 1747 she experienced severe outbreaks of scurvy while on patrol duty in the English Channel. During the second outbreak Lind conducted a clinical trial which, however perfunctory it may appear by later standards, was an advance on what had gone before. Twelve sailors suffering from scurvy were put on the same general diet, but each pair was given a different daily supplement. The supplements were elixir of vitriol; vinegar; seawater; two oranges and a lemon; cider; and a medicinal paste accompanied by a barley-water and tamarind juice mixture. The first two treatments were the favoured ones in the navy of this period; but Lind recorded that 'the most sudden and visible good effects' were noticed in the two patients given the oranges and lemon each day. In 1753 Lind published his *Treatise of the Scurvy* (dedicated to Anson), in which the results of his trial were set in the context of 400 pages of general, philosophical and historical material on the disease. Although Lind's researches, both at sea and later at the Haslar Naval Hospital, drew him towards the discovery – or rather rediscovery – of the antiscorbutic properties of lemon juice, he believed that just as outbreaks of scurvy were multicausal, so should be its treatment. He stressed the importance of cleanliness and good air, together with a planned, antiscorbutic diet that included lemon juice, onions, sauerkraut and greens such a cress and lettuce grown on board. Lemon juice, he advised, could be kept for long periods in tightly corked bottles under a thin layer of olive oil. But Lind had no influential patron, and Anson, though he may have had a part in his appointment to Haslar Hospital in 1758, seems to have shown no particular interest in Lind's work on scurvy. The post-Anson Admiralty of the 1760s and 1770s was sceptical about the potency of lemon juice or rob once it had been stored for any length of time, and listened instead to the Dublin physician, David MacBride, an enthusiastic advocate of malt wort as an antiscorbutic. It was to take the rest of the century for Lind's recommendations to be officially accepted, but they marked the beginning of an experimental and clinical approach to the problem of scurvy.

In some sections the *Voyage* looked to the future as it recommended surveys of the Falkland Islands, Tierra del Fuego and the west coast of Patagonia to make access into the South Sea easier for future expeditions. The Falklands in one ocean and Juan Fernández in the other were seen as likely way-stations both for trading ventures in time of peace and for predatory expeditions in wartime. The same theme was followed in Chapter XIV, 'A brief account of what might have been expected from our squadron, had it arrived in the South-Seas in good time'. This postulated a summer passage round the Horn with little damage to the ships and their crews; the seizure of Valdivia and other Spanish ports, which might have been followed by an Indian rising in Chile, and then, perhaps, by a war of independence throughout Spanish America. This unabashed piece of special pleading, which blamed Anson's misfortunes on his late start, provoked Horace Walpole into a response that had at least an element of justification. 'He sets out with telling you that he had no soldiers sent with him but old invalids without legs or arms; and then in the middle of the book there is a whole chapter to tell you, what they

ord Anson, 1755. This oil painting by Joshua Reynolds shows Anson in Admiral's full dress, a
more imposing (and portly) figure than the reflective-looking naval officer of the time of the
oyage round the world (*see frontispiece*).

would have done if they had set out two months sooner; and that was no less than conquering Peru and Mexico with this disabled army.'

Walpole's was a rare critical voice amid a general chorus of approval for Anson's conduct, both on the voyage and after. He soon overcame the damage he seemed to have done to his career with his resignation letter of June 1744. His retirement as a captain on half-pay was short-lived, for in December of that year the Board of Admiralty lost office, and the new board, headed by the Duke of Bedford, included Anson. In April 1745 he was promoted to Rear-Admiral of the White, and by 1746 he was at sea again. In May 1747 his defeat of the French fleet off Cape Finisterre in the first major naval victory of the war resulted in his ennoblement as Baron Anson of Soberton. Among the captains of his ships that day were Saumarez, Brett and Denis (the latter, appropriately, in command of the *Centurion*). At the peace celebrations of 1748 Anson was promoted Admiral of the Blue, and in 1751 he became First Lord of the Admiralty, a position he held (with one brief interlude) until his death in 1762. As he moved into the highest circles of politics and administration, Anson paid particular attention to those young officers who had sailed with him to the South Sea. Nine became captains before the end of the war in 1748: Philip Saumarez, Charles Saunders, Peircy Brett and Peter Denis (lieutenants at the outset of the voyage); John Campbell, Augustus van Keppel, Hyde Parker and Thomas Saumarez (midshipmen); and Justinian Nutt (warrant officer). All except Philip Saumarez (killed in October 1747), Thomas Saumarez and Justinian Nutt reached flag rank, and Saunders became First Lord of the Admiralty in 1766. Among those who became captains later was the young Charles Proby, first to sight the *Covadonga* on the morning of 20 June 1743. Most distinguished of all the survivors from the voyage was Richard Howe, who had sailed as a fourteen-year-old midshipman on the *Severn* with Legge – the inauspicious beginning of a career which saw him become Admiral of the Fleet, Earl Howe KG, victor at the 'Glorious First of June' in 1794.

During his years on the Board of Admiralty there can be little doubt that Anson's reforming zeal was given a keener edge by the memory of those galling experiences that had delayed and handicapped his expedition. In some instances the link between cause and effect was a direct one. So the act passed in 1749 'for extending the discipline of the navy to the crews of his Majesty's Ships, wrecked, lost, or taken, and continuing to them their wages upon certain conditions' owed much to the problems faced by Captain Cheap of the *Wager* after his ship was lost. The Order in Council of 1755 establishing a permanent Corps of Marines (to become the Royal Marines in 1802) may well have had something to do with Anson's dismay at the wretched condition of the raw marines sent on board his ships in 1740, almost all of them to die before they ever saw the South Sea. Other measures were a response to the standard litany of complaints by seagoing officers against the naval dockyards and other departments in England. A system of annual inspections introduced soon after Anson joined the Board of Admiralty did something to improve matters. In the heyday of Whig patronage he argued that appointments to the navy should be made on grounds of efficiency, with preferment going to those who had fought 'on equal terms with the enemy'. For his own part, Anson was happier on deck than behind his desk at the Admiralty. In 1755 he longed to be at sea with the Western Squadron, 'but when I mentioned it to the Duke of Newcastle, he asked me what was then to become of the Admiralty'. Three years later his chance came, and at the age of sixty-one Anson, to his unfeigned delight, took the Western Squadron to sea for an arduous summer of patrol duty against the French. As he wrote to Hardwicke, 'The command of a squadron at sea has always been my principal object and passion.' Years after his death William Pitt paid tribute to Anson's role at sea and on land in the triumphs of the Seven Years War. 'To his wisdom, to his experience and care the nation owes the glorious successes of the last war.'

The journals, letters and orders from Anson's circumnavigation bring us little closer to him personally. After almost three years on the *Centurion* in close proximity to Anson, Lieutenant Peter Denis wrote a long letter from Macao to his brother in England describing the events of the voyage, but he could only apologise for his inability to say anything perceptive about his captain – 'To give you a character of him would require a more masterly pen'. Throughout Anson's career his character was tantalisingly difficult to assess. He was a taciturn man who left behind little private correspondence, awkward at 'ceremony and correspondence', as he once admitted. At first sight he is a self-effacing figure in later life, moving unobtrusively among the great Whig oligarchs of his day, perhaps remembered too often by the jibe that 'he had been around the world, but was never in it'. Yet his steady progress to the height of his profession indicates that Anson was not quite the disingenuous sailor some of his contemporaries may have thought. A more revealing comment by a modern student of naval administration asserts that Anson 'had a talent for politics without having the appearance and inclinations of a politician'. Every now and again his letters reveal a flash of humour, a hint that he may have been a more sardonic observer of things and persons than many realised. The day before Lady Anson died in 1760 he wrote to Hardwicke with the doctors' latest prognosis on her illness, but then added: 'I don't understand their jargon, and always feel, when I have any of them in the house, as I always did when I had a Pilot; being ignorant myself, I always doubted whether my pilot knew as much as he ought to do; but in both cases there is nothing else to trust to.' Underneath the reserve there was a proud and touchy man, as Page's journal on the vicissitudes of Anson's stay at Canton in 1743 had revealed. And if he appeared to his colleagues as colourless, then those closest to him would have glimpsed the inner steel. This was the commander of the voyage which, he hoped, would make his reputation; who had lost all his ships except one; whose men had died in their hundreds; but who never gave up, never wavered in his determination to carry out as much of his task as he could. Yet Anson was no martinet. He was a humane commander, who in times of danger worked alongside his men, hauling ropes, chopping wood, nursing the sick. What they made of this we have no way of telling, except that Anson's ability to forget rank when the occasion demanded some more muscular contribution was stressed in all the accounts. One sign that he kept the respect of his men despite the disappointments and hardships of the long voyage was that he was never confronted with a serious threat of mutiny.

Evidence has now emerged that indicates that Anson used his position as a Lord Commissioner of the Admiralty to urge a follow-up expedition to the South Sea in the first year of peace. In January 1749 he reported to his colleagues on the Board of Admiralty (where the Earl of Sandwich was First Lord) that the King had agreed that two sloops should be sent 'on Discoverys' into southern latitudes. By the end of February the sloops had been chosen, and John Campbell (who had been with Anson on the *Centurion*) was appointed to command the expedition. By now the Spanish government had got wind of the venture, and its ambassador in London demanded further details. These came from Sandwich, who explained to the Duke of Bedford, Secretary of State for the Southern Department, that in the South Atlantic the vessels were to survey Pepys Island (allegedly discovered by Ambrose Cowley in 1684, but never subsequently sighted) and the Falklands, and then sail round the Horn into the South Sea. After watering at Juan Fernández they were to follow a traverse course across the Pacific between latitudes 25°S. and 10°S. for at least 3,000 miles. Sandwich assured Bedford that no settlements would be made, and that if necessary he would be willing to abandon the second, or Pacific, part of the voyage. In Madrid the Spanish foreign minister continued to express concern, warning that 'neither He nor any one else could be a Stranger to the Rise and Intent of such an Expedition, since it was so fully explained in the printed Relation of Anson's Voyage'. Benjamin Keene, Britain's special envoy to Spain at this time, was also uneasy at the prospect of Anson's voyage leading to new British discovery ventures in the South Sea that would make his task more difficult. By June British ministers, anxious not to upset delicate diplomatic negotiations with the Spanish government on the asiento and other issues, ordered the Admiralty to drop the expedition 'for the present'.

The matter did not end there, for Anson seems to have tried to redirect the aborted expedition. The attempt sprang from the realisation, after the failure of two expeditions (in 1741–2 and 1746–7) to find a Northwest Passage through Hudson Bay, that a discovery voyage to locate its Pacific entrance might be more feasible. The idea was not new: it dated back to Grenville and Drake in Elizabethan times, and had been advocated by Dampier in the late seventeenth century. The notion of a Pacific approach had been given a new lease of life by the rediscovery in the 1740s of a bizarre report, first printed in 1708, of a voyage supposedly made in 1640 by a Spanish admiral, Bartholomew de Fonte, north from Lima to the coast of (modern) British Columbia. There he claimed to have found a network of straits and rivers leading east towards the Atlantic. The entry point of these waterways was the Archipelago of San Lazarus. In February 1749 the first chart purporting to show the Fonte discoveries was published. This was included in a detailed analysis of the Fonte account by T. S. Drage, who had sailed to Hudson Bay on the unsuccessful Northwest Passage expedition of 1746–7, and on his return published an account of the voyage under the pseudonym of 'the Clerk of the California'. Central to Drage's thesis was his identification of Fonte's Archipelago of San Lazarus with the entrance of the Strait of Anian, the long-sought waterway between America and Asia that would provide a sea route between the Atlantic and the Pacific. According to Drage, the location of the southern part of the archipelago was the same as that of the south shore of the Strait of Anian in latitude 51°N., longitude 141°47'W. He did not acknowledge the source of such a precise location for the Strait of Anian, but it came from Pascoe Thomas's *True and Impartial Journal* of Anson's voyage. At the end of the book Thomas appended, without comment, a list captured from the Spaniards of the latitudes and longitudes of various places in the South Sea; and this included 'the Point of Suesta del Estrech Danian' in latitude 51°N., longitude 141°47'W. The exactness of this location, contained in an otherwise mundane table of observations, further strengthened the long-standing suspicion in Britain that the Spaniards had discovered the Strait of Anian, but had kept its location secret for fear of another Anson expedition, this time coming through the Northwest Passage.

In September 1749, four months after the original expedition to the Falklands and beyond was cancelled, newspapers noted that one of the sloops involved was again being made ready for the South Sea. Further reports described meetings held at the end of the year between the Admiralty and Henry Ellis. He had sailed as agent on the Northwest Passage expedition of 1746–7, had written a book on the voyage in which he held out continuing hopes of a passage, and was soon to publish a pamphlet arguing that the next attempt on the passage should be made from the Pacific side. Anson, the reports continued, was much involved in the

matter. There may have been some wishful thinking in all this. The
Admiralty records make no mention of such meetings, although this does
not necessarily mean that they did not take place. That some sort of
northern expedition was under consideration is suggested by the later
evidence of a retired merchant named Cramond. He recorded that in
about 1750 he had discussed such an expedition with Anson, who thought
that the two vessels originally destined for the South Pacific might be
used, under the command of Captain John Campbell and Captain Peter
Denis. Progress was slow, according to Cramond, because of the doubts
about the expedition raised by the East India Company, always jealous
of its monopoly rights; and then the growing war clouds in Europe put
an end to the project.

Of the instructions intended for the naval expedition of 1749, the
most significant was the proposed track of the two sloops west into the
Pacific from Juan Fernández for 3,000 miles, steering 'a traverse course'
between latitude 10°S. and latitude 25°S. If followed long enough, this
would have taken the vessels into the heart of Polynesia (Tahiti lies in
latitude 17°30'S.). It is unlikely that Anson or his colleagues on the Board
of Admiralty had any premonition of the Society Islands, but they may
have read the accounts in print in English translation of the track of the
Dutch explorer, Roggeveen, through the northern Tuamotus in about
latitude 15°S. A more likely influence was Henry Hutchinson, who had
fallen on hard times since his return as agent-victualler from Anson's
voyage. He remained an indefatigable memorialist, and among his papers
which found their way to the Admiralty is one entitled 'Colony in South
America'. The document is undated, and could have been written any
time after his return to England on the *Centurion* in 1744. Once again,
Hutchinson advocated the establishment of a settlement in Chile, with
trade links extending across the Pacific to the East Indies in one direction
and China in another; but a more intriguing note was struck by the
paper's claim that the Spaniards had discovered 'Good Islands' far out in
the ocean west of Peru, whose existence they had kept secret. This was
not the first time this rumour had appeared, but Hutchinson's acquaintanceship with Anson makes it more likely that this report found its way
onto the admiral's desk.

Whatever the motives and reasoning behind the planned expedition of 1749, there were no discovery voyages from Britain to the South Sea for twenty years after Anson's return. As the Seven Years War battered the nations of Europe and their overseas empires, the nearest British approach to the Pacific came with a scheme for the capture of Manila, approved by Anson as First Lord of the Admiralty shortly before his death. Sitting through three days of meetings in January 1762, Anson would have heard echoes of the discussions of the autumn of 1739 as he listened to the advantages that would follow the seizure of Manila and the establishment of a British base on Mindanao, from which 'the Spanish provinces in the South Seas, both of South and North America may with great success be insulted and plundered on the part of Great Britain.' In the event, there were to be other resonances from Anson's voyage about this operation, for in October 1762 British warships captured the *Santissima Trinidad*, one of the last and greatest of the Manila galleons.

Only at the end of the Seven Years War did ministerial thoughts again turn to seaborne exploration, and in 1764 the first discovery expedition of George III's reign, commanded by Commodore John Byron, sailed for the Pacific. Perhaps because of the new reign, perhaps because an account of it appeared in Hawkesworth's *Voyages* in company with the journals of Wallis, Carteret and Cook, Byron's expedition has conventionally been linked with the subsequent discovery voyages. In reality it was a throwback to an earlier period; it was the abortive 1749 expedition writ large. Byron had been a midshipman on the *Wager*, so it was appropriate that he was to command an expedition whose aims would be familiar to Anson and to Anson's generation. Anson had died in June 1762, still regretting (a ministerial colleague recorded) that he had not pressed ahead with the earlier project. In a sense Byron took up the torch that Anson laid down. His expedition was anti-Spanish in character; the links were with the voyages of Drake, Dampier and Anson rather than with the more dispassionate and scientific approach that would come with James Cook and his contemporaries. The First Lord of the Admiralty, the Earl of Egmont, told his cabinet colleagues on hearing of Byron's arrival in the Falklands, that the islands were 'the Key to the whole Pacifick Ocean'. Their possession, he continued, 'will render all our Expeditions to those parts most lucrative to ourselves, most fatal to Spain'. But Byron's successors in the Pacific were men of peace rather than of war. His voyage represented the last dying echo of those clamorous and often ill-conducted British predatory ventures into the South Sea. Of those, Anson's voyage was the most celebrated, but in time perceptions of it changed. Increasingly, it became seen as an object-lesson in Admiralty mismanagement, its crews victims rather than heroes.

To have survived the voyage was achievement enough, and brought its own claim to modest fame. Among those listed in the *Centurion*'s muster book for the years 1740 to 1744 was James Steward(t), able seaman. He was not mentioned in any of the journals or accounts of the voyage, but his unobtrusive service was not quite forgotten. On 13 June 1768 the *Lloyd's Evening Post* of London printed among the week's deaths: 'Saturday last, suddenly, Mr. James Steward, of South Benfleet Hall, Essex, who made the Voyage round the World, with Lord Anson in his Majesty's Ship *Centurion*'.

A Literary Puzzle: The Authorship of
Anson's *Voyage Round the World*

The authorised account of *A Voyage Round the World by George Anson* was one of the more notable publishing successes of the eighteenth century. The first edition, published in May 1748 by John and Paul Knapton of Ludgate Street, London, was a handsome quarto volume printed on royal paper. It went through another four editions before the end of the year, and by 1776 no fewer than fifteen editions, mostly in the cheaper octavo or duodecimo formats, had appeared. It was regarded as a model of its kind, and when in 1771 the Admiralty approached Dr John Hawkesworth with a commission to put into book form the Pacific journals of James Cook and his contemporaries, his immediate response was: 'I would do my best to make it another *Anson's Voyage*.' At the latest count, there have been about ninety reprints of the book, including editions in French, Dutch, Italian, Spanish, German, Polish, Swedish and Russian.

The importance and popularity of the *Voyage* make the four-year delay in publication and the uncertainty about the book's authorship the more puzzling, although it now appears that the two matters were linked. The title-page of the first edition is clear enough. The book, readers were told, was 'Compiled From Papers and other Materials of the Right Honourable George Lord Anson, and published under his Direction, by Richard Walter, M.A. Chaplain of his Majesty's Ship the *Centurion*'. Walter's name appeared again at the end of the fulsome dedication of the book to the Duke of Bedford. Nor does the fact that the chaplain left the *Centurion* at Canton in December 1742 to return home necessarily rule him out as the author. In the book the writer noted that several officers returned to England in East India Company ships and that he went with them. At this point all first-person references disappear and the narrative becomes more summary – precisely what one would expect. And it was presumably the chaplain Pascoe Thomas had in mind when he accused 'a certain Honourable Gentleman' on the *Centurion* of stealing some of his notes, and then leaving the expedition early to write an account of the voyage that he intended 'to publish by Authority (an effectual Method to discourage others)'.

Yet soon after publication doubts were expressed about Walter's right to be regarded as sole author of the *Voyage*. For example, a note accompanying the first instalment from the book printed in the *Gentleman's Magazine* for September 1749 attributed 'the chief hand' in the work to 'Mr Robins, F.R.S.' Benjamin Robins was a talented and versatile mathematician, engineer and pamphleteer. Among his scientific publications were several mathematical discourses, numerous papers read before the Royal Society (which awarded him its Copley Medal in 1747), and his best-known work, *New Principles of Gunnery* (1742). His interest in naval gunnery, and the association with Anson which that expertise brought, led him in 1747 to publish his *Proposal for increasing the strength of the British Navy by changing all the guns from eighteen-pounders downwards into others of equal weight but of a greater bore*. But his writings were not confined to technical treatises. As early as 1739 he was writing (anonymously) political pamphlets, often with a strong anti-Spanish tinge, such as his *Observations on the Present Convention with Spain* of that year. Robins was appointed engineer-general to the East India Company in 1749, arrived at Madras in July 1750, and died there a year later.

In 1761 a volume appeared containing Robins's *Mathematical Tracts*. In his preface the editor of the volume, James Wilson, claimed that Robins had replaced Walter as the main author of *Anson's Voyage*. He went on to say that although Anson had originally commissioned Walter to write the account of the voyage, when Robins at Anson's request inspected Walter's manuscript he found that it consisted mainly of material taken from the shipboard logs – 'the wind and weather, the currents, courses, bearings, distances, offings, soundings, moorings . . .' Robins added as much again in the way of general remarks and observations 'in his own style and manner'. Wilson stated that he had in his possession a copy of an indenture between the Knaptons and Robins that treated the latter as 'the sole proprietor' of the book. He also printed a letter from Anson to Robins of October 1749 which regretted that the latter's departure for India would prevent him completing a second volume on the voyage; this implied, though it did not state directly, that Robins had written the first. Wilson's claims on behalf of his dead friend were accepted by some contemporary reference works, including Andrew Kippis's *Biographica Britannica*, which in its second edition of 1778 mentioned the Anson voyage and the 'excellent account that has been written of it by the late Mr. Robins'.

Walter was still alive (although seriously ill at this time), but he made no attempt to refute these statements. It was left to his widow, Jane, four years after his death in 1785, to write to a relative, John Walter the Charing Cross bookseller, recalling the long hours Richard had spent writing the book in the months before they were married. She remembered her husband-to-be working for hours each day and then waiting on Anson at 6 a.m. the next morning to show him 'every sheet that was written'. Robins had been involved, she said, but only to give advice on the illustrations in the volume; and some months before publication he had gone to Flanders in connection with siege works there. In rebuttal of James Wilson's assertion that he had in his possession an indenture in Robins's name, the daughter of Richard and Jane Walter later sent a bill to Sir John Barrow, secretary of the Admiralty and author of a biography of Anson that appeared in 1839. He had aroused the ire of the Walter family by writing that 'Walter drew the cold and naked skeleton, and that Robins clothed it with flesh and muscles'. The bill apparently showed an agreement in which the book's publishers paid Richard Walter the sum of £750, but unfortunately it was never returned to the Walter family.

One of the problems with these claims and counter-claims is that they date from the period after the book's publication, when its huge success might tempt those who had some share in its making to inflate their contribution. In recent years evidence has been found which, though not entirely conclusive, throws more light on the sequence of events between Anson's return and the belated publication of the book. A hint of Anson's dissatisfaction with Walter comes in the recollections of the Revd Alexander Carlyle, a young man at the time of the *Centurion's* return. Among his friends was Captain Cheap of the *Wager*, who had arrived back in England in April 1746 and 'was employ'd by Ld Anson to look out for a Proper Person to write his voyage, the Chaplain whose Journal furnish'd the Chief Materials being unequal to the work'. Whether Walter actually kept a journal on the voyage as implied here is open to doubt. There are only a few personal references to him in the entire book published under his name. On 22 May 1741 the *Centurion* was in such desperate straits off the coast of Chile that only 'the Master and myself' were at the wheel. At Chequetan on the coast of Mexico in April 1742 torpedo fish gave shocks to anyone who touched them, and 'I myself had a considerable degree of numbness conveyed to my right arm, through a walking cane which I rested on the body of the fish'. The chaplain also recorded that when the *Centurion* was driven off Tinian in September 1742, 'I was then on board'. Finally, there was the departure for Europe from Canton in December 1742 of Saunders and others, when 'I, having obtained the Commodore's leave to return home, embarked with them'. These references, though few, show that Walter's part was not simply that of assembling navigational data. On the other hand, one of the curious lacunae in *Anson's Voyage* is that it never mentions the spiritual role of the chaplain. There is no reference to religious services on board the *Centurion*, nor any expression of gratitude to the Almighty for the several deliverances of the voyage.

The most important evidence supporting Robins comes in the correspondence between a learned clergyman, the Revd Thomas Birch, F.R.S., F.S.A., and the Hon. Philip Yorke, eldest son of Lord Hardwicke, and from 1748 Anson's brother-in-law. Birch wrote each week from London to Yorke at his country residence at Wrest in Bedfordshire with the news of the day. From the time of Anson's return to England in 1744 Birch frequently mentioned the celebrated voyage (a subject in which Yorke was naturally interested), and the progress of the account being written of it. Birch knew Robins, whom he seems to have often met in London, and he passed on to Yorke the information he picked up from Robins about the forthcoming book. In September 1744 he described the unauthorised narratives of the voyage then being rushed off the presses as 'despicable fictions', and told Yorke that Anson was 'determined to give the world an account himself'. There is then a gap of almost two years before Birch returned to the subject, first with news in August 1746 that Robins had been to see Anson at Portsmouth, and then the next month with something more definite: 'Mr. Anson has now put his papers into the hands of Mr. Robins, Mr. Walter, the first undertaker, having made scarce any progress in the work.' Robins's visit to Portsmouth had been to consult Anson and other officers from the voyage, and to bring back relevant papers. Among these were presumably journals kept on the voyage; for the book's descriptions of Santa Catarina and Juan Fernández, for example, owe much to the entries in the journal kept by Philip Saumarez.

Two years further on the *Voyage* had been published, and Birch's letters are full of news about its reception. Among 'the general applause and admiration' were criticisms also: from disgruntled officers of the *Gloucester*, deprived as they saw it of their fair share of the prize money; from divines shocked by 'the total absence of piety and religion'; and from Anson's political enemies who saw the work as 'a gross panegyric' and alleged that the admiral had given Robins £1,000 to write just that. What is consistent in Birch's letters is the assumption that Robins, and Robins alone, was the author. Robins is shown arguing at the dinner table with Charles Stanhope about the book's depiction of the Chinese, meeting in London French missionaries just back from China who apparently agreed with his criticisms of the fashionable 'aggravated and romantic representations' of the Chinese, corresponding with Voltaire about the book, and finally accepting an offer from the East India Company which put an end to any thought of a second volume. The book, Birch told Yorke, had made a great deal of noise – 'pamphlets will be writ of course, scribblers must dine, and the author is not one jot worse for them'.

The matter cannot be allowed to rest quite there. Difficulties remain: in particular the appearance of Walter's name, linked with Anson's, on the title-page, and Jane Walter's testimony. Her assertion that Robins was in Flanders before the publication of the book is confirmed by Birch's letters. Robins left England in August or September 1747, and although the date of his return is uncertain he must have been away for much of the time that the book, published the following May, was in the press. His contribution to the book was clearly made over the period of twelve months from the late summer of 1746 to the late summer of 1747, enough time for someone who was in a sense a professional writer. Despite the fact that Robins was not on the voyage it is in some ways easier to accept that a writer of his skill was responsible for a best-seller than that it was the work of a man who apparently never used his literary gifts before or after the success of 1748. Apart from providing the framework of the voyage that Robins was to clothe with 'dissertations' (Wilson's term), it seems feasible that Walter also saw the book through the press in Robins's absence on the continent, and that proof-reading and correcting formed the main burden of those labours remembered by his widow more than 40 years later. There is a significant sentence in Jane Walter's letter to John Walter in which she remarked that before the book's publication 'I have frequently seen Mr. Walter correct the proof sheets for the printer'. If the evidence suggests that the literary style of the book derived from Robins's pen, this takes nothing away from Anson's overseeing of the project. The fact that the co-author (at least) had not been on the voyage, Birch's note that Anson had originally intended to write an account himself (unlikely in the event, given Anson's known aversion to pen and ink), and Jane Walter's memory of Anson's close scrutiny of the work in progress, all point to the *Voyage* as being in everything except stylistic terms Anson's own interpretation of events. It is valuable not as an impartial account – for that was never its purpose – but as a narrative that reflects the views of the expedition's commanding officer.

APPENDIX II

Sources

ABBREVIATIONS AND LOCATIONS

Add.MS	Additional Manuscripts, British Library
Adm	Admiralty records, Public Record Office
ADM	Admiralty records, National Maritime Museum
Audiencia de Filipinas	Archivo de Indias, Seville
Corr.Pol.	Correspondance Politique, Archives du Ministère des Affaires Etrangères, Paris
Guernsey MSS	Philip Saumarez Papers, Sausmarez Manor, Guernsey
IOR	India Office Records, British Library
HAR 4	Hartwell Papers/4, National Maritime Museum
HCA	High Court of Admiralty records, Public Record Office
NMM	National Maritime Museum
OHS	Oregon Historical Society, Portland
SP	State Papers, Public Record Office
Wager MSS	Sir Charles Wager Papers, Vernon-Wager Collection, Library of Congress, Washington DC
WO	War Office records, Public Record Office

GENERAL

(For printed books the place of publication is London unless otherwise stated.)

A prime source for Anson's voyage remains the authorised account published under Richard Walter's name in 1748 as *A Voyage Round the World in the Years MDCCXL, I, II, III, IV By George Anson, Esq* (hereafter referred to as *Anson's Voyage*). On the vexed question of its authorship see Appendix I above. Among other contemporary books on the voyage the earliest, a brief, anonymous *Authentick Account ... Taken from a private Journal*, was published in August 1744.

This was followed in September by *An Authentick Journal of the late Expedition under the Command of Commodore Anson* by 'John Philips', a full-length account that seems to have been based on one or more genuine logs. This book appeared, with some changes of wording and arrangement, in several pirated editions: *An Authentic and Genuine Journal ... Published from the Journals of several of the principal Officers* (1744); *A Voyage to the South-Seas ... By Commodore Anson. By an Officer of the Fleet* (1745); *A Voyage to the South Seas ... By Commodore Anson* (1745). 1745 also saw the publication of the much superior account by Pascoe Thomas, 'Teacher of the Mathematicks on board the *Centurion*', *A True and Impartial Journal of a Voyage to the South Seas and Round the Globe in His Majesty's Ship the Centurion* (1745), hereafter cited as Thomas, *Journal*. The several books on the fate of the *Wager* are listed under Chapter III.

There are biographies of Anson, all containing chapters on the voyage, by Sir John Barrow, *The Life of Lord George Anson* (1839); Walter Vernon Anson, *The Life of Admiral Lord Anson, the Father of the British Navy, 1697–1762* (1912); and S. W. C. Pack, *Admiral Lord Anson* (1960). A full-length account of the expedition based on published sources was written by Vice-Admiral Boyle Somerville, *Commander Anson's Voyage into the South Seas and around the World* (1934). The present writer edited primary source material on the voyage in *Documents relating to Anson's Voyage round the World 1740–1744* (Navy Records Society, 1967). Leo Heaps, *Log of the Centurion: Based on the original papers of Captain Philip Saumarez on board HMS Centurion* (1973), contains lengthy extracts from the journals of Philip Saumarez.

More than twenty manuscript log books or journals survive from the voyage. Most are brief, and where they have useful information are cited in the source material for particular chapters below. Three, however, contain exceptionally full individual accounts of the voyage, and have been used throughout (with specific citations only where the location in the journal of a reference is not clear from the text). Captain Matthew Michell's log of the *Gloucester*, 3 Nov. 1740 to 16 Aug. 1742 is in Adm 51/402, with an additional section up to 20 Dec. 1742 covering his time as a supernumerary on the *Centurion*. The journals of Lieutenant (later Captain) Philip Saumarez exist in at least two copies, but both pose problems of accessibility. His journal from 20 Dec. 1739 to 21 June 1743 is in ADM/L/C/ 301, but the fading of the ink entries means that many of them are, at best, only partly legible. The present writer consulted another copy, together with 'Historicall Remarks' and other documents, at Sausmarez Manor, Guernsey, in the 1960s, and made transcripts of much of this material. The journal seems to have left the possession of the de Sausmarez family in the early 1970s, and its present whereabouts is not known to the writer. Finally, Lawrence Millechamp, purser at different times on several of the ships of the squadron, wrote on his return 'A Narrative of Commodore Anson's Voyage into the Great South Sea' that he presented to Earl Fitzwalter, one of the Lords Commissioners for Appeals in Prize Cases. This journal is in NMM MS 9354/JOD 36, and since it has no page numbers, and few dates, all references to it are taken from the version, printed in sections, in Williams, *Documents*, pp. 65–82, 111–38, 186–94.

CHAPTER I : *A South Sea Venture*

For parliamentary insistence on attacking the Spanish West Indies see William Cobbett, *The Parliamentary History of England*, XI (1812), espec. cols. 16–19, 24, 87, 93–4, 138, 152, 251–2, 286. A detailed narrative of Vernon's and other naval campaigns in the first year of the war is contained in H. W. Richmond, *The Navy in the War of 1739–48*, I (Cambridge, 1920), supplemented by a more recent study by Richard Harding, *Amphibious Warfare in the Eighteenth Century: The British Expedition to the West Indies 1740–1742* (Woodbridge, Suffolk, 1991). For the exploits and writings of English seamen in the Pacific from Narborough to Shelvocke see Glyndwr Williams, *The Great South Sea: English Voyages and Encounters 1570–1750* (1997), chs. 3–5. Evidence of earlier interest in the South Sea by Norris and Wager is in Add.MS 28,140, fo. 27v., and William Coxe, *Memoirs of the Life and Administration of Sir Robert Walpole* (London, 1798), II, p. 514. Details of the careers of Hubert Tassell and Henry Hutchinson are scattered through Add.MSS 25,510 and 25,558; their letter to ministers in Sept. and Oct. 1739 are in Add.MS 32,694, fos. 47, 88–93, and in SP 42/88, fos. 37–41. Sir John Norris's daily 'Journal of My Proceedings', with its verbatim reports of ministerial discussions, is in Add.MS 28,132. Details of James Naish's career with the East India Company are in IOR: Court Minutes 43–58; his proposals for a Manila expedition are set out in Wager MSS, fos. 45846, 46216–7, 46984–5, and in Add.MS 19,030, fo. 450. His copy of *Anson's Voyage*, annotated with his comments, is in the British Library (Printed Books: 10025, fo. 8). For Anson's early career see Adm 1/1438, Section IV (Captains' Letters: Anson); Pack, *Anson*, ch. 2; Edgar K. Thompson, 'George Anson in the Province of South Carolina', *Mariner's Mirror*, LIII (1967), pp. 279–80; *The Private Character of Admiral Lord George Anson by a Lady* (c.1747). Anson's letter of 14 Nov. 1734 to Norris is in Add.MS 28,156 (no p. no.). His instructions for the voyage are in SP 42/81, fos. 293–8 (draft), SP 42/88, fos. 2–10 (31 Jan. 1740), fos. 12–13 (19 June 1740). The draft manifesto for distribution in Spanish America is in Add.MS 19,030, fos. 470–72. For Wager's involvement with the Northwest Passage scheme see William Barr and Glyndwr Williams, eds., *Voyages to Hudson Bay in Search of a Northwest Passage 1741–1747: I, The Voyage of Christopher Middleton 1741–1742* (1994), section 1.

Dimensions and other details of Anson's ships are summarised in David Lyon, *The Sailing Navy List* (1993), pp. 44, 46, 47, 53, 201. The exchange of letters between Anson, the Lords of the Admiralty, and the Navy Board on the preparations for the voyage fill many pages of: Adm 1/1439, Section III (Captains' Letters: Anson); Adm 3/43, 44 (Admiralty Minutes); Adm 2/201 (Lords of the Admiralty: Out-Letters); Adm 106/916 (Navy Board: In-Letters); Adm 106/2178 and ADM/B/111, 112 (Navy Board: Out-Letters). Details about the state of affairs on the *Cambridge* are in *Manuscripts of the Earl of Egmont*, III (Historical Manuscripts Commission, 1923), p. 163. Details about Chaloner Ogle's manning problems, and conditions at Gosport Hospital, are given in Daniel Baugh, *British Naval Administration in the Age of Walpole* (Princeton, 1965), pp. 179–86. Walpole's reactions to the manpower shortage are recorded in Romney Sedgwick, ed., *Some Materials Towards Memoirs of the Reign of King George II by John, Lord Hervey*, III (1931), pp. 933, 937. William Robinson Crusoe makes his brief appearance in Adm 36/4456 (*Wager*'s muster book), fo. 57.

Lt.-Col.Cracherode's instructions regarding his five companies of invalids are in SP 42/88, fo. 43. The personal histories of many of the invalids sent to Anson's ships are in WO 116/2, 3; the sad story of their arrival at Portsmouth is told in Adm 1/4109, docs. 42, 43, Add.MS 35,406, fo. 223, Adm 3/44, 14 Aug. 1740, Adm 1/1439, 16 Aug. 1740. The minute book of the Board of Chelsea Hospital, WO 250/470, contains the memorial from its secretary (p. 229), the petitions from invalid deserters (pp. 227, 229, 239, 240), and the Secretary at War's decision on the petitions (p. 236). The muster books of the *Centurion* are in Adm 36–554, 555, 556; the *Gloucester*'s in Adm 36/1385. The offhand comment (by the Secretary at War) about marines is reported in Cobbett, *Parliamentary History*, XI, col. 158. Complaints by Cavendish and Norris about the marines at Portsmouth are in Adm 1/903, 904, April–July 1740. The whole tangled business of Tassell and Hutchinson's appointment as victualling agents can be followed in Adm 111/26, minutes of the Victualling Board, 28 April–11 June 1740; and Adm 110/12, Victualling Board Letters, pp. 122, 124.

Anson's untidy departure from Spithead is described in Philip Saumarez, 'Historicall Remarks', Guernsey MSS (also printed in Williams, *Documents*, pp. 56–60). The 'Will Wimble' reference is taken from Philip Woodfine, 'Ideas of naval power and the conflict with Spain, 1737–1742', in Jeremy Black and Philip Woodfine, eds., *The British Navy and the Use of Naval Power in the Eighteenth Century* (Leicester, 1988), p. 77. Details of French and Spanish knowledge of Anson's expedition are in Adm 1/1695, fos. 271–3, SP 42/88, fo. 61, Add.MS 32,802, fo. 209, Corr.Pol./Espagne/460, fos. 46, 192, /462, fos. 119, 149, 238v.

CHAPTER II : *The Ordeal Begins*

Anson's report of the deaths of the invalid officers is in Add MS 15,855, fo. 44; while fos. 47v–48 contain the captains' reports on sickness on their ships in November 1740. Michell's acount of his arrival on the *Gloucester* is in Adm 51/402, fo. 2. For the casualty rates on Ogle's squadron see Harding, *Amphibious Warfare*, pp. 83–5, 149. Samuel Sutton's encounter with Jacob Acworth is described in his book, *A New Method for extracting the foul Air out of Ships* (1749), pp. 6–9. Two slightly different versions of Dandy Kidd's death-bed speech are given in Anon., *A Voyage to the South-Seas . . . By an Officer of the Fleet* (1745), pp. 20, 273. Lt. Salt's report of his encounter with Pizarro's ships is in Adm 1/2099, section 3, 8 July 1741, and Anson's instructions to his captains before they left Port St Julian in Add.MS 15,855, fo. 63.

Lt. Saumarez's problems on the *Tryal* are reported by him in ADM/L/C/301, log entries 27 Feb.–13 March 1740. The master mariner's description of rounding Cape Horn is by Alan Villiers, *Captain Cook, The Seamen's Seaman* (Harmondsworth, 1969), pp. 130–31. Details of scurvy in the 16th and 17th centuries are taken from Kenneth J. Carpenter, *The History of Scurvy and Vitamin C* (Cambridge, 1986). For health problems generally in the navy in this period see Christopher Lloyd and J. L. S. Coulter, *Medicine and the Navy*, III, 1714–1815 (Edinburgh, 1961). The consultations about antiscorbutics between the Admiralty, the Navy Board, the College of Physicians, and Anson, are in Adm 106/2178, pp. 307–8; Adm 106/916, 6 July, 15 July 1740; *London Magazine* (1740), p. 403. The descriptions of the first outbreak of scurvy on the voyage are in *Anson's Voyage*, pp. 100–103; Thomas, *Journal*, p. 142; Michell log, Adm 51/402, fo. 28. The reference to scurvy on da Gama's voyage comes from James Watt, 'Medical Aspects of the Long Voyages of Exploration', Mário Gomes Marques and John Cule, eds., *The Great Maritime Discoveries and World Health* (Lisbon, 1991), p. 23. For the most recent of his several writings on health issues on the Anson voyage see James Watt, 'The Medical Bequest of Disaster at Sea: Commodore Anson's Circumnavigation 1740–1744', Journal of the Royal College of Physicians of London, 32 (Nov./Dec. 1998), pp. 572–9.

The conditions on the individual ships during their passage round the Horn and into the Pacific are described for the *Centurion* in *Anson's Voyage*, pp. 76–83, and Thomas, *Journal*, pp. 22–4; for the *Gloucester*, Michell log, Adm 51/402, fos. 14–16; for the *Pearl*, Adm 1/2040, Section 11; for the *Tryal*, Saumarez log, ADM L/C/301, 8–31 March 1741 (his draft letter of complaint to Anson is in Guernsey MSS, and has been printed in Heaps, *Log of the Centurion*, p. 96), and Millechamp, 'Narrative', pp. 77–8. Together with the Saumarez and Michell logs for 13, 14 April 1741, Anson's log of the *Centurion* (ADM L/C/300, same date) should be consulted for the unexpected sighting of land. A. F. Frézier's warning is in his *Voyage to the South-Sea* (1717), p. 42. For Shovell's disaster, and Harrison's early chronometers, see Dava Sobel, *Longitude* (1996), pp. 11–13, 16–17. Keppel's narrow escape in 1758 is described in Thomas Keppel, *The Life of Augustus Viscount Keppel*, I (1842), p. 271. Anson's complaint about the sluggishness of the *Gloucester* is in NMM HAR 4: 'Case heard before the Lords Commissioners for Appeals in Prize Causes', April 1747, p. 6. Anson's order to his captains to keep close to the *Centurion* is in Add.MS 15,855, fo.72v; fo.63v has his instructions that give an incorrect location for Juan Fernández. George Shelvocke's comments on Juan Fernández are in his account, *A Voyage Round the World by Way of the Great South Sea* (1726), ch. VII. The description of Richard Walter is by his Cambridge friend, William Cole, printed in *Notes & Queries*, 7th series, VIII, p. 517. For conditions and casualties on the ships when they reached Juan Fernández, to the accounts above should be added the muster books, Adm 36/556 (*Centurion*), Adm 36/1385 (*Gloucester*), and Adm 36/4348 (*Tryal*). The explanation for the health of the boys comes in a personal communication from Sir James Watt, 15 January 1999; for information on ships' boys generally in this period see Nicholas Rodger, *The Wooden World: An Anatomy of the Georgian Navy* (1986), espec. pp. 26–8, 266–8. The only account of the *Anna*'s survival is in *Anson's Voyage*, pp. 138–45. For Sandwich's later remarks on her see J. C. Beaglehole, ed., *The Journals of Captain James Cook*, II (Cambridge, 1961), p. 714.

CHAPTER III : *The Missing Ships*

Crucial documents for the turning back of the *Severn* and *Pearl* are the ships' logs and muster books (*Severn*: Adm 51/888, Adm 36/3562; *Pearl*: Adm 51/723, Adm 36/2406). Edward Legge's letters on the incident are in Adm 1/2040, section 2, George Murray's in Adm 1/2099, section 3. Lt. Innes's log of the *Severn* is in ADM/L/S/237. For contemporary comments on the captains' conduct see Thomas, *Journal*, p. 24; *Anson's Voyage*, pp. 364–5; *London Magazine* (April 1742), p. 207; Thomas Anson to Anson, 30 Nov. 1743, Add.MS 15,957, fos. 28–9; Henry Legge to Anson, 4 Sept. 1748, in Add MS 15,956, fo. 211v. Later comments are in Somerville, *Anson's Voyage*, pp. 43–5; A. C. Murray, *An Episode in the Spanish War 1739–1744* (1952), espec. chs. VII, VIII, and p. 44 for the family tradition of Anson's gift of a gold watch to Captain George Murray; and Watt, 'Medical Bequest of Disaster at Sea', p. 574.

The logs and other official documents for the *Wager* disappeared with the wreck of the ship (the log in Adm 51/1082 and muster book in Adm 36/4456 extend only to Nov. 1740). The events that followed the wreck must be pieced together from the books written by the survivors: John Bulkeley and John Cummins, *A Voyage to the South-Seas, In the Years 1740–1. Containing, a Faithful Narrative of the Loss of His Majesty's Ship the Wager* (1743), 2nd edn. (1757), with additional material on Cheap; Alexander Campbell, *The Sequel to Bulkeley and Cummins' Voyage to the South-Seas* (1747); Isaac Morris, *A Narrative of the Dangers and Distresses which Befel Isaac Morris and Seven More of the Crew* (1751); John Byron, *The Narrative of the Honourable John Byron* (1768), which includes on pp. 2–3 Byron's recollections of the *Wager* at the outset of the voyage. His instructions of 1764 to search for survivors of the *Wager* are in Robert C. Gallagher, ed., *Byron's Journal of his Circumnavigation, 1764–66* (Cambridge, 1964), p. 7. Cheap's letters about the shipwreck and subsequent events are in Add.MS 35,396, fos. 192–6 (to Richard Lingley, 26 Feb. 1744), and Add MS. 15,955, fo. 214 (to Anson, 12 Dec. 1745). Legge's report to Anson that Alexander Campbell had joined the Spanish service is in Add.MS 15,956, fos. 182v.–183. Recent studies are S. W. C. Pack, *The Wager Mutiny* (1964), which prints (pp. 226–42) a transcript of the court martial proceedings of April 1746; Peter Shankland, *Byron of the Wager* (1975); and Philip Edwards, *The Story of the Voyage: Sea-Narratives in Eighteenth-Century England* (1994), ch. 4.

CHAPTER IV : *'To Distress and Annoy the King of Spain'*

An account of the misadventures of Pizarro's ships is in *Anson's Voyage*, Book I, Ch. III; see also C. Fernández Duro, *Armada Española*, VI (Madrid, 1900), pp. 286–8, and Jorge Juan and Antonio de Ulloa, *A Voyage to South-America* (1758), pp. 2–3, 194–5, 203–9, 237, 293–4. This latter, an English translation from the Spanish *Relación Histórica* of the same date, also has information on the measures taken in Peru against Anson's squadron. The fortunes of Anson's ships once they sailed from Juan Fernández can be followed in the published accounts and ships' logs cited under 'General' above, together with some specific references to the following matters: the ill feeling between Michell and Anson, Michell log, Adm 51/402, 19 Sept. 1741, 2 Feb. 1742; prize-money disputes, Thomas, *Journal*, pp. 52, 63–4 ; unofficial account of attack on Paita, 'Philips', *Authentick Journal*, p. 85; Captain Hall's experiences in Peru, Basil Hall, *Extracts from a Journal written on the Coasts of Chili, Peru and Mexico in the Years 1820, 1821, 1822* (Edinburgh, 1824), II, p. 99.

The published accounts of the Mexican coast consulted by Anson were William Dampier, *A New Voyage Round the World* (1697) and George Shelvocke, *A Voyage Round the World* (1726). For the captured Spanish charts on the *Centurion* see Saumarez log, ADM/L/C/301, 10, 13 Feb. 1742. The standard account of the galleons remains W. L. Schurz, *The Manila Galleon* (New York, 1939); see also Peter Gerhard, *Pirates on the West Coast of New Spain 1575–1742* (Glendale, CA, 1960). The description of a galleon's cargo is taken from 'Philips',

Authentick Journal, pp. 107–8. For accounts of earlier attacks on the galleons see Williams, *Great South Sea*, pp. 41–3 (Cavendish), 139–40 (Dampier), 152–3 (Rogers). The officers' hopeful estimates of the galleon's treasure are in *Gentleman's Magazine* (June 1743), pp. 325–6 (Denis), and 'Abstract of a Journal', 7 Dec. 1742 (Saumarez). Anson's note on Louis Leger is in the *Centurion's* log, ADM/L/C/300, 14 April 1742; the entry for 19 April 1742 describes Brett's skirmish with Spanish horsemen. Brett's own account is in ADM/L/C/83, 19 April 1742. There is a considerable amount of material on the destruction of the *Tryal Prize*. Anson's own orders are scattered through Add MS. 15,855, fos. 111, 114v.; HCA 42/41, Part I; NMM HAR 4, 'Written Depositions', p. 10. See also Michell log, Adm 51/402, 29 March 1742, and Saunders log (of the *Tryal Prize*), ADM/L/T/53, 15 April 1742. Millechamp gathered together the most important documents in his 'Narrative', pp. 116–19.

CHAPTER V : *'Words Cannot Express the Misery'*

The most detailed accounts of the voyage across the North Pacific are in Michell log, Adm 51/402, and Saumarez log, ADM/L/C/301. Anson's admission is in NMM HAR 4, 'Case . . .', p. 12. A translation of Gemelli Careri's account was printed in Awnsham and John Churchill, *A Collection of Voyages and Travels*, IV (1732), pp. 457–77. The accounts of earlier crossings of the North Pacific by English ships are in Dampier, *New Voyage*, pp. 276ff., Shelvocke, *Voyage*, pp. 414, 432ff.; Woodes Rogers, *A Cruising Voyage Round the World* (1712), pp. 356ff. The comments by Anson's men on the difficulty in finding the trade winds come from Millechamp, 'Narrative', p. 124; Lt. Patrick Baird log, ADM/L/G/53, 15 May 1742; Saumarez, ADM/L/C 301, 13 June 1742. James Naish's comments are written in his copy of *Anson's Voyage*, p. 224. Pascoe Thomas's description of scurvy, and his note on the ineffectiveness of Ward's pills are in his *Journal*, pp. 141–4. Anson's order to Michell of 24 July 1742 was copied into Millechamp, 'Narrative', p. 125. The reference to men dying 'like rotten sheep' is in the *Universal Spectator*, 25 Aug. 1744. For Anson's emphasis on oranges as an antiscorbutic see Anon., *Authentick Account*, p. 49, and Thomas, *Journal*, pp. 173, 175. Saumarez's later description of his command of the *Centurion* when she was blown off Tinian is in his 'Abstract of a Journal', 7 Dec. 1742, Guernsey MSS. For the doubts about Anson's plans expressed by those stranded on Tinian see Millechamp, 'Narrative', p. 133; Thomas, *Journal*, p. 159; *Anson's Voyage*, pp. 322, 325. Details of the *Centurion's* lost anchor were given in *The Times*, 24 Aug. 1829, cited in *Life of Keppel*, I, p. 55.

Anson's unfinished letter to James Naish from Canton is now in the Staffordshire Record Office: D615/P(5)/1/10/4A. His official report to Newcastle, 7 Dec. 1742, is in SP 42/88, fos. 77–85. News of Anson's squadron was published from time to time in *London Magazine* (July 1741), pp. 361, 363; (Nov. 1741), p. 567; (April 1742), pp. 204, 207; (May 1742), p. 256; (Aug. 1742), p. 411; *Gentleman's Magazine* (April 1742), p. 218; (June 1742), p. 330; (July 1742), p. 387; (Sept. 1742), pp. 496–7. Vernon's letters to Newcastle of Feb–April 1742 with reports on Anson are in SP 42/92, fos. 42, 80, 92v.–93, 128–9, 147. Anson's letter to Captain Cheap is in Add.MS 15,855, fo. 133. Leger's account is in *London Magazine* (April 1743), pp. 202–3. The account of his pay is recorded in Adm 33/383, *Centurion's* pay book. For Leger's reassurance about Philip and Thomas Saumarez's health see Havilland de Sausmarez, *Captain Philip Saumarez 1710–1747 and his Contemporaries* (Guernsey, 1936), p. 7.

The standard work on the East India Company at Canton is H. B. Morse, *Chronicles of the East India Company trading to China 1635–1834*, I (Oxford, 1926). The disruption to the Company's trade in 1744 by Spanish warships is covered in IOR: Correspondence Committee, Memoranda/12, Miscellaneous In-Letters/ 32. The only surviving parts of the supercargoes' China Diary from 1742 relating to Anson's visit is in IOR: Factory Records, China II, 3, pp. 11–17, 37–40. Naish's comments on French and Dutch obstructiveness are written in his copy of *Anson's Voyage*, p. 57. Six letters from Anson to Saumarez, 24 Nov.–6 Dec. 1742 in Guernsey MSS, are printed in Williams, *Documents*, pp. 148–52. Anson's request to the East India Company captains for men, and his criticism of their attitude, are in Add.MS 18,855, fos. 130v, 161. Saunders's final entry in his log of the *Tryal Prize* is in ADM/L/T/53, 1 May 1742. Anson's letter to the viceroy is in Add.MS 15,855, fo. 131v.

CHAPTER VI : *The Prize of All the Oceans*

For the low spirits of the crew see the first paragraph of Lt. Denis's letter from Macao, 1 Dec. 1742, printed in *Gentleman's Magazine* (June 1743), pp. 325–6, and Thomas, *Journal*, p. 278. Anson's letter to Hardwicke is in Add.MS 35,359, fo. 360. Information about Joseph Allen at Macao is in NMM HAR/4, p. 18; evidence of Collet's help comes from Thomas, *Journal*, p. 288. Anson's letter to the governor of Batavia is in Add.MS 15,855, fo. 135v. The problem of the gunpowder is recounted in Millechamp, 'Narrative', p. 186. The full commands for firing a cannon are listed in Brian Lavery, ed., *Shipboard Life and Organisation, 1731–1815* (Aldershot, 1998), pp. 90–91. All the accounts of the voyage have a description of the taking of the *Covadonga*; the fullest is by Saumarez in his journal entry for 20 June 1743. For Montero's earlier career see Schurz, *Manila Galleon*, p. 206. The hiding places for treasure on the galleon are described in Millechamp, 'Narrative', p. 190.

The reports (unsigned) from Canton to the governor of Manila about Anson are in Audiencia de Filipinas/256, docs. 4, 5. For the identity of the informant, and also the fitting out of the *Pilar*, and events on board the *Covadonga*, see Juan de la Concepción, *Historia General de la Philipinas*, XI (Madrid, 1791), pp. 124, 132–9, 152–61. A contemporary English translation of the log of the *Covadonga*'s pilot is in NMM: 36 MS.0827 Log F/7. Details of the great *Santíssima Trinidad* are in Schurz, *Manila Galleon*, p. 340. For the size of the *Covadonga* and her crew see 'Deposition made by Montero', 21 July 1743, in HCA 32/135 Bundle A; and Thomas, *Journal*, Appendix, p. 7. The galleon's 'Plan de Guerra' was originally seen by the present writer in the Guernsey MSS; there is a photograph of it in Heaps, *Log of the Centurion*, p. 231. Anson's description of the damage to the galleon is in his letter to Newcastle, 14 June 1744, in SP 42/88, fo. 87. The report of the fire on the *Centurion* appeared in the *Universal Spectator*, 25 Aug. 1744; the description of a smoke-blackened Anson is taken from Anon., *Authentick Account*, p. 54.

Chapter VII : *Confrontation at Canton*

Thomas, *Journal*, pp. 294, 302–3, 304, 306, 313, has material on the chase of the French vessel, Montero's 'stolen' sword, Anson's insistence on his dignity, and the initial distribution of the prize money. For Lt. Denis's hostile reception in Canton see Millechamp, 'Narrative', p. 189. The Chinese interpretation of Anson's surrender of his prisoners is set out in Arthur Waley, *Yuan Mei* (1956), pp. 205–9. The order from the chuntuck restricting movements on the Canton River is in Add.MS 15,855, fo. 7. Nutt's reference to the Canton fire is in ADM/L/C/83. For Anson's visit to the chuntuck see Anon., *Authentick Account*, p. 58; his own report on the visit is in SP 42/88, fos. 87–8. The reference to the live animals taken on board comes, predictably, from purser Millechamp's 'Narrative', p. 193.

The documents relating to the relationship at Canton between Anson and Edward Page are in the Library of the Oregon Society: OHS MS 2893, nine letters, dated Sept.–Dec. 1743, from Anson to Page; OHS MS 2892, seven letters in reply from Page to Anson; OHS 2894, a 73-page manuscript by Page, 18 Nov. 1765, 'A little Secret History of Affairs at Canton in the year 1743 when the *Centurion* Comodore Anson was lying in the River'. For Page's earlier career with the East India Company see OHS 2894, p. 16, and Morse, *Chronicles*, I, pp. 174–5. Colin Campbell's experiences at Canton are described in Paul Hallberg and Christian Koninckx, eds., *A Passage to China: Colin Campbell's Diary of the First Swedish East India Company Expedition to Canton, 1732–33* (Göteborg, 1996).

Eighteenth-century European interest in China has produced a huge literature; Hugh Honour, *Chinoiserie: The Vision of Cathay* (1961) remains a good introduction. For reactions to the criticism of the Chinese in *Anson's Voyage*, see Add.MS.35,397, fos. 104, 111, 145, 163. Voltaire's views are set out in *Oeuvres Complètes de Voltaire*, XXVIII (Paris, 1826), p. 295.

CHAPTER VIII : *Homecoming: Acclamation and Recrimination*

Details of the Spanish search expeditions are in Juan and Ulloa, *Voyage*, II, p. 294, and Audiencia de Filipinas/256, doc. 1 (governor of Manila to King of Spain, 5 July 1744, NS). The description of the mixed crew of the *Centurion* is in Add.MS 35,396, fo. 217. Differing estimates of the treasure are in *Daily Post*, 16, 18 June 1744, and *General Advertiser*, 16 June 1744. Newcastle's reaction is in SP 42/88, fo. 89; Anson's letter to Hardwicke in Add.MS 35,359, fo. 360. The dispute between Anson and the Admiralty is outlined in Adm 1/1440 Captains' Letters: Anson) and Add.MS. 35,396, fos. 205v.–206; there is a section on the matter in Pack, *Anson*, pp. 22–6.

The descriptions of Anson's reception in London are taken from issues of the *Daily Post, General Advertiser, Daily Advertiser, Penny London Morning Advertiser* for June–Aug. 1744. The assessment of Anson is by 'an officer' (Lt. Denis) in the *Universal Spectator*, 15 Aug. 1744. Walpole's comment is in W. S. Lewis, ed., *The Yale Edition of Horace Walpole's Correspondence*, XXX (New Haven, 1961), p. 53. The Admiralty note on the deaths of warrant officers on the *Centurion* is in ADM/L/C/300, flyleaf. Letters describing the health problems of Anson and his officers are in SP 42/88, fos. 87–8 (Anson, 14 June 1744), Adm 1/2465 (Saunders, 18 Jan. 1747), Adm 1/1603 (Cheap, 15, 18 Jan. 1747), Saumarez (Guernsey MSS, printed Heaps, *Log*, pp. 258–9). Saumarez's part in designing a naval uniform is described in de Sausmarez, *Captain Philip Saumarez*, pp. 12–15.

On the prize-money dispute Saumarez's letter to his brother is in Guernsey MSS, 15 Aug. 1744. The most important of the official documents on the dispute are in HCA 42/41, part 1 (including Anson's evidence of 19 Feb. 1745); HCA 32/135, bundle A (including Montero's deposition, 21 July 1743); HAR 4, Case heard before the Lords Commissioners for Appeals in Prize Causes, April 1747, including written depositions (pp. 6–24), copies of orders on the voyage (pp. 24–35), depositions of the respondents' witnesses (pp. 36–63), and summary of the cases of both sides (pp. 64–76). For the celebrations in London on news of Anson's victory off Cape Finisterre see *Morning Advertiser*, 18–20, 20–22 May 1747. Estimates of the amount of the prize money are in SP 42/88, fos. 87–8 (Anson), ADM L/C/83, 23 Oct. 1743 (Nutt), Thomas, *Journal*, pp. 306, Appendix, pp. 4–5. For the exchange rates at this time see John J. McCusker, *Money and Exchange in Europe and America* (Chapel Hill, 1978), pp. 8, 98–9. The original of Philip Saumarez's will is in Guernsey MSS, together with a note by him of 23 Sept. 1747 showing the amount of prize money he had received. For the comparable Woodes Rogers prize-money case see Williams, *Great South Sea*, pp. 158–60. Anson's pay for the voyage is shown in the *Centurion*'s pay book, Adm 33/383. Saumarez's final words on the matter are in Heaps, *Log*, p. 255, Millechamp's in 'Narrative', p. 194.

CHAPTER IX : *Past and Future*

For 'lucky Anson' see C. H. Firth, ed., *Naval Songs and Ballads* (1908), p. 196. Thomas Anson's request for the Spanish standard is in Add.MS 15,955, fo. 55; the saga of the *Centurion*'s figurehead in *Gentleman's Magazine*, XXX (Feb. 1749), p. 69. The relevant passages from John Campbell are in his *Navigantium atque Itinerantium Bibliotheca*, I (1744), pp. 364–5, II (1748), pp. 399–404, 1039–41; see also [Stephen Whatley], *A Complete System of Geography*, II (1747), p. 799. Henry Legge's letter to Anson is in Add.MS 15,956, fo. 211.

For contemporary comments on scurvy in relation to the Anson voyage see Richard Mead, *A Discussion of the Scurvy* (1749), pp. 97, 111, 114–15, 117, 119; James Lind, *A Treatise of the Scurvy* (Edinburgh, 1753), pp. 149–53. For modern investigations see Watt, 'Medical Bequest', and more generally Carpenter, *History of Scurvy*.

Walpole's criticism is in Lewis, ed., *Walpole's Correspondence*, IX, p. 53. Anson's work at the Board of Admiralty is covered in Pack, *Anson*, espec. ch. XIII; see p. 253 for Pitt's tribute. His letters on the Western Squadron are in Eg.MS 3444, fo. 46 and Add.MS 35,359, fo. 413. Anson's admission of awkwardness is printed in Barrow, *Life*, p. 401. For the opposing views on Anson see Lord Holland, ed., *Memoirs of the Reign of George II by Horace Walpole* (2nd edn., 1847), I, p. 194, and Baugh, *British Naval Administration*, p. 504. Anson's letter to Hardwicke on Lady Anson's health is in Add.MS, fo. 428v.

There is considerable documentation on the proposed Pacific expedition of 1749, especially in Adm 3/60, 19 Jan., 28 Feb. 1749; Adm 2/214, fos. 265, 301, 321, 353, 399; Add.MS 43,423, fo. 81; SP 94/135, fos. 177–8, 265–9, 271–2, 330. The more important documents are printed in a recent article by the present writer with Alan Frost, 'The Beginnings of Britain's Exploration of the Pacific Ocean in the Eighteenth Century', *Mariner's Mirror*, 83 (1997), pp. 410–18. Keene's comment is in Richard Lodge, ed., *The Private Correspondence of Sir Benjamin Keene* (Cambridge, 1933), 29 May 1743. The location of the assumed Strait of Anian is given in Thomas, *Journal*, Appendix, p. 36. Cramond's recollections are in J. C. Beaglehole, ed., *The Journals of Captain James Cook*, III (Cambridge, 1967), p. li. For the Manila meetings of Jan. 1762 see N. P. Cushner, ed., *Documents Illustrating the British Conquest of Manila 1762–1763* (1971), p. 12. Hutchinson's memorial is in Add.MS 47,014C, fo. 122. For evidence of Anson's regret about the abandoned 1749 expedition see Helen Wallis, ed., *Carteret's Voyage Round the World 1766–1769* (1965), II, p. 309. Egmont's memorandum is printed in Gallagher, *Byron's Journal*, pp. 160–61.

APPENDIX I : *A Literary Puzzle: The Authorship of Anson's Voyage Round the World*

Hawkesworth's comment is in J. L. Abbott, *John Hawkesworth: Eighteenth-Century Man of Letters* (Madison, 1982), p. 144; Pascoe Thomas's accusation in his *Journal*, p. 10. For James Wilson's assertions on the authorship question see his edition of *The Mathematical Tracts of the late Benjamin Robins, Esq; Fellow of the Royal Society and Engineer-General to the Honourable the East India Company* (1761), Preface. Jane Walter's letter of June 1789 is printed in *Notes & Queries*, 8th series, II (1892), pp. 86–7; the story of the lost bill is in ibid., 7th series, VIII (1899), p. 14. Sir John Barrow's verdict is in his *The Life of George Lord Anson* (1939), p. 14. For Cheap's evidence see James Kinsley, ed., *Anecdotes and Characters of the Times* (Oxford, 1973), p. 99. Birch's letters to Yorke on the matter are in Add.MS. 35,306, fo. 258; Add.MS. 35,397, fos. 16v, 20, 104, 108v–109, 111, 112v–113, 120v, 145, 163, 197v.

INDEX

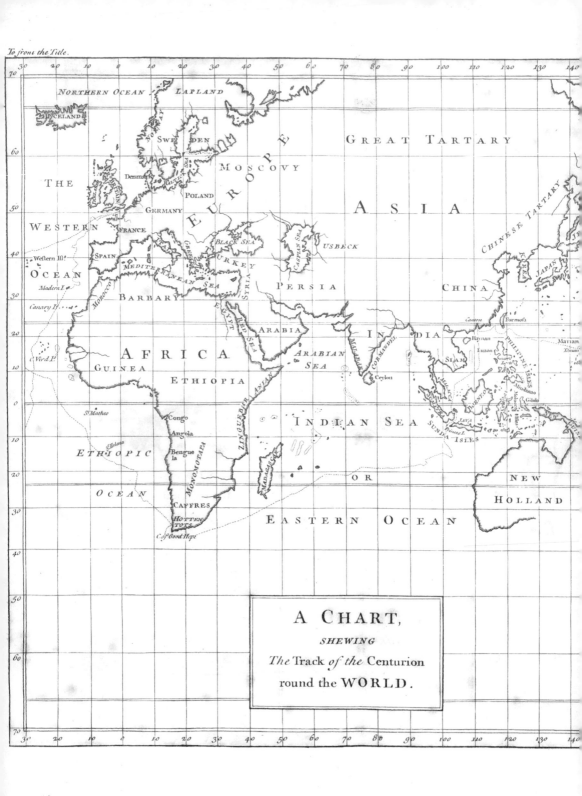

NORTHERN OCEAN   LAPLAND

ICELAND

SWEDEN

GREAT TARTARY

THE

MOSCOVY

Denmark

WESTERN

POLAND

GERMANY

EUROPE

ASIA

FRANCE

BLACK SEA

CASPIAN SEA

USBECK

CHINESE TARTARY

KOREA

JAPAN

Western Isl.

SPAIN

ITALY

MEDITERRANEAN SEA

TURKEY

SYRIA

PERSIA

CHINA

Madera I.

OCEAN

Morocco

BARBARY

EGYPT

RED SEA

Canary Is.

ARABIA

INDIA

Canton   Formosa

C. Verd I.

AFRICA

ARABIAN SEA

MALABAR

COROMANDEL

Haynan

Luzon

PHILIPPINE ISLES

Marian

GUINEA

ETHIOPIA

Ceylon

SIAM

St. Matheo

ZINGUEBAR

ANIAN

INDIAN SEA

BORNEO

MOLUCCA

Minhano

Gilolo

Congo

Angola

SUNDA

ISLES

ETHIOPIC

Helena

Bengue la

MONOMOTAPA

MADAGASCAR

OR

JAVA

Prince I.

NEW

OCEAN

CAFFRES

HOLLAND

HOTTEN TOTS

EASTERN   OCEAN

C. of Good Hope

A CHART,

SHEWING

The Track of the Centurion

round the WORLD.